Fish and Fowl Decoys of the Great Lakes

Donna Tonelli

Schiffer Publishing Ltd
4880 Lower Valley Road, Atglen, PA 19310 USA

Dedication

This book is dedicated to the early Midwest decoy collectors who gathered up these hunting and fishing artifacts, identified their makers, and researched their origins, thus preserving the decoy from obscurity, and often destruction, guaranteeing its status as an important American folk art. These men and women followed their quest for decoys into boathouses, sheds, barns, attics, and basements, traveling hundreds of miles at the drop of a hat in hopes of finding another decoy for their collection and at the same time gathering information about the carvers and the waterfowling traditions that surround this sport to share with other collectors. There was camaraderie among these folks who shared a love of decoys and the lore that surrounded them. They treasured decoys like memories of a great day of duck hunting.

This dedication is made in memory of Joseph A Tonelli's grandfather, Arthur "Heck" Tonelli and father, Joseph Rokar Tonelli who shared their hunting and fishing experiences with him from an early age, instilling a passionate love of the out-of-doors that led to Joe's interest in waterfowling, and fishing memorabilia and history which is the basis of this book.

Arthur Tonelli (1900-1954): Joseph R. Tonelli (1924-1999) with Joe Tonelli (1946-present)

Library of Congress Control Number: 2002104972

Designed by Sue
Type set in WindsorBT/Humanist521BT

ISBN: 0-7643-1643-5
Printed in China
1 2 3 4

Title page photo: Canvasback drake, Joseph Sieger (1872-2959), Tustin, Wisconsin, circa 1920. $15,000.

Published by Schiffer Publishing Ltd.
4880 Lower Valley Road
Atglen, PA 19310
Phone: (610) 593-1777; Fax: (610) 593-2002
E-mail: Schifferbk@aol.com
Please visit our web site catalog at **www.schifferbooks.com**
We are always looking for people to write books on new and related subjects. If you have an idea for a book please contact us at the above address.

This book may be purchased from the publisher.
Include $3.95 for shipping.
Please try your bookstore first.
You may write for a free catalog.

In Europe, Schiffer books are distributed by
Bushwood Books
6 Marksbury Ave.
Kew Gardens
Surrey TW9 4JF England
Phone: 44 (0) 20 8392-8585; Fax: 44 (0) 20 8392-9876
E-mail: Bushwd@aol.com
Free postage in the U.K., Europe; air mail at cost.

Contents

Preface

Belonging to the sporting fraternity should teach that the genuine sportsmanship is based upon honor, generosity, obedience to the law and a scrupulous willingness to perpetuate for those who come after them the recreation they themselves enjoy.
- Grover Cleveland

Collecting waterfowling and spearing decoys and the myriad of related artifacts is one very important way to preserve our sporting traditions for future generations. Were it not for collectors much of this folklore would have been lost. The collectors who searched for this folklore were not scholars, but people who loved the out-of-doors and sought to bring mementos into their homes to help them recapture the days of wonder they had experienced in the wild.

This book is the result of a lifetime of hunting in the field for game and in boathouses, barns, garages, flea markets, and antique shops for decoys that were replaced by newer, more practical, inexpensive plastic, or paper decoys. Joe Tonelli grew up on the Illinois River, where his father and grandfather shared their love for hunting and fishing with him. By the time he was a teenager, wooden decoys were being phased out. He brought in a few old birds to decorate the family's basement game room and soon learned he could pick up spending money by selling old decoys to his neighbor, Murray Crowder, an outdoors writer and field tester for Sears and Roebuck. His collecting changed when he began to correspond with Hal Sorenson, who sent Joe a copy of *The Decoy Collectors Guide*, which was quickly confiscated by one of his high school teachers when he was caught studying it instead of his algebra. By the time we were married in 1965, Joe had accumulated at least a thousand decoys, which he kept in fifty-five gallon drums. Willis Pennington knocked at our door one day and gave Joe his first lesson in decoy haggling. Pennington left the house with six original-paint Ben Schmidt decoys and Joe was the proud owner of a pair of Charlie Perdew mallards repainted by Cline McAlpin. A whole new world had opened for us.

Our free time was spent looking for decoys. An afternoon drive down the river would usually mean coming home with a trunk full of them. We spent hours sitting in the workshops of Charlie Perdew, Bob Weeks, Fred Destri, Fred Coleman, and Hector Whittington, listening to their tales about the good old days while they carved and painted their decoys. The real thrill of collecting was poking around an old boathouse, garage, or barn and seeing a gunnysack hanging from the rafters. You just knew there were wooden decoys inside.

There were many times Joe wished he could go back. One day in 1967 he had called on Charles Schoenheider, Jr., in his workshop, hoping to be able to pick up a decoy or two. "Tell you what Kid, see those old geese up in the rafters? You can have them all for $1,000 or $100 each." Joe could make out Canada goose heads and metal feet sticking up into the air. What he found when he stood on a ladder was twelve Charles Schoenheider, Sr., Canada goose decoys; ten standing full-bodied ice decoys, and two floaters. His heart was thumping but that was a lot of money when your weekly paycheck was $75 and you had a pregnant wife and a toddler; so Joe bought two. Came home, sold one for $150 and kept the other for his collection. That was how we built our collection: buy a group of decoys and sell most of them so we could afford to keep one or two of the best.

During the next 35 years we developed lifelong friendships with people from every state and walk of life. This strange passion for decoys broke down all the barriers of age, position, education, and wealth. Rarely a week went by when a collector wasn't stopping by to visit and swap decoys. The decoy shows became our social contact with true friends and the folks that would become the icons of decoy collecting, Joe French, Bill Mackey, Will Pennington, Gene Konopasek, and Hal Sorenson. As decoys have evolved into a major American folk art genre, they often command prices that would stagger the early collectors. Sadly, in many cases the provenance and folklore of a decoy is lost in the frenzy of high prices. Fortunately, although most of the shows and now major decoy auctions have grown into to huge functions, there is still a wonderful underlying camaraderie among collectors who are willing to share their wealth of information with new collectors to perpetuate the nostalgia of their sporting collectibles. Recognizing the need to discourage unscrupulous vendors who will misrepresent the quality of a particular decoy or sell out-and-out fakes, veteran collectors will graciously identify and evaluate decoys if asked. They take seriously a statement of purpose which is found in the by laws of most collecting organizations:

> "The purpose of the Midwest Decoy Collectors is to foster the hobby of decoy collecting by attracting new collectors, seeking out and preserving the old decoys, gathering information about old carvers and their methods for historical records, and to hold an annual show for decoy collectors and carvers for the exchange of information about their origin."

Acknowledgments

When I decided to do another book on decoys, it only seemed natural to combine waterfowling decoys with fish decoys, because their basic function is the same to lure game to the sportsman. Today both types of decoys also lure collectors and it was the collectors who made this book possible. I can't begin to thank everyone who influenced the outcome of this project, yet several deserve a special word of thanks. First and foremost is Joe Tonelli, my partner in life and best friend. His patience and knowledge made an arduous task a lot easier. Because of his ability to recall information about hundreds of decoys and decoy carvers instantly, he is an invaluable source of information on waterfowling traditions and hunting clubs.

Several friends have been stanch supporters of my work since I started to document decoys and their makers. Joseph B. French, our dear friend and one of the first decoy collectors we met many years ago, shared his priceless decoy archives without hesitation. Most of the photographs of the old decoy collections and carvers came from him. Barbara Sorenson, who gave me free access to her late husband Hal's *Decoy Collectors Guide* files including original photographs, unpublished articles, also provided moral support that only another woman can do. Dottie Pennington who at 90 continues to support the Midwest Decoy Collector Association and attends the show each year also shared her late husband Willis's personal files, where he recorded all of the information he had uncovered and kept copies of anything he found in print about decoys and their makers. Becoming seriously involved in decoy collecting during the 1970s, Jim Cook hired Joe Tonelli as a decoy consultant and together they have built one of the finest collections in the world. Jim and his wife, Diane, had many of their Midwest decoys photographed for this project. I will always remember that it was Alan Haid, author of *Decoys of the Mississippi Flyway* and co-author of *Mason Decoys*(with Russ Goldberger), who first assured me that I was capable of writing a decoy book. He and his wife, Elaine, opened their collection and supplied numerous illustrations for this project. George and Miriam VanWalleghem graciously allowed Doug Congdon-Martin, my editor, to invade their home to photograph their exquisite collection of Michigan fish and duck decoys. Gene and Linda Kangas, authors of *Decoys-A North American Survey* and *Decoys*, have always been quick to help, supplying their own decoys and photographing birds for other collectors. To the other collectors, Ron Koch, author of *Decoys of Winnebago Lakes* (Wisconsin decoys), Tim Godard (Schroeder decoys), Gary Lane Meister (Lane decoys), Jim Wierzba (Wisconsin decoys), George Rader (Heddon fish decoys), Dan Yundt (Ohio decoys), Tom Schumaker (Michigan decoys), Gregory Braun. (Ohio decoys), Keith J. Snider (Schmidt decoys), Joseph Engers (photography), Ron and Kathy Fritz, author of *Michigan's Master Carver- Oscar W. Peterson* (Michigan fish decoys), Jim Marsh (Michigan shooting clubs), Jim & Patti Aitkin (Michigan decoys), Don Cassini (Indiana decoys), Lou Schifferl (artwork), Robert Christensen, author of *Duck Calls of Illinois* (duck calls), Herb Desch (Wisconsin decoys), the Dashners, Shirley, Joe and Dean (Wisconsin decoys), Randy and Judy Mayers (Illinois decoys), Christine McAlpin (McAlpin photographs), William Taylor, Jr., (Gromme photographs), Roy Gromme (Gromme decoys), John Redshaw (Redshaw photograph),Tom Whitlock (Ohio decoys), Rosemary Adamson (fish decoys), Bill Klein (Illinois decoys), Fritz and Lori Neuschel (Koehler decoys), Charles Bruno (Illinois decoys), Malcolm Clark (vintage photographs), Carter Stenburg (Minnesota decoys), LeRoy Jarl (vintage photographs), Gary Rieker (duck Calls), and Frank Baron (fish decoys), David Henderson (Minnesota decoys), and Steve Hutton (Perdew photos).Thanks for helping preserve our hobby!

As collectors we owe a special thanks to the following early decoy collectors for their contributions to our hobby:

Willis and Dottie Pennington, co-founders Midwest Decoy Collectors Association

Ralph Loeff, co-founder Midwest Decoy Collectors Association,

Hal and Barbara Sorenson, co-founders Midwest Decoy Collectors, Association, publisher/editor *Decoy Collectors Guide*, co-founder Great Mississippi Valley International Decoy Contest,

Joseph B. French, decoy historian and benefactor,

Alan and Elaine Haid, decoy historian and collector, author, Board Member, Midwest Decoy Collectors Association,

Gene and Shirley Konopasek, President, Midwest Decoy Collectors, Association

Paul Paramlee, decoy historian and collector,

Forrest Loomis, decoy historian and collector, author

Lou Schifferl, unofficial artist for Midwest Decoy Collectors Association, and *Decoy Collectors Guide*

Phyllis Elliston, decoy historian and collector

Ed DeNavarre, decoy historian and collector

Bill Brauer, founder, Wisconsin Decoy Collectors Gathering

Dick Brust, co-founder, Minnesota Decoy Collectors Club

Bob Michaelson, co-founder, Minnesota Decoy Collectors Club, Chairman, Great Mississippi Valley International Decoy Contest,

Hy Dahlka, decoy historian and collector,

Don and Elmira Clark, decoy historian and collector, Founder Henry Decoy Show,
Bill Green, decoy historian and collector, co-founder, Ohio Decoy Carvers and Collectors show,
Ron Koch, author
Gene and Linda Kangas, decoy historians and collectors, authors, past editors Ohio Decoy Carvers and Collectors Newsletter
Barney Crandall, Decoy Historian, collector, author
Ron and Kathy Fritz, author
Art, Annie, and Scott Kimball, decoy historian and collectors
Frank Baron, decoy historian and collector, founder The Great Lakes Fish Decoy Carvers and Collectors Club
John Shoffner, decoy historian and collector, founder The American Fish Decoy Association,
Donald J. Peterson, author

To any collector who I may have inadvertently omitted and their families I offer my sincere apologies.

A note about prices

One of the hardest parts of writing this book was assigning values. Many of the examples used here are in pristine condition, often the finest known, and most collectors wouldn't consider selling their favorite pieces for any price. When a good collectible is sold, many factors influence the price: rarity, condition, regional preferences, auction sales, and ever-changing market trends. With this in mind, the values represent a guideline for collectors and dealers.

Early Midwest Collecting History

Midwest decoy collecting started in earnest during the 1960s by a small group of collectors who gradually discovered that there were others who appreciated the old wooden blocks that were discarded by hunters throughout the country as lighter, cheaper, plastic and paper decoys came on the market. They preserved thousands of decoys that would have been burnt or buried in landfills. Mostly hunters themselves, these early collectors perceived decoys differently than most folk art collectors. Decoys were mementos of an era long past when waterfowl darkened the skies. Those were simpler times when a man didn't spend his day cooped up in an office, when he could join his friends for a day of hunting. Rising before dawn to a hearty breakfast, he would load his wooden decoys, gun, and a lunch into his boat and make his way to his favorite duck hunting spot. There he would watch the sunrise, scan the sky for ducks, and gaze over his rig of decoys gently rocking in the water before him.

As individual collectors realized that they weren't the only ones who collected decoys they began to gather to trade extra decoys and to share the information they found about the carvers and old hunting clubs. Certain men were instrumental in advancing the hobby of decoy collecting in the Midwest. The enthusiasm that Willis Pennington, a La Grange, Illinois traveling salesman, had for decoy collecting was infectious. His route took him throughout the Illinois River Valley where he stopped at every hardware store, barbershop, and local café asking if anyone had any old decoys. This often led him to other collectors. Pennington kept detailed records of every collector he met. Hal Sorenson, a advertising man from Burlington, Iowa, started his pet project, *The Decoy Collector's Guide* during the early 1960s. In 1963 he published the first issue with the help of his wife, Barbara, doing all of the layout work, editing, and much of the writing themselves. For many years, this was the only periodical devoted exclusively to decoys. Joseph B. French, of St Louis, Missouri, was the first major Midwest decoy collector who documented many of the master decoy carvers while they were still alive, capturing them in their workshops on film. French also photographed many of the major decoy collections throughout the country. These records are invaluable today.

During the early days of collecting, collectors in their search for decoys found themselves rummaging through old boathouses, barns, garages, and basements, places where old decoy rigs were stowed and forgotten. If one lived in an area that was hunted extensively, like the Detroit area, the Illinois River Valley, or central Wisconsin, he could amass lots of duplicates. Collectors began to gather to trade these extras. A Charlie Perdew decoy was traded for a Mason decoy, and so on. The first decoy shows were small local gatherings. In 1966, Willis Pennington, Ralph Loeff, and Hal Sorenson decided to organize a formal decoy showing and formed the Midwest Decoy Collectors Association. Invitations were sent out to Sorenson's *Decoy Collectors Guide* mailing list and to Pennington's personal collectors address list. 74 collectors gathered in a meeting room at the Ottawa Holiday Inn, Ottawa, Illinois. From this humble beginning the Association has grown into an international organization, which sponsors an annual convention hosting thousands of collectors, dealers, and a major decoy auction by Guyette and Schmidt Inc., West Farmington, Maine. The Midwest Decoy Collectors' Directory lists collectors from every state of the Union, Canada, the Netherlands, and United Kingdom. The directory is cross-referenced by location so collectors can visit other private collections if they happen to be in the area.

Other annual major decoy functions also developed in other regions and continue to grow: The Pointe Mouille Duck Hunters' Tournament and Decoy Show (Michigan); The Ohio Decoy Collector's Carvers and Collectors Show; The Wisconsin Decoy Collectors' Gathering; and The Minnesota Decoy Collector's Decoy Show. Smaller decoy shows are still popular in most major waterfowling areas. Local events, like the Henry Decoy Show (Illinois), The Edgerton Decoy Show (Wisconsin), and Chillicothe's Optimist Club's Decoy Show (Illinois), are held at school gymnasiums and city parks and retain the flavor of the old decoy gatherings, drawing area hunters and everyday folks who enjoy the local waterfowling lore.

It is only in the past decade that fish decoys have begun to develop as a collecting field. For many Midwest collectors it is deja' vu. Fish spearing began as a very localized sport; the need for thick ice formations on lakes that can support the weight of the fishermen and their shanties means that it remains so. Because of the perceived threat to other forms of sport fishing, winter spearing was never popular in the outdoor life media; therefore there was little documentation on the sport or the fish decoy. In our own experience, Joe and I started spending our entire summers in northern Minnesota in 1980. Our attempts to find hunting decoys in this area were futile. What we did find at the garage sales and local auctions were delightful fish carvings that began another quest for more decoys and information. As we had in the 1960s, we visited with old-timers who shared their local lore. We were able to meet master fish carvers like Chuck Hall and Chet Sawyer. Soon we found others who collected fish decoys, men like Art Kimball, and his sons who authored several books on vintage fishing tackle and fish decoys; Ron Fritz, who documented Michigan grand carver Oscar Peterson's work; Frank Baron, organizer the Great Lakes Fish Decoy Collectors and Carvers; John Shoffner, who spearheaded The American Fish Decoy Association; and Jim and Mary Richards, Minnesota fish collectors. Local pickers and antique dealers became sources for darkhouse boxes filled with decoys and information about the makers. Many of them, like John Goperude, John Banhauser, Ron Adamson, the Meyers brothers (Peter, Michael, Steve and Ben), Ron Holloway, Frank Pasiewicz, Don Peterson, and Joe Tonelli went on to become the core of fish decoy collecting.

Hal Sorenson, Burlington, Iowa, was best known as the publisher of *Decoy Collectors' Guide*, which was the message board for decoy collectors. He encouraged collectors to write down the information they were uncovering about decoys. Hal often organized their rough notes and wrote the articles himself. With the help of his wife, Barbara, Hal edited and did all the layout work, and handled all the distribution. Sorenson was a founding member of the Midwest Decoy Collectors Association and co-organizer of the organization's first show. He also convinced the Greater Mississippi Valley Fair, Davenport, Iowa to host a decoy carving contest. It became a meeting place for decoy collectors and a major annual international competition for contemporary decoy carvers, supported by the old masters like Hector Whittington and Harold Haertel. Judges included notables like Owen Gromme and William Mackey. *Photograph courtesy Joseph B. French.*

Joseph B. French, St Louis, Missouri, was the first major Midwest decoy collector. As early as the mid 1950s, he traveled throughout the country visiting other collectors and many of the master carvers. French recorded his encounters on film and has recently created video presentations based on these visual images. In his attempt to secure the decoy's place as an American art form, French has donated many fine decoys to various museum collections. He also wrote many early articles for *Decoy Collectors Guide, Decoy Magazine,* and *Waterfowl Carving and Collecting. Photograph courtesy Joseph B. French.*

Willis Pennington, LaGrange, Illinois, was one of the major forces that propelled decoy collecting throughout the Midwest. As a traveling salesman, he was the "link" among the small number of early collectors in the Midwest and in many cases the first collector that a novice collector met. Pennington freely shared the information he gleaned about the carvers in numerous articles published in *Decoy Collectors Guide*. He was instrumental in the formation of the Midwest Decoy Collectors' Association, spearheading the organization's first decoy show held in Ottawa, Illinois 1966 and serving as first co-chairman. *Photograph courtesy Joseph B. French.*

DECOY
COLLECTOR'S GUIDE
and Trading Post

No. 1, JANUARY-MARCH 1963 Single Copy 75c

There are many ways of displaying decoy collections. One simple, but effective method is a mass display on open shelving. Shelves are held in place on adjustable brackets.

IN THIS ISSUE

•DECOYS ALONG THE MISSISSIPPI •MASON MALLARDS
•MASTER DECOY MAKERS: LLOYD J. TYLER and W. O. EWINGER
•DECOY DETECTIVE •BOOK REVIEW •THE DELTA MARSH CANVASBACK
•AND MUCH, MUCH MORE

Premier Issue *Decoy Collectors Guide*, Hal Sorenson, Publisher/Editor. Bi-monthly publication 1963-1965, three annuals 1966-67, 1968, 1977.

Finding a crow hunting rig usually meant one owl decoy, at least one crow call, and an assortment of crow decoys. Owl, John Hyatt, Pekin, Illinois; crow decoys by Charles Perdew.

John Ziggly, a Peoria architect hunted over his rig of Perdew decoys, which Tonelli bought out of Ziggly's attic years after Ziggly switched to plastic decoys.

Responding to newspaper ad, Joe Tonelli was able to purchase this rig of Bert Graves decoys, still in gunnysacks, that were stored in the rafters of a Peoria garage.

Buying a pair of old working mallard decoys that were donated to a local Ducks Unlimited chapter's fund raising auction, gave Joe Tonelli a valuable lead to the identity of a previously undocumented Illinois River decoy carver, Douglas Moseley, Princeton, Illinois. Moseley's rig of decoys which included his own carvings, and decoys by Henry Holmes and Charles Shelstrom, had been kept in an attic window seat since his death in 1924.

Ralph Leoff, Hal Sorenson, and Joe French (left to right) discuss the merits of Joe's shorebird display at the first Midwest Decoy Collectors Show held at the Ramada Inn, Ottawa, Illinois, 1966.

Exhibition catalog, *The Wild fowl Decoy- An American Folk Art Tradition*, Rockford Art Association, February-March 1965. Described as: "An unusual. Collection of over 150 exceptional waterfowl decoys assembled from collectors of the Illinois and Wisconsin area.".

Rockford Art Association exhibition *The Wild fowl Decoy An American Folk Art Tradition* 1965.

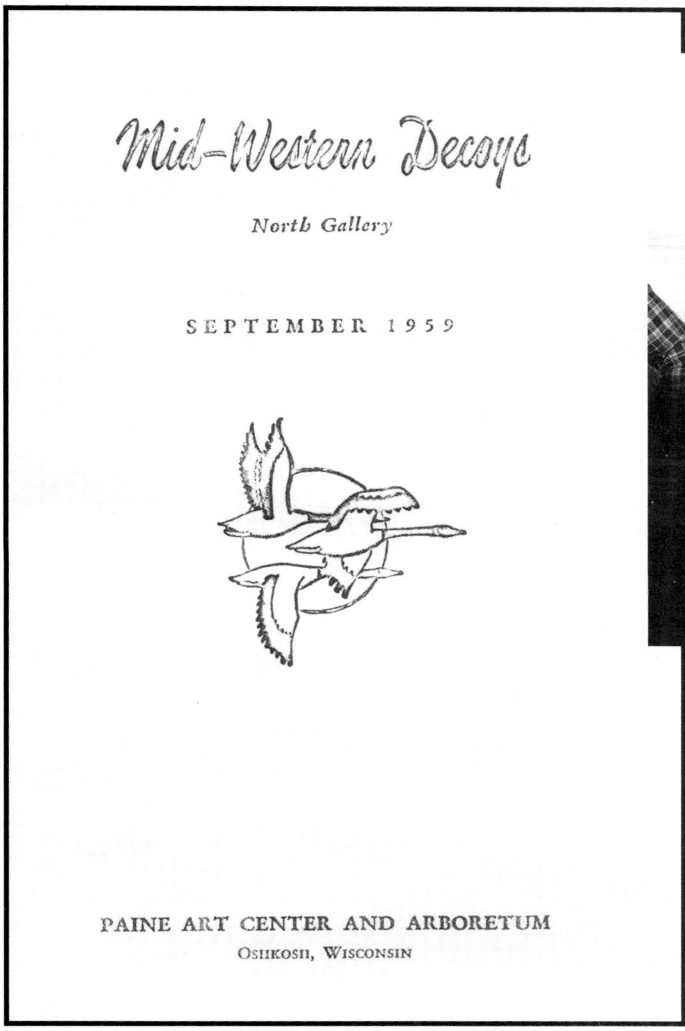

Mid-Western Decoys

North Gallery

SEPTEMBER 1959

PAINE ART CENTER AND ARBORETUM

Oshkosh, Wisconsin

Exhibition catalog, *Mid-Western Decoys*, September 1959, Paine Art Center and Arboretum.

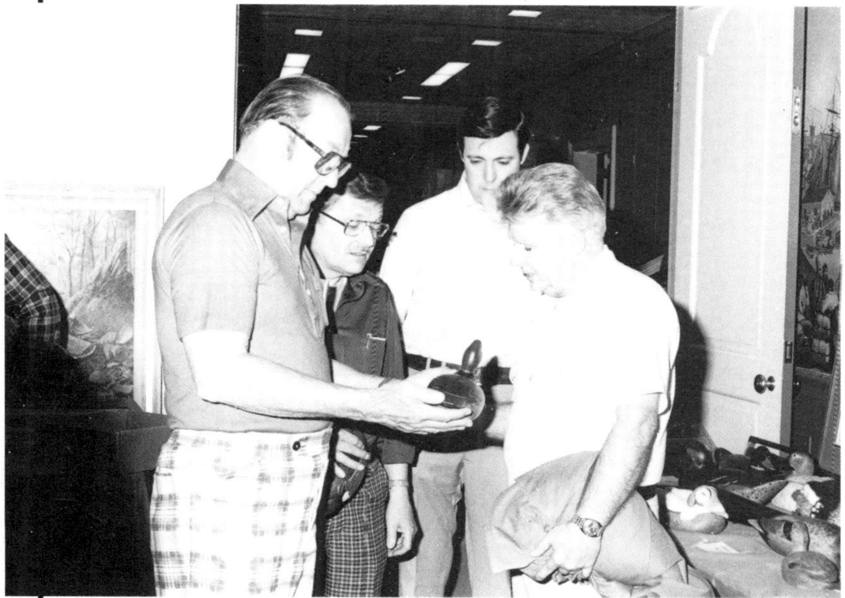

Edward Moore, Gene Konopasek, Richard Clark, and Jim Foote admire a Mason decoy at the 1972 Midwest Decoy Collectors Show at the Drake Oakbrook, Oakbrook, Illinois that would become the home base for the organization's annual show for the next 12 years.

Right and below:
Mid-Western Decoys Exhibition included examples from Illinois, Wisconsin, and Michigan. Decoys were from the collections of Joe French and Lou Schifferl
Photographs by Norman Getchel and courtesy of Joseph B. French.

The Collectors, pre-1975

The following is understandably an incomplete list of the early Midwest decoy collectors from the Great Lakes states. To the collectors that I have inadvertently omitted and their families I offer my sincere apologies. Collectors who have an asterisk beside their name attended the first Midwest Decoy Collectors' Show in 1966.

Illinois

Allen, Mel
Anderlik, Joseph
Billings, Bob
Bruno, Charles
Bill and Rose Claussen
Carr, William *
Clark, Don *
Cole, Robert
Destri, Fred
Dunham, John *
Glick, Herman
Glick, Merle
Haertel, Harold
Humbracht, William
Junker, Gerald *
Klopp, Charles & Isabelle *
Konopasek, Gene & Shirley *
Lashbrook, Virgil *
Leoff, Ralph *
Randy and Judy Mayers
Moore, Charles
Moore, Edward
Paul Paramlee
Pennington, Willis *
Peterson, Donald
Pitt, Harold
Pogemueller, Earl
Reagan, Penn
Ries, Al
Root, Randy
Schmidt, Sandy *
Shaw, Les & Bernice
Siloski, Jerry
Silverman, Donald
Slack, Jim and Pat
Tonelli, Joseph *
Tyler, Bud *
Weeks, Robert
White, Howard *
Zidek, Ladd
Zmuda, Walter

Minnesota

Adamson, Ronald
Banholzer, John
Brust, Richard
Gene Dankowski
"Digger"
Goperude, John
Green, William
Holloway, Ronald
Jarl, Leroy
Jordan, William
Kieser, Jack
Leiferman, Robert
Lindgren, John
Meyers Peter
Meyers, Ben
Meyers, Michael
Meyers, Stephen
Michaelson, Robert *
Olsen, Ollie
Pasiewicz, Frank
Richards, Jim & Mary
"Stan, the man"
Typell, Richard

Wisconsin

Appel, Bud
Balzer, Jim
Belonger, Brian
Bosworth, Marion and Robinson Jr.
Buffmire, Al *
Brauer, William
Clark, Malcolm
Cole, Don
Dashner, Dean
Dashner, Joe and Shirley
Edwards, Dennis
Gromme, Owen
Hanson, Arthur *
Johnson, William & Norma
Kimball, Arthur & Annie
Kimball, Scott
Koch, Ronald
Koebel, Gary
Ludwig, Roger
Markam, Grigsbee *
Neil, Jim
Personius, Robert
Schifferl. Lou
Schultz, Paul
Schultz, William
Shostak, Ben
Spengler, David *
Whaley, Kirt

Ohio

Bednaick, Karl
Dwyer, Robert
Feasal, William
Glassmeyer, Stan
Green, William
Haid, Alan & Elaine
Kangas, Gene & Linda
Meder, Richard
Potter, Colonel
Price, Robert
Purvis, John
Simmons, Al
Wiesenberger, David
White, David
Winstel, Thomas
Yundt, Dan

Indiana

Cassini, Don
Delph, John
Giaçoletto, Bernard
Schaffer, Paul

Michigan

Adams, Jerry
Aitkin, Jim
Barron, Frank
Bowman, Edward M.D. *
Carnighi, Len
Catana, Jerry,
Childs, Edward
Crandall, Barney
Dahlka, Hy
Dekoniack, Charles

DeNavarre, Edward *
Elliston, Phyllis *
Foote, Jim
Fritz, Ron
Hall Julie
Hall, Gary
Hall, Michael
Jackson, Lowell
Jones, John & Midge
Kane, F.J.
LeZott, Edward
Shoffner, John
Seitz, Harry
Swanson, Ron
Van Walleghem, George & Miriam
Votens, Abner
Walsh, Clune

Left:
Charles Klopp, Palatine, Illinois and his wife Isabelle hosted a typical informal gathering of decoy collectors at their home each year. At this backyard picnic, the men would spread out their extra decoys on the grass and picnic tables and proceed to trade decoys. *Photograph courtesy Joseph B. French.*

Gene Konopasek, a well-rounded sportsman, never limited his collecting to waterfowl decoys. At any Midwest flea market or collector show, he could be seen buying decoys, original cover art, advertising posters and calendars, game plates, fishing reels, fish decoys, vintage tackle and outboard motors, advertising buttons, Ducks Unlimited pins, black powder tins, and anything else that might be related to hunting and fishing. He and his wife, Shirley, used his collections to decorate their home in Fox River Grove, Illinois. In 1976 he was elected president of the Midwest Decoy Collectors Association and continued to serve as the chairman of their annual convention until 1995. *Photograph 1982, courtesy Shirley Konopasek.*

Bill Brauer used this photo of himself and Donna Tonelli with one of her contemporary carvings to promote The 1978 Wisconsin Decoy Collectors Gathering held each spring at the Pioneer Inn Resort on Lake Winnebago, Oshkosh, Wisconsin. The show started out as a small gathering of decoy collectors held in the back room of a Fond du Lac tavern on a Sunday afternoon. With help of fellow Wisconsin collectors, Roger Ludwig, Gary Koebel and Tom Beardsley, Bill built the show into a major Midwest decoy collectors' event.

Edward Moore, DeKalb, Illinois, served as co-chairman of the second Midwest Decoy Collectors Association decoy show held in DeKalb, in 1967 with Bud Tyler, and Donald Silverman, also of DeKalb. Like most of the early decoy collectors he loved duck hunting and always welcomed other collectors into his home. *Photograph courtesy Joseph B. French.*

Right:
Lou Shifferl, who started to collect decoys in 1958, was one of the first Wisconsin decoy collecters. Also one of the state's premier artists, Shifferl used his artwork to support the decoy collecting community, giving countless original ink and ink drawings, first to Sorenson's *Decoy Collectors Guide* and now the Midwest Decoy Collectors Association.

Bill Green, shown with a William Enright Canada goose decoy, was present in 1978 when fourteen fellow collectors met at the Cleveland Museum of Natural History. Together they laid the ground-work of the Ohio Decoy Collectors Association. Green served as the chairman of the association's annual decoy carvers and collectors show for many years. *Photograph courtesy Tom Whitlock.*

Paul Parmalee took on a major project with Forrest Loomis during the mid-1960s. Commissioned by the state of Illinois, they attempted to document all of the decoys and decoy carvers of the state. They blanketed the state with questionnaires and compiled the data into *Decoys and Decoy Carvers of Illinois*, which remains one of the most comprehensive books on decoys ever published. *Photograph courtesy Joseph B. French.*

Although relatively unknown to contemporary collectors, Al Simmons, Cleveland, Ohio, was the first Ohio decoy collector. Before his death, he compiled one of the finest collections in the country and donated many of his decoys to Cleveland Museum. *Photograph courtesy Joseph B. French.*

Don Clark is the founder and organizer of the Henry (Illinois) Decoy Show, first held in 1968 only blocks away from the home of Charles and Edna Perdew. The show continues to be strongly supported by locals and decoy collectors alike and has been able to retain the social atmosphere of the early decoy shows. A personal friend of Charles Perdew, Clark donated a Perdew decoy to the Shelbourne Museum, the first in their collection. *Photograph courtesy Joseph B. French.*

Right:
Phyllis Elliston was Michigan's first serious decoy collector. Her collection, which was housed in a converted church, included 1,000 decoys. Phyllis was one of the few early collectors who concentrated part of her collecting on fish decoys. Like many veteran collectors she welcomed and encouraged new collectors. *Photograph courtesy Joseph B. French.*

Edward DeNavarre, Detroit, Michigan, was a major force among the Michigan decoy collectors. In his search for decoys DeNavarre located and handled more great Michigan decoys than any other decoy collector and became an ardent student of St. Clair Flats waterfowling folklore. An avid duck hunter, he was involved with the establishment of the Michigan Decoy Show and the Pointe Mouille Duck Hunter's Tournament and served as the show chairman for over 15 years. *Photograph courtesy Joseph B. French.*

Jim Aitkin, collecting since the early 1970s, has been able to build one of the finest collections of decoys from his home state of Michigan and serves on the Midwest Decoy Collectors Association's Board of Directors.

Right:
Jim Foote worked with the Michigan State Wildlife Department. He excelled as a collector and a professional wildlife artist. His carved working and decorative waterfowl and fish decoys, as well as doing flat artwork. His decoy knowledge was well respected and he was often called upon to serve as a judge in the different carving competitions. Foote's impressive Michigan decoy collection includes great waterfowl and fish decoy. *Photograph courtesy Joseph B. French.*

Hy Dalka and Jim Foote worked together organizing the Monroe Michigan Decoy Show and the contemporary decoy carving competition held in conjunction with the Pointe Mouille Duck Hunter's Tournament held at the Pointe Mouille State Refuge. Dalka knew the hunting areas around his home like the back of his hand and was able the acquire thousands of decoys; he was a major source for top quality Michigan decoys. He became a living legend among collectors who were always welcome in his basement as long as they waited until afternoon to call. *Photograph courtesy Joseph B. French.*

Dick Brust, Minneapolis, helped many Minnesotans to develop their decoy collecting hobby. Together with Robert Michaelson, Brust organized the Minnesota Decoy Collectors Club and served as co-chairmen at the clubs first annual decoy show. Specializing in collecting teal decoys, Dick is one of the few men who can say he never sold a decoy. *Photograph courtesy Joseph B. French.*

Robinson Bosworth (left) and son, Tom, show off their geese shot at The Island Club, Lake Butte des Morts, Wisconsin, 1967. Photograph courtesy T. Thompson Bosworth.

Stan Glassmeyer was a quiet man who helped men like Alan Haid when they first collecting. Cincinnati, Ohio.

Colonel & Mrs. Potter, Columbus, Ohio.

Robert Michaelson, a major force among the Midwest decoy collectors. Michaelson, a contemporary and friend of nationally renowned decoy collector William Mackey, was responsible for bringing Mackey as a guest speaker at the early Minnesota decoy shows. *Photograph courtesy Joseph B. French.*

Alan Haid, author of *Decoys of the Mississippi Flyways* , *Mason Decoys* and numerous articles, Cincinnati, Ohio, presently Darien, Connecticut.

Left:
Grigsbee Markam, Milwaukee, Wisconsin helped build the impressive Milwaukee Public Museum decoy collection by securing a major purchase of outstanding decoys from William Mackey during the late 1960s. At the Museum's wetlands exhibition in 1969 room-sized dioramas, designed and painted by William Schultz, showcased these decoy acquisitions This collection of waterfowling decoys, which has been is storage for the last 30 years was exhibited with the help of a second generation collector Tom Bosworth, son of Robinson Bosworth.

Bill Cox and his wife proudly pose with his exquisite decoy collection.

Right:
John Delph, an early Indiana collector, now lives in Ponte Vedra Florida. He has authored two major books on decoys, *New England Decoys*, and *Factory Decoys~ Mason, Stevens, Dodge, & Peterson.*

Virgil Lashbrook, Pekin, Illinois, is one of the last surviving makers of classic Illinois River hunting decoys. During the early days of collecting, one could always find a nice selection of good Illinois River decoys in his personal collection.

Dr Ed Bowman, was one of the earliest Michigan decoy collectors, Grosse Pointe, Michigan.

As a young man, Randy Root built one of the finest Mason Decoy collections in the country and unquestionably the great Midwest duck hunting area, Mallard Farms, Metamora, Illinois.

Gene and Linda Kangas provided collectors with priceless documentation on duck and fish decoys through their numerous articles and books. They were actively involved with the Ohio Decoy Carvers and Collectors Association and edited the club's newsletter for years.

Gene Schmidt, Rockford, Illinois, at one time owned the finest group of decoys branded G.K. Schmidt (no relation), including Charles Perdew decoys of various species and pristine Premier Grade Mason decoys, which were found stored in a Midwest bank vault, circa 1965.

Left:
Fellow collectors, Ron Adamson and LuAnn Forbes haggle out a deal on fish decoys at the Midwest Decoy Collectors Association convention, 2000. Before his untimely death, Adamson, a veteran Minnesota picker turned collector, was a great source for decoys and information and actively promoted Minnesota decoys. His greatest find was Leroy Howell's forgotten inventory of fish decoys, which were stored in an outhouse on the family farm, circa 1980.

Frank Baron, Livonia, Michigan has authored, *Bud Stewart, Michigan's Legendary Lure Maker*, *One Fish, Two Fish, Green Fish, Blue Fish*, and *Commercial Fish Decoys*, as well as numerous articles. He is a driving force in the fish decoy collecting field and co-founder of the Great Lakes Fish Decoy Collectors & Carvers Association.

John Shoffner, Michigan was instrumental in the forming of the American Fish Decoy Association, which sponsors an annual show and fish decoy carving competition each fall and publishes a regular newsletter. Shoffner's decoy shows are widely supported by fish decoy collectors and contemporary carvers.

Art Kimball and his son, Scott, penned and self-published the first books devoted exclusively to the fish decoy with the help of Art's wife, Annie. Their three volume edition of *The Fish Decoy* is considered the fish decoy collector's bible. Their groundwork inspired other collectors to document their decoys. Living in the north woods of Wisconsin, the Kimballs are a driving force not only among collectors of vintage decoys, but also contemporary fish decoy carving. The Kimball's remain actively involved with all facets of fish decoy carving and collecting.

John Goperude is one of the largest dealers in vintage Minnesota fish decoys and vintage fishing tackle. Long before fish decoy collecting became popular John was picking up decoys. Collectors anxiously await his mailings, which list decoys he has for sale.

Introduction Fish & Fowl Decoys of the Great Lakes

The Midwest has always been a major center for waterfowling and spear fishing, especially in the regions surrounding four of the Great Lakes; Lake Michigan, Lake Superior, Lake Huron, and Lake Erie. The lakes began to form eons ago. During prehistoric times lava flowed creating a rock basin that lies beneath the lakes. In the course of the great Ice Age, massive glaciers spread and receded through this region smashing and grinding up everything in their path and transforming the landscape. Many geologists believe the Great Lakes were carved out by a mighty ancient river system that once flowed into Hudson Bay or down the St. Lawrence River. As the ice sheets ripped up the surrounding terrain, natural dams and dikes were formed that altered the river's drainage and produced the Great Lakes. This same movement of ice was also responsible for creating thousands of Midwest lakes, wetlands, and marshes. The ice scooped out lakebeds, many of which gradually filled in with peat to become fertile marshes. These great marshes surrounding the Great Lakes were teeming with wildlife.

Rose Ignoski, of Wisconsin poses with her catch of the day on Lake Winnebago, circa 1950. Small fish decoys were used to lure large prey fish like this sturgeon within striking distance. *Photograph courtesy Rose Ignoski.*

The native peoples of the continental North America learned how to tap into this rich resource. Accounts and diaries of the earliest trappers and explorers of this new land told of Native Americans using lures to facilitate their hunting and fishing.

Natives used several types of fish and waterfowl decoys. They were usually quickly made and disposable: A tree branch with a profile that resembled a duck or goose head was stuck into a body form shaped out of mud or the head of a dead bird was propped up with a forked stick. A notable exception was the Tule Decoys, found in a cave nestled in Nevada's Humboldt Sink in 1924. Bundled in a rush mat hidden in the bottom of a seed-storage pit under a false bottom were 11 finely crafted canvasback decoys and two bundles of snares made of string and twigs. The earliest known hunting decoys, they are believed to be from the Lovelock Culture circa 1100 A.D. Now housed at the Smithsonian Institute, the canvasback Tule Decoys were fashioned out of tightly woven and tied native marsh grasses called tule. The decoys were stained with berry juices and decorated with duck feathers.

Since a fish decoy was small, it could be easily carried on one's person. Fish decoys were durable but simple fish forms of bone, shell, or wood. Wood fish decoys were formed out of small sticks that were stained or decorated with burnt markings. Bits of leather or yarn were added as attractors. Small stones added the weight needed to submerge the decoy. Although present day collectors would like to believe that the fish decoy originated in North America, archaeologists have found prehistoric fish decoys in the Neolithic sites of southeast Siberia. Since use of fish decoys and spearing has been documented throughout most of northern Asia, it is probable that ancient peoples brought the knowledge of luring fish with a decoy with them as they migrated across the Bering Straits into North America. Small prehistoric shellfish forms believed to be decoys have been unearthed as far south as Fulton County, Illinois.

As Europeans of every nationality settled in North America, they brought with themselves the crafts of their native lands. These skills were assimilated with the Native concept of decoying waterfowl and fish. Since the lifestyles of the new settlers was less mobile, the decoys they developed were more detailed and used year after year. These decoys are now recognized as functioning folk art forms. Made as tools to enhance the sportsman's success, decoys embody the individual maker's interpretations of what would attract his prey. Waterfowl tend to flock together, feeding and resting in groups. Waterfowl decoys are attempts to recreate the natural settings of the birds they are meant to attract. The spear fisherman on the other hand needed to provide bait to attract large fish of prey. His decoys represented small baitfish and critters. A notable exception to this rule is sturgeon decoys. Sturgeon will congregate so they are attracted to other sturgeon, so a larger sturgeon decoy is used. The large sturgeon decoy sometimes served a second purpose. Government regulations set size limits on sturgeon as a conservation method to protect breeding stock. To comply with this rule, fishermen would sometimes use a large sturgeon decoy to gauge the size of the fish that came into their hole.

Waterfowling in the Great Lakes regions was mostly limited to duck and goose hunting, but the methods of hunting varied as much as the terrains of each state. The decoys produced in the various hunting locales reflect these differences. Although there recently has been a growing interest in early molded paper mache and plastic decoys, generally speaking most collectible hunting decoys are carved of wood and painted. Decoy heads were carved separately and attached to the body. Bodies were carved of wood and sometimes cork. Depending on the type of waterfowling setting, the decoy bodies were either solid or hollow to reduce the weight of the decoy. A rig of decoys could contain as few as six or as many as several hundred, depending on the type of waterfowling. For example a lone hunter who was jump shooting mallard or teal along a river in Ohio may throw out a few decoys in a widening of the river while someone who was shooting diver ducks on large open waters of Lake St. Clair, could position a layout boat amid a raft of hundreds of canvasback and bluebill decoys.

Because the natural hunting conditions dictated the design of the decoy certain common traits created identifiable decoy carving schools in most hunting areas like Illinois River Decoys, St. Clair Flats Decoys, etc. There are also several different categories of decoy carvers. While some hunters made decoys for their own use and limited local distribution, others made their livelihood producing decoys, game calls, and hunting boats for paying customers. There were also a number of factories that manufactured extensive lines of decoys.

Game calls were another important tool used by Midwest waterfowlers. Developed especially for the hunter, duck, goose and crow calls added alluring sounds to a hunter's decoy spread. Here again the maker's creativity and skill created beautifully turned wooden reed instruments. There are two classifications of callers: tongue-pinchers; and barrel calls with separate tone board and reed. The tongue-pincher call lent itself well to making the purring calls of diving ducks or loud caws of the common crow. With its broader range of notes, the barrel call enabled a duck hunter to recreate the varying calls used by the mallard, a popular game bird. Some game calls reflect the ingenuity of the makers, moving them clearly into the area of folk art. The form of a call often has more to do with the value of a particular call than the quality of the sounds it makes. Some call makers used exotic woods laminated into geometric designs. Checkering similar to the techniques used by gunsmiths to decorate their gunstocks and forearms was also a common form of decoration on game calls. Other call makers sculpted the barrels of their calls, added metal bands, or grooved rings. The most elaborate game calls involved relief carved scenes, and personalizing carved initials on the call's barrel.

In the northern states of Michigan, Wisconsin, and Minnesota, spearing through the ice was a popular method of fishing. Locals would spear game fish indiscriminately in the little shanties on the frozen lakes. On the larger lakes, fish buyers would pull their sleds out onto the ice, buying fish directly for pennies a pound. As the number of sport fishermen using bait casting lures and flies increased, they began to notice their catches becoming smaller. They lobbied for restrictions and limits to protect the fish populations. Although winter spear fishing is still practiced today, it is severely limited.

Unlike the more popular bait casting and fly-fishing, spear fishing was the sport of the hearty locals. Most carved their own fish decoys. As with any folk art form, some carvers excelled in their craft and soon began supplying other fishermen with decoys creating a small cottage industry. Yet even the most ambitious decoy makers marketed their decoys in a limited area, often selling them at local taverns, bait shops, and hardware stores. Although a few major commercial tackle companies offered limited fish decoy product lines, fish decoys were mostly a regional art form and as such offer extensive variety and form to the collector.

In the following chapters, the reader will see hundreds of examples of true Americana. As a collector, the author realizes that other collectors want to see as many examples as possible to help them identify and recognize the various makers. With this in mind, *Fish and Fowl of the Great Lakes* is a pictorial history of Midwest waterfowling and spear fishing decoys. Since the physical terrain and population of each locality strongly influenced the types of decoys that were used and produced, this text will be organized by states. Keeping in mind that the identities of certain decoy carvers may never be known, the unknown decoy will also be covered. Some of these anonymous artists created delightful pieces of Americana with their own recognizable styles. This has enabled collectors to labeled unknown works with fictitious names, which have become accepted and will be used in this text as attributed to. Other carvings by unknown makers can only be documented and dated by their owners as to where they were used. Many such examples will be included in this text because of quality and artistry they represent and in the hope that some will be recognized and identified correctly.

Although most ice shanties were compact and left little extra room for more than one fisherman, there were usually other shanties close by so spear fishermen could share their experiences. Here Bob Hendrickson, holding his decoy, poses with a fishing buddy in front of his darkhouse on the Mississippi River at La Crosse Wisconsin, circa 1935. *Photograph courtesy Bob Hendrickson.*

Ohio and Indiana

By the mid-1800s, hunting and fishing were just beginning to change from subsistence activities to sporting pastimes. Many still actively pursued market hunting as a part-time occupation. Most market hunters shot heavily for a short period, when the great masses of waterfowl were in their areas, then they returned to their daily farming activities. As the Industrial Revolution came into full swing, businesses needed more and more people to work in the factories and offices instead of working the land. Work schedules became relatively fixed and uniform, creating blocks of leisure time for the worker. Improvements in guns and ammunition made it easier for the average man to own an accurate firearm and become a fairly good shot. The development of railroad systems made it possible for a sportsman to travel in relative comfort to a good hunting area. In time sportsmen realized the need to preserve and protect the wetlands. They banded together in organizations forming managed wetland areas to entice waterfowl and set up shooting hours and rest areas to ensure the return of the game.

Ohio and Indiana waterfowling history began long before the other Midwestern states. Hundreds of marshes along the northern shores of Lake Erie in Ohio once formed a chain of feeding and resting places that supported great migrations of waterfowl. And the Grand Marsh of the Kankakee River in Indiana originally contained approximately 500,000 acres of prime waterfowling habitat. Wetlands and prairie habitats were continuously intertwined with the Kankakee River as it meandered its way from South Bend Indiana to the Illinois state line, taking a 240-mile winding trek to cover the 75-mile distance. Unfortunately progress came early to these regions. With it came the farmer who viewed the wetlands as wasted grounds. These great watershed systems fell to ambitious drainage projects that would convert waterfowling paradises into fertile farmland.

Initial efforts to drain the Grand Kankakee Marsh began as early 1873. By 1917, the great winding 240 mile Kankakee River was reduced to a 88 miles of dredged channel. The white man had conquered the land early surveyors described as "The Land that God Forgot." Prior to this, hunters came to the Kankakee for superb shooting at clubs like the Louisville Kentucky club, the Columbian Hunting Club, named in honor of the Columbian World Fair, and the Hovey Lake Hunting Club. Most enjoyed pass shooting or hunted over live decoys and obviously had little need of wooden decoys. Consequently there are only rare examples of true Indiana decoys

Waterfowl crisscross the northern part of Ohio funneling into the Mississippi Flyway. Although most of the Lake Erie marshes are gone today, hunters preserved parts of this once vast wetland by forming hunting clubs as early as 1857. Some of the better-known clubs are Cedar Point Club, the Toussant Club (est. 1885), the McGee Marshes (originally known as the Crane Creek Club), the Ottawa Club (est. 1871, originally known as the Hones Club), and Winous Point Club (est. 1857). These clubs have been forced over the years to maintain extensive water-control levees and dikes to protect the aquatic plant life, which is often replanted each year at great cost. Granted, their acts were self-motivating, but considering the cost of waterfowling, today's club members have inherited a heavy responsibility to save the traditions of this grand shooting sport for future generations. In some cases the government has stepped in to take over their tasks, but without the foresight of these early waterfowling gentlemen, the entire wetlands may have been lost.

What has also been lost in many cases is the information about the men who carved the great Ohio decoys. Few have been identified and sadly it is doubtful that anyone can document these carvers because of their age, most being active before 1900. In many cases, matching the brands and markings used by individual hunters to identify their hunting rigs with old club records has dated Ohio decoys. Still these decoys are characterized by a form and style found in true sculpture. The artistry of these unknown carvers is easily appreciated.

Although spear fishing has rarely been considered a sport in Ohio or Indiana, both states were home to major tackle companies, Creek Chub Bait Company, South Bend Tackle Company, and Pflueger's Enterprise Manufacturing Company. These companies each offer at least one style of fish spearing decoy in their product lines.

Mallard drake, Frank Davis, New Philadelphia, Ohio, circa 1946. $200. *Collection of and photography by Gregory Braun.*

Black duck, rare calling style, William T. Enright (1913-1979), Maumee Bay, Toledo, Ohio, circa 1940. $700. *Collection of Dan and Karen Yundt.*

Pintail drake, cork body, wooden head, William T. Enright. Toledo, circa 1940. $500. *Collection of and photography by Gregory Braun.*

Pintail drake, William Enright, Toledo, Ohio, circa 1948. $500. *Collection of Dan and Karen Yundt.*

Canvasback drake; with canvasback drake "stick-up" heads used in mud or shallow marsh grass along shore, Ferdinand Going, Marblehead, Port Clinton, noted market gunner, circa 1880. Stick-ups, $250 each; decoy. $500. *Collection of Dan and Karen Yundt.*

Canvasback pair, sleepers, William T. Enright, Toledo, Ohio, circa 1940. $600. *Collection of Alan and Elaine Haid. Photography Alan Haid.*

Background: canvasback drake, wooden; $850. Foreground: canvasback, rare cast iron wing duck. It weighed down a sink box so its platform was just at the water's level. One of three known examples; Fred Harris, Port Clinton, Ohio, circa 1900. $1,500. *Collection of Dan and Karen Yundt.*

Canvasback drakes, hollow, Ned J. Hauser, circa 1850. $2,000. *Collection of Gene and Linda Kangas. Photography by Gene Kangas.*

Mallard hen, raised carved wings, Robert Haldeman, Bolivar, Ohio, circa 1948. $500. *Collection of and photography by Gregory Braun.*

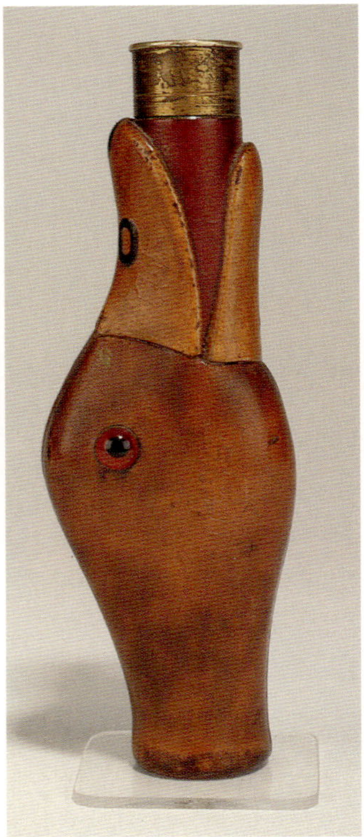

Duck call, carved duck head with shot shell in mouth, C.L.V. Kinney and William F. Harlow, Newark, Ohio, circa 1890. Leather is stretched over the wooden duck head. Kinney & Harlow is stamped into the brass casing of the shot shell. Extremely rare limited production call. A similar call sold for a world record price of $60,000 at the Guyette & Schmidt Inc/ Sotheby's Inc auction of Dr. James McCleery's collection in 1999. $35,000.

Canvasback drake, only known example, solid, Ned John Hauser (1826-1900), Sandusky, Ohio, who is the earliest documented decoy carver from Ohio, circa 1880. $2,000. *Collection of and photography by Gregory Braun.*

Guns, from $2.50. Rifles, from $4.00. Send for Catalogue.

MEM. FROM
B. KITTREDGE & CO.
CINCINNATI, O.

DECOY DUCKS OF HEART STOCK,
WHITE CEDAR.

NATURAL FORM—FOUR COAT OIL PAINTED.

Cincinnati, ______ 188

Dear Sir:

Yours of ______ received Enclosed Bill ______ Bill Lading Catalogue mailed if called for.

Letterhead, B. Kitteredge & Company, Cincinnati, Ohio, circa 1880. Although nothing has surfaced about this company to date, the graphics illustrate a high quality decoy line. Similar to Dodge Decoy Company, this could be the maker of early Dodge -style decoys used at Ohio hunting clubs like Winous Point and Ottawa Club.

Canvasback drake, high head style, C. Klopping, Point Place (Toledo), Ohio. Klopping decoys are branded under their keel "C. Klopping," suggesting this was the maker not owner of the decoy, circa 1930. $1,000. *Collection of Dan and Karen Yundt*.

John Fredrick "Jack" Rider (1881-1967), Middle Harbor, Port Clinton, Ohio circa 1940. *Photograph courtesy Shirley, Joe, and Dean Dashner*.

Canvasback drakes, used at Barr Creek Hunting Club, Charles Redding, Fremont, Ohio, circa 1930. $400 each. *Collection of Dan and Karen Yundt*.

Redhead drake, John F. Rider, Port Clinton, circa 1940. $500. *Collection of Alan and Elaine Haid. Photography by Alan Haid.*

Great horned owl, exceptional one-of-kind decoy and, without question, the finest decoy ever produced in the state. Jack Rider, Middle Harbor, Port Clinton, Ohio, circa 1930. $50,000. *Collection of Jerry Catana.*

Canada goose, "Watch Gander," John F. "Jack" Rider, circa 1920. $3,000. *Collection of Dan and Karen Yundt.*

Assorted miniatures, John Fredrick "Jack" Rider, Middle Harbor, Port Clinton, Ohio, circa 1940. $700 each. *Collection of Alan and Elaine Haid. Photography by Alan Haid.*

Mallard pair, hen sleeper, John Sharon, Toledo, Ohio. $500 pair. *Collection of Dan and Karen Yundt.*

Bluebill drake, used on Sandusky River, "Yorky" Sting, Fremont, Ohio, circa 1925. $350. *Collection of Dan and Karen Yundt.*

Canvasback drake, unknown maker, branded "Sellers," founding member Hones Point/Ottawa Shooting Club, circa 1870, Port Clinton, Ohio, $1,500; shot shell box, Quick Shot Loaded Shells, 10 gauge, Peters Cartridge Company, Cincinnati, Ohio, circa 1920, $1,000.

Redhead drake, unknown maker, Blair School, found and used at hunting club near Sandusky, Ohio, circa 1880. $4,000. *Collection of Alan and Elaine Haid. Photography by Alan Haid.*

Mallard hen, hollow, unknown maker, Blair School, Port Clinton, Ohio, circa 1880, $1,500; shot shell box, Popular Shot, 10 gauge, Peters Cartridge Company, Cincinnati, Ohio, extremely rare, circa 1910. $1,000.

Bluebill hens, unknown maker, Sandusky Bay, Ohio, early Dodge Decoy Company style, circa 1880, $500 each; shot shell box, Peters Referee, 12 gauge, Peters Cartridge Company, Cincinnati, Ohio, circa 1920. $450. *Collection of Dan and Karen Yundt.*

Green-winged teal, unknown maker, Blair School, used at Winous Point Shooting Club, circa 1870. $2,500. *Collection Gene and Linda Kangas. Photography by Gene Kangas.*

Canvasback drake, "bull neck" style, unknown maker, Sandusky Bay, Port Clinton, Ohio, branded "CLARKE," member Winous Point Gun Club 1878, circa 1870. $2,000. *Collection of Tom Burrier.*

Mallard drake, unknown maker, Sandusky Bay, Ohio, early Dodge Decoy Company style, circa 1880, $1,000; shot shell box, Quick Shot Crimped shells, 10 gauge, Peters Cartridge Company, Cincinnati, Ohio, circa 1910. $1,000.

Redhead drake, unknown maker, Sandusky Bay, Port Clinton, Ohio, branded "W. H. Harris," Winous Point Shooting Club member 1870. $2,500. *Collection of Dan and Karen Yundt.*

Black duck, hollow exact rig mate to decoys captured in a 1864 daguerreotype photo taken at Winous Point Shooting Club, unknown maker Sandusky Bay, Port Clinton, Ohio, circa 1850. $1,000. *Collection of Dan and Karen Yundt.*

Redhead, unknown maker, J. H. Porter Rig, Winous Point Shooting Club, circa 1870. $2,000. *Collection of Gene and Linda Kangas. Photography of Gene Kangas.*

Black duck, unknown maker, Port Clinton, Ohio, stamped G. A. S. for George Stanley, same unknown maker as pintail preener decoy in Winous Point Shooting Club collection, circa 1857. $3,000. *Collection Dan and Karen Yundt.*

Black duck, hollow, unknown maker, J. H. Porter Rig, Winous Point Shooting Club, circa 1870. $3,000. *Collection of Gene and Linda Kangas. Photography of Gene Kangas.*

Canvasback drake, unknown maker, George Stanley Rig, Winous Point Shooting Club, circa 1870. $1,500. *Collection of Gene and Linda Kangas. Photography Gene Kangas.c*

Background: bluebill drake, hollow; foreground: mallard drake, hollow; unknown maker, Port Clinton, Ohio: circa 1870. This maker's decoys have been found in rigs owned by J.H. Biter and George A. Stanley, founding members of the prestigious Winous Point Shooting Club. $1,000 each. *Collection of Dan and Karen Yundt.*

Blue-winged teal, unknown maker George Stanley Rig, Winous Point Shooting Club, circa 1870. $2,000. *Collection of Gene and Linda Kangas. Photography of Gene Kangas.*

Minnow, 7", early model with no fins, soft rubber, which hardened and became very brittle with age, thus few survived; patented 1882 Pflueger (Enterprise Manufacturing Company), Akron, Ohio, circa 1895. $2,500.

Blue-winged teal, unknown maker, R. White, Winous Point Shooting Club, circa 1880. $1,500. *Collection of Gene and Linda Kangas. Photography by Gene Kangas.*

Background: green-winged teal, $2,000. Foreground: mallard drake, $2,000; rig mates, branded "Worthington," member Winous Point Shooting Club, 1874, unknown maker, Port Clinton, Ohio, John Blair style painting, circa 1874. *Collection of Dan and Karen Yundt.*

Canvasback drake, John Vickers, Maumee Bay, Toledo, Ohio, circa 1930. $1,000. *Collection of Tom Burrier.*

Minnow, 7", finned model, soft rubber, Pflueger (Enterprise Manufacturing Company), Akron, Ohio, circa 1895. $2,500. *Photograph courtesy of Frank Baron.*

Minnow, wooden model, Pflueger (Enterprise Manufacturing Company), Akron, Ohio, listed in pre-1900 Pflueger catalogs but not illustrated, extremely rare. $4,000. *Photograph courtesy of Frank Baron.*

Blue-winged teal, Paul Lipke, Whitting Indiana, circa 1940. $5,000. *Collection of James R. and Diane Cook.*

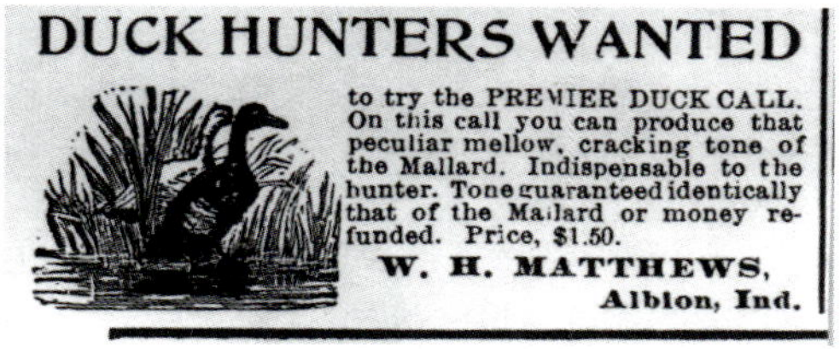

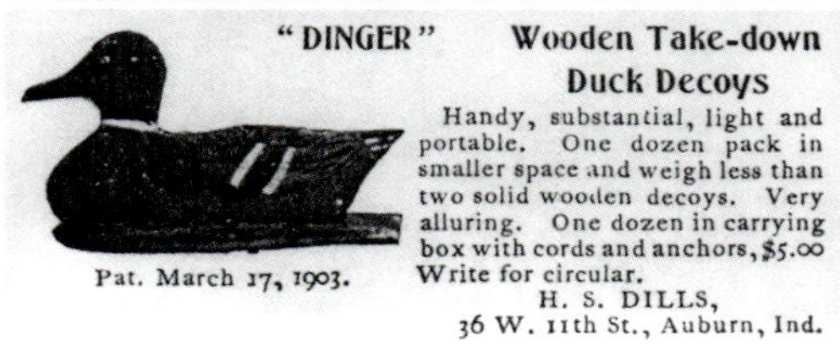

The only records of some early decoy producers are the ads that are found in old sporting magazines. Examples: H.S. Dills, Auburn, Indiana; the "Dinger" folding silhouette decoys; Boyd Martin Decoy Company, Delphi, Indiana, crow hunting set, which included stuffed canvas owl with flappable wings, three stuff crow decoys, and walnut crow call; W.H. Matthews, Albion, Indiana, Premier Duck Call.

Hoosier Crow Call, George H. Garrison, Delphi, Indiana, circa 1940. $200.

Bernard E. Ohnmacht, (1889-1975), Lafayette, Indiana, proudly posed with his decoys and a day's bag, circa 1960. Ohnmacht returned to his home state and settled in Lafayette, Indiana, building an extensive aviary where he raised ducks and geese to sell to other bird lovers.

Mallard pair, overlain cork bodies with wooden heads, Bernard E. Ohnmacht, Lafayette, Indiana, circa 1940. $2,500 each. *Collection of Donald Cassini. Photograph courtesy of Donald Cassini.* (Unfortunately the original photo had darkened with age. This is an attempt to restore the image, but does not capture the beauty of the decoy or Mr. Cassini's photography.)

Canada goose pair, overlain cork bodies with wooden heads, Bernard E. Ohnmacht, Lafayette, Indiana, circa 1940. $3,000 each. *Collection of Donald Cassini. Photograph courtesy of Donald Cassini.*

Mallard drake, Dewey's Metal Folding Decoys, Outing Manufacturing Company, Elkhart, Indiana, metal silhouette on wooden base and collapsible stake so decoy could be used on water or in the field. Note the specially designed anchor weight, which was notched so it could be wedged between the bill and breast for storage, circa 1920. $300.

Advertisement, Dewey's Metal Folding Decoys, Outing Manufacturing Company, Elkhart, Indiana, *Outdoors America*, September 1924.

Minnow, 5-1/4", green scale pattern, #258SF, South Bend Bait Company, South Bend, Indiana, circa 1920. In original box. $3,500. *Photograph courtesy of Frank Baron.*

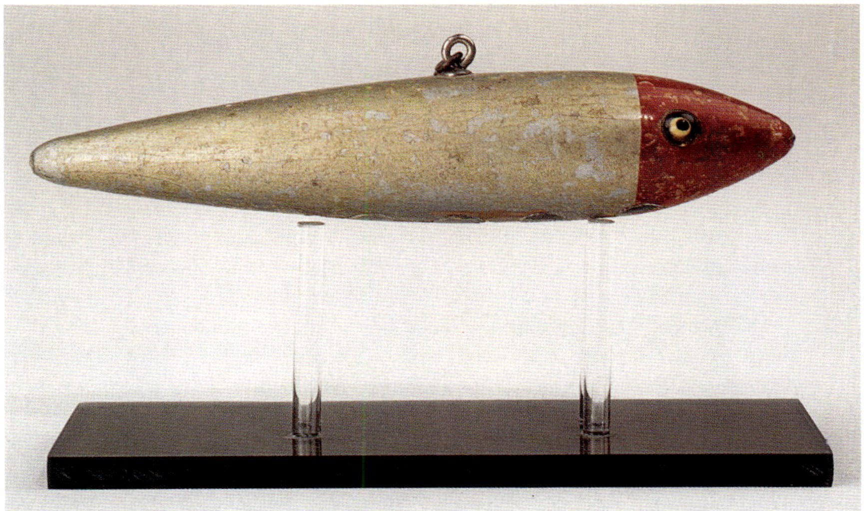

Minnow, 5-1/4", red head, silver body pattern, #258HA, South Bend Bait Company, South Bend, Indiana, circa 1920. $2,000.

Fish decoy, 5", "Dace" color pattern, Creek Chub Bait Company, Garret, Indiana, circa 1895, extremely rare. $5,000. *Photograph courtesy of Frank Baron.*

Michigan

As ducks and geese leave their spring nesting grounds in northern Canada, they funnel down into the Mississippi Flyway over Michigan and afford the sportsman a broad diversity of waterfowl hunting experiences. The natural terrain included vast expanses of marshland interlaced with small creeks, potholes, and bays. Large lakes are fringed with abundant aquatic feed and cover. The big waters of Lake Huron and Lake Erie compare to the oceanfront hunting areas of the coastal regions. As early as the mid-1870s sportsmen recognized the potential of the marshlands along Lake Huron's Saginaw Bay, the adjoining Lake St. Clair, and Lake Erie. Grand resorts were built, which offered a wide variety of recreational sports, swimming, boating, fishing, and of course waterfowling. Hunting clubs, like the Detroit Hunting and Fishing Association and the Marshland Club, were headquartered at such resorts during the late-1800s. Others, like the Lake St. Clair Fishing and Shooting Club, Erie Shooting Club, Point Mouille Shooting Club, and the Monroe Marsh Company, built their own smaller clubhouses that could accommodate weeklong stays by the members. Local hired help provided meals, and guides, called punters, maneuvered small double-bowed boats (punts) through the thick marsh grasses using a long push pole and helped with the day's hunt.

Within the boundaries of the state, waterfowlers could shoot diving ducks, puddle ducks, sea ducks, and geese. This variety of hunting situations required very different types of hunting decoys, ranging from the St. Clair School flat-bottom decoys, which often eggshell thin, hollowed out bodies, to the massive cedar diver decoys used on the big waters of the Lake Huron and Lake Houghton in central Michigan. To the delight of the decoy collector, many Michigan carvers excelled in creating wonderfully sculptured and painted working decoys. Carvers, like Nate Quillin, Ben Schmidt, and Ferdinand Bach, have become icons, in the annals of waterfowling because they made decoys not as art but as tools for the hunter.

Michigan was also home to most of the major commercial decoy factories, including Peterson Decoy Company, J.N. Dodge Company, and Wm. J. Mason decoys. George Peterson started his decoy factory on the second floor of the Mellus Saw Factory in 1873 and produced a line of wooden decoys turned on a multiple-spindled lathe. His decoy design was discontinued when Jasper N. Dodge purchased the Peterson Decoy Company in 1884. Although Dodge used the same equipment, he advertised that he would reproduce any decoy a customer sent him. As a result Dodge decoys are difficult to categorize. Most Dodge bodies have high wide shoulder area and a blunt tail. The William J. Mason factory enjoyed the most success of the Detroit-area decoy factories. Starting in 1882, Mason produced of an extensive decoy line, which included most species of ducks, shorebirds, geese, and brants in five grades. After William's death in 1905, his son, Herbert, carried on the decoy operation, continuing it until 1924. At that time he switched to the paint-making business, supplying Detroit's new booming industry, automobile production. Another short-lived Michigan decoy making factory was the Sibley Decoy Company. For years the Sibley decoy was identified as an unknown Illinois River decoy. It was only recently that collectors learned that this uniquely designed decoy with replaceable bill and internal lead ballast weight was actually produced in Whitehall, Michigan from 1899-1901. George Sibley, a wealthy man, discarded his decoy-producing project and moved to Denver, Colorado in 1901. There is also evidence of another decoy and call manufacturer, the A.W. Wilson Company, White Pigeon, Michigan. Company flyers and a letter dated 1885 describes their decoys but to date no one has been able to document a Wilson decoy.

Michigan is also known for its mass-produced fish decoys. James Heddon & Son Tackle Company, Dowagiac, is a major producer of fishing lures, reel and rods. They also offered their customers a line of decoys for winter spear fishing as early as 1913. The Moonlight/PawPaw Bait Company, PawPaw, Michigan manufactured an extensive line of wooden fish decoys that would rival the Heddon decoys, as well as a line of duck decoys. Other minor fish decoy companies, like the K & E. Company producers of the Bear Creek Ice King, would come on the scene later. One notable commercial fish decoy producer was the Rhodes Brothers. Their hollow-cast aluminum decoy was patented in 1917. This decoy is so rare it is doubtful if many were ever produced. Other makers, like Oscar Peterson, Ken Bruning, and Hans Janner, stir the hearts of the fish decoy collector.

Michigan is one of the few states that still allow winter spear fishing. Many sportsmen who often consider spearing a greater sport than fishing with a hook and line still carry on this tradition. Just as in olden days, they position a small shanty over a 2-3 foot hole cut in the ice. Inside the shanty, a small heater keeps the fisherman warm while he watches the scene below. By blocking out all the daylight, the fisherman is able to see everything below while remaining invisible to the fish. Imagine the anticipation he must feel as he watches a large fish circling below his decoy. The weighted decoy was suspended into the water on a string, which allows the fisherman to jerk the line causing the decoy to circle and swim like its live counterpart. He readies his 3-5 tined spear, weighted so it will pierce the water swiftly and straight when thrown. The large prey fish below may continue his slow approach or strike the decoy with a flashing ferocity. The fisherman may have waited hours for just this moment. If his aim is true, his spear will plunge into the fish behind the neck killing the fish instantly. If not he will have to wrestle the fish, sometimes weighting as much as 20-30 pounds, on his roped spear to bring it onto the ice.

While trout decoys were most popular among Michigan spear fishermen, the interpretation of the craftsmen who carved the decoys is as varied as the carvers' personalities. Water conditions also influence the style of a fish decoy. Aside from the obvious choice of abstract or realistic rendition of a species, fish also look different at deeper depths. A colorful trout will appear simply a glowing green color in very deep waters. Since much Michigan spear fishing is done in extreme depths, carvers often painted their fish this color. As a rule Michigan fish decoys are larger than fish decoys produced in other states, averaging 8 - 10 inches long, but decoys that where used on frozen rivers were usually smaller, 4-6 inches with straight bodies.

Master Michigan decoy carvers: seated, left to right: Ferdinand Bach, Benjamin Schmidt, Charles Pozzini; standing, left to right: Thomas Schroeder, Ralph Johnston. *Photograph Frank M. Cowger, 1967. Courtesy of Barbara Sorenson.*

Monroe Marsh Company, the first game preserve in the Northwest, circa 1872. Owner William Sterling became the only resident of Monroe County to hold a membership in the newly form Point Mouille Shooting Club when he sold his game preserve of 5000 acres, including 5-1/2 miles of lake frontage to the newly formed club in 1880. *Photograph courtesy of James Marsh.*

Early contemporary Michigan competition decoy carvers: seated left to right: Jeffery H. Merril, Birmingham; Edward de Navarre, Detroit; James Foote, Trenton; standing left to right: Charl E. Greene, Brooklyn; James McIlhenny, Rockwood; William C. Pierce, Lansing; Nicholas Purdo, Detroit. *Photograph by Frank M. Cowger, 1967. Courtesy of Barbara Sorenson.*

Erie Shooting Club, circa 1940. In response to "outsiders" gaining control of so much of their hunting grounds, the local sportsmen and farmers owning marshland banded together. They put all their marsh lands, totaling roughly 4,000 acres, into one preserve and formed the Bay Point Shooting Club in 1878. This club was later reorganized under the name the Erie Shooting Club, circa 1889. *Photograph courtesy of James Marsh.*

Harold Harrison Ackerman (1891-1982), Lincoln Park, Michigan, circa 1977. *Photograph: The Museum, MSU Folk Art Division. Courtesy Tom Schumaker.*

Redhead drake, Ferdinand Bach, Lake St. Clair, Michigan, one of three known examples, circa 1930. $20,000. *Collection of James R. and Diane Cook.*

Autographed portrait of Ferdinand Bach (1888-1967), St.Clair Shores, Michigan, which appeared in Detroit New March 18, 1956. *Photograph staff photographer Ternes. Courtesy Barbara Sorenson.*

Blue bill pair, Ferdinand Bach, Lake St.Clair, Michigan, best known example, circa 1930. $40,000. *Collection of Jim and Patti Aitkin.*

American merganser drake, Ferdinand Bach, solid cedar, only known example, circa 1930. $25,000. *Collection of James R. and Diane Cook.*

Canvasback drakes, Ferdinand Bach. Top: standard size; bottom: oversized, circa 1930. $15,000, each. *Collection of James R. and Diane Cook.*

Bluebill hen, J. N. Dodge Decoy Company, Detroit, Michigan, circa 1880. $1,000.c

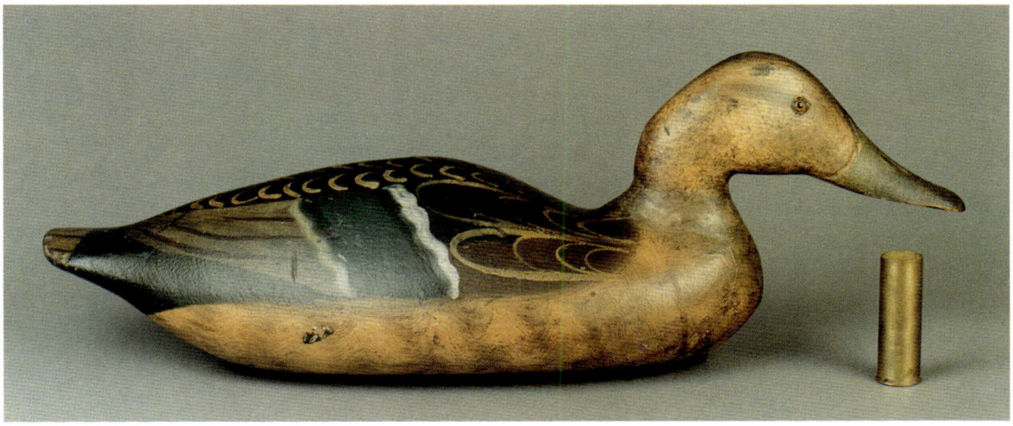

Mallard hen, J. N. Dodge Decoy Company (1884-1894), Detroit, Michigan, extremely rare, circa 1880. $1,500. *Collection of Alan and Elaine Haid. Photograph by Alan Haid.*

Mallard drake, J.N. Dodge Decoy Company, Detroit, Michigan, circa 1880. $1,000.

Widgeon drake, J. N. Dodge Decoy Company, Detroit, Michigan, circa 1880. $4,000. *Collection of James R. and Diane Cook.*

Plover, J. N. Dodge Decoy Company, Detroit, Michigan, circa 1880. $2,500. *Collection of Alan and Elaine Haid. Photography by Alan Haid.*

Blue-winged teal drake, John Finch, Port Huron, Michigan, Lake St. Clair School, circa 1940. $3,000. *Collection of George and Miriam Van Walleghem.*

Curlew, J. N. Dodge Decoy Company, Detroit, Michigan, circa 1880. $3,000. *Collection of Alan and Elaine Haid. Photography by Alan Haid.*

Black duck, John Finch, Port Huron, Michigan, Lake St. Clair School, circa 1940. $2,000. *Collection of George and Miriam Van Walleghem.*

Mallard drake, Western style, J.N. Dodge Decoy Company, Detroit, Michigan, circa 1880. $1,500.

Canada goose, canvas over wire frame body, wooden head, Jackson Industries, Kalamazoo, Michigan, circa 1940. $500.

Redhead pair, "One-Arm" Kellie, Monroe Michigan, circa 1915. $2,500. *CollectionS of Tom Schumaker/Jack Wilkie. Photograph by Tom Schumaker.*

Mallard drake, rare example, "One-Arm" Kellie, Monroe Michigan, circa 1915. $1,000. *Collection of Tom Schumaker/Jack Wilkie. Photograph by Tom Schumaker.*

Redhead pair, "One-Arm" Kellie, Monroe, Michigan, circa 1915, $2,500. *Collections of Tom Schumaker/Jack Wilkie. Photograph Thomas Shumaker.*

Canvasback drake, "One-Arm" Kellie, Monroe Michigan, circa 1915. $1,200. *Collections of Tom Schumaker/Jack Wilkie. Photograph by Tom Schumaker.*

Canvasback drake, "One-Arm" Kellie, Monroe Michigan, circa 1915. $1,200. *Collections of Tom Schumaker/Jack Wilkie. Photograph by Tom Schumaker.*

James Kelson (1888-1968), Mount Clemens, Michigan, circa 1946. *Photograph by staff photographer, John Herrmann, Detroit News. Photograph courtesy of Thomas Shumaker.*

Canvasback drake, Edward "One Arm" Kellie, Monroe, Michigan, solid cedar, circa 1940. $1,500. *Collection of George and Miriam Van Walleghem.*

Canvasback hen, Edward "One-Arm" Kellie, Monroe, Michigan, circa 1915. $1,500. *Collection of George and Miriam Van Walleghem.*

Canvasback drake, James R. Kelson, Mount Clemens, Michigan, balsawood, circa 1940. $1,000. *Collection of George and Miriam Van Walleghem.*

Canvasback drake, James R. Kelson, Mount Clemens, Michigan, balsawood, circa 1940. $1000. *Collection of George and Miriam Van Walleghem.*

Catalog Mason Decoy Company, Detroit, Michigan, 1915.

Catalog, Mason Decoy Company, Detroit, Michigan, circa 1915.

A happy hunter posed for this studio photograph with his Mason decoys. Mason decoys were very popular with waterfowlers throughout the United States and Canada. Founded by William James Mason in 1889, the company remained operational until 1924. The Mason Decoy Company produced most species of waterfowl in several Grades; Premier, Challenge, Standard (Detroit) glass eye, Standard (Detroit) tack eye, and Fourth Grade painted eye models. Shorebird decoys were offered with glass eye or tack eyes. The earliest models had wooden bills and later models had iron bills. *Photograph courtesy of Shirley, Joe and Dean Dashner*.

Catalog, Deluxe gold embossed cover, Mason Decoy Company, Detroit, Michigan, 1910, includes offering of Mason Premier wood duck decoy.

Detail slide 12/10, Original Premier Grade stamp on bottom of mallard drake.

Catalog Mason Decoy Company, Detroit, Michigan, 1905. Features early slope breasted models, low head sleeper decoys, and Chesapeake Bay Model Canvasbacks.

Standard Model Glass Eye Decoys

Any Specie $12.00 per dozen

F. O. B. Detroit

Mason's Decoy Factory

5971-5975 Milford St. and P. M. R. R.

DETROIT, MICHIGAN

PRICE LIST

All Quotations F. O. B. Detroit

Subject to change without notice

Premier Model (Hollow) - -	$21.00	per dozen
Mammoth Canvas Back (Solid)	21.00	" "
Canada Brant - - - - - - -	30.00	" "
11 W.-Weedless Anchors - -	2.00	" "
11 BS-Brass Shank Anchors -	2.00	" "
11 BW-Oval Body Weights -	1.50	" "
11 BWX-Oval Body Weights (Extra Heavy) - - - -	1.75	" "
11 RHL-Rawhide Loops - -	.30	" "
11 SE-Screw Eyes - - - -	.15	" "
11 AC-Anchor Cord - - - -	.50	" "
1 FS-Lead Balance Weight -	1.50	" "
1 J-Iron Loop Anchor - - -	2.00	" "
1 G-Iron Loop Anchor - - -	2.25	" "

These prices for immediate acceptance only

MASON'S DECOY FACTORY

5971-5975 Milford St. and P. M. R. R.

DETROIT, MICHIGAN

Price list for Mason Decoy Factory, circa 1919.

Mallard pair, Premier Grade, Mason Decoy Company, Detroit, Michigan, circa 1910. $8,000.

Mallard drakes, hollow, Challenge Grade, Mason Decoy Company, Detroit, Michigan, circa 1920. $2,000, each.

Mallard hen, snaky head, Premier Grade, Mason Decoy Company, Detroit, Michigan, circa 1905, G.K. Schmidt Rig mate to slide 12/13. $10,000.

Mallard drake, snaky head style, Premier Grade, Mason Decoy Company, Detroit, Michigan, circa 1905. Originally part of the famous G.K. Schmidt Rig of Perdew and Mason decoys found stored in a bank vault in 1966. $7,500.

Mallard pair, rare hollow models, Challenge Grade, Mason Decoy Company, Detroit, Michigan, circa 1900. $5,000.

Mallard pair, Detroit Grade, Mason Decoy Company, Detroit, Michigan, circa 1920. $800.

Black ducks, Mason Decoy Company, Detroit, Michigan. Top: Premier Grade, circa 1920, $4000. Bottom: Challenge Grade, circa 1920, $5,000.

Black duck, rare slope-breasted model, Premier Grade, Mason Decoy Company, Detroit, Michigan, circa 1890. $5,000.

Advertisement, Mason Decoy Company, Detroit, Michigan, circa 1910.

Pintail pair, Premier Grade, Mason Decoy Company, Detroit, Michigan, circa 1905. $15,000.

Pintail drake, Fuller Rig, Challenge Grade, Mason Decoy Company, Detroit, Michigan, circa 1890. $10,000. *Collection of James R. and Diane Cook.*

Green-winged teal pair, Premier Grade, Mason Decoy Company, Detroit, Michigan, circa 1905. $25,000, pair. *Collection of James R. and Diane Cook.*

Pintail drake, Premier Grade, Mason Decoy Company, Detroit, Michigan, V.L. & A. stamp, Chicago, Illinois on bottom, circa 1900. $20,000. *Collection of James R. and Diane Cook.*

Pintail drake, rare slope-breasted model from Dupee Rig, Premier Grade, Mason Decoy Company, Detroit, Michigan, circa 1890. $7,500.

Blue-winged teal, pair, Premier Grade, Mason Decoy Company, Detroit, Michigan, circa 1910. $8,000.

Blue-winged teal drake, Premier Grade, early sloped breasted, Mason Decoy Company, Detroit, Michigan, circa 1890. $5,000.

Blue-winged teal pair, Detroit Grade, Mason Decoy Company, Detroit, Michigan, circa 1905. $3,000, pair.

Blue-winged teal pair, early snaky head style, Premier Grade, Mason Decoy Company, Detroit, Michigan, circa 1910. $12,000.

Blue-winged teal pair, Challenge Grade, Mason Decoy Company, Detroit, Michigan, circa 1905. $7,000.

Blue-winged teal pair, Fourth Grade, Mason Decoy Company, Detroit, Michigan, circa 1920. $3,000, pair.

Widgeon drake, Premier Grade, Mason Decoy Company, Detroit, Michigan, circa 1900, best known example. $25,000. *Collection of James R. and Diane Cook.*

Bufflehead drake, Detroit Grade, Mason Decoy Company, Detroit, Michigan, circa 1905. $4,000.

Bufflehead hen, Challenge Grade, Mason Decoy Company, Detroit, Michigan, circa 1900. $10,000.

Bufflehead pair, Challenge Grade, Mason Decoy Company, Detroit, Michigan, circa 1900. $30,000. *Collection of James R. and Diane Cook.*

Bluebill drake, early slope-breast style, from Fuller Rig, Premier Grade, Mason Decoy Company, Detroit, Michigan, circa 1920. $7,000. *Collection of James R. and Diane Cook.*

Bluebill pair, Premier Grade, Mason Decoy Company, Detroit, Michigan, circa 1900. $4,000, pair.

Bluebill pair, special-order low head sleeper with small body, Premier Grade, Mason Decoy Company, Detroit, Michigan, circa 1900. $8,000.

Bluebill pair, special order Nathaniel Quillen model, Fuller Rig, Premier Grade, Mason Decoy Company, Detroit, Michigan, circa 1900. $10,000.

Bluebill drakes, low head sleeper style, Challenge Grade, Mason Decoy Company, Detroit, Michigan, circa 1900. $4,000 each.

Bluebill pair, Challenge Grade, Mason Decoy Company, Detroit, Michigan, circa 1910. $2,500.

Bluebill drake, Detroit Grade, Mason Decoy Company, Detroit, Michigan, circa 1910. $500.

Canvasback drake, Seneca Lake Model, Premier Grade, Mason Decoy Company, Detroit, Michigan, circa 1905. $1,500.

Canvasback pair, Premier Grade, Mason Decoy Company, Detroit, Michigan, circa 1905. $5,000. *Collection of James R. and Diane Cook.*

Canvasback pair, Chesapeake Bay Model, Premier Grade, Mason Decoy Company, Detroit, Michigan, circa 1900. $5,000.

Canvasback drake, early slope-breasted model, stamped "V. L. & A., Chicago," Premier Grade, Mason Decoy Company, Detroit, Michigan, circa 1900. $10,000. *Collection of James R. and Diane Cook.*

Redhead drake, Premier Grade, Mason Decoy Company, Detroit, Michigan, circa 1910. $2,500.

Redhead drake, low head, Premier Grade, Mason Decoy Company, Detroit, Michigan, circa 1890. Only know original example. $10,000. *Collection of James R. and Diane Cook.*

Redhead drake, Premier Grade, Mason Decoy Company, Detroit, Michigan, circa 1900. $5,000. *Collection of James R. and Diane Cook.*

Redhead pair, Challenge Grade, Mason Decoy Company, Detroit, Michigan, circa 1900. $10,000. *Collection of James R. and Diane Cook.*

Golden-eye drake, Premier Grade, Mason Decoy Company, Detroit, Michigan, circa 1900. $10,000. *Collection of James R. and Diane Cook.*

Golden-eye pair, Premier Grade, Mason Decoy Company, Detroit, Michigan, circa 1920. $8,000.

American Merganser pair, Premier Grade, Mason Decoy Company, Detroit, Michigan, circa 1905. $25,000, pair. *Collection of James R. and Diane Cook.*

Golden-eye drake, Challenge Grade, Mason Decoy Company, Detroit, Michigan, extremely early example, circa 1890. $7,000. *Collection of James R. and Diane Cook.*

Grey coot, Challenge Grade, Mason Decoy Company, Detroit, Michigan, circa 1900. $4,000.

American merganser pair, Challenge Grade, Mason Decoy Company, Detroit, Michigan, circa 1905. $20,000, pair.

Grey coot, fresh-water, Challenge Grade, Mason Decoy Company, Detroit, Michigan, circa 1900. $3,500.

Brant, Challenge Grade, Barron Rig, Mason Decoy Company, Detroit, Michigan, circa 1900. $5,000.

Atlantic brant, Challenge Grade, Mason Decoy Company, Detroit, Michigan. $5,000. *Collection of James R. and Diane Cook.*

Canada goose, Premier Grade, Mason Decoy Company, Detroit, Michigan, circa 1910. $7,000. *Collection of Alan and Elaine Haid. Photograph Alan Haid.*

Black-bellied plover, Mason Decoy Company, Detroit, Michigan, circa 1890, special order model. $12,000. *Collection of James R. and Diane Cook.*

Early style wooden bill shorebirds, extremely rare, Mason Decoy Company, Detroit, Michigan, circa 1900. Left: dowitcher, $15,000. Right: snipe, $20,000. *Collection of Alan and Elaine Haid. Photography Alan Haid.*

Long-billed curlew, extremely rare, Mason Decoy Company, Detroit, Michigan, circa 1900. Left: special order model patterned after William Bowman decoy with raised relief carved wings, $20,000. Right: standard two-piece Glass-eye Grade curlew, $20,000. *Collection of Alan and Elaine Haid. Photography Alan Haid.*

Early style wooden bill shorebirds, extremely rare, Mason Decoy Company, Detroit, Michigan, circa 1900. Left: robin snipe, $12,000. Right: ruddy turnstone, $12,000. *Collection of Alan and Elaine Haid. Photography Alan Haid.*

Ruddy turnstone, wooden bill, split tail, extremely rare, Mason Decoy Company, Detroit, Michigan, circa 1900. $15,000. *Collection of Alan and Elaine Haid. Photography Alan Haid.*

Andrew A. Meyers (1872-1960) owned a parcel of marshland on the west shore of Lake Huron where he hunted, trapped and fished all his life.

Duck calls, Reelfoot Lake-style, John "Sandy" Alexander Morrow (1880-?), Flint, Michigan, circa 1930. $1,000 each.

Canvasback drake, hollow big water stylized keel, Andrew Meyers, Flint, Michigan, circa 1925. $1,500.

Ringbill pair, Paw Paw Bait Company, Paw Paw, Michigan, circa 1930. $500.

Black duck, Peterson Decoy Factory, Detroit, Michigan, circa 1885. $3,000.

Advertisement, Peterson Decoy Company, circa 1880.

Bluebill hen, Peterson Decoy Company, Detroit, Michigan, circa 1885. $2,500. *Collection of James R. and Diane Cook.*

Blue-winged teal drake, Peterson Decoy Factory, Detroit, Michigan, circa 1885. $3,500.

Mallard pair, Peterson Decoy Factory, Detroit, Michigan, circa 1885. $5,000 pair.

Widgeon drake, Dr. Miles Pirnie (1898-1976), East Lansing, Michigan, circa 1945. $4,000. *Collection of James R. and Diane Cook.*

Rig of Nathaniel Quillen used and found at Pointe Mouille Marsh, circa 1965 by early Michigan decoy collector, Hy Dalka.

Redhead pair, Nathaniel Quillen, Rockwood, Michigan, circa 1880. TOP: hen, Helmet-style tucked head sleeper. This unique head form conformed to a hunter's hand for easier handling Top: W. T. Barber Rig, $7,000. Bottom: drake, regular low head sleeper style, Flint Rig, $7,000.

Blue-winged teal drake, Nathaniel Quillen, Rockwood, Michigan, circa 1880 Many collectors feel this drake and its mate are the finest known examples of Michigan decoys. $25,000. *Collection of George and Miriam Van Walleghem.*

Hy Dalka, Pointe Mouille, holding pair of Quillen blue-winged teal, the only known examples on the day that he found them.

Blue-winged teal hen, Nathaniel Quillen, Rockwood, Michigan, circa 1880. $20,000. *Collection of George and Miriam Van Walleghem.*

Bluebill drake, Nathaniel Quillen (1839-1908), Rockwood, Michigan, circa 1880. $3,000. *Collection of George and Miriam Van Walleghem.*

Pintail drake, Nathaniel Quillen, Rockwood, Michigan, circa 1880. $5,000. *Photograph courtesy Alan Haid.*

Bluebill hen, Nathaniel Quillen, Rockwood, Michigan, circa 1880. $4,000. *Collection of George and Miriam Van Walleghem.*

Pintail pair, Nathaniel Quillen, Rockwood, Michigan, circa 1880. $10,000. *Photograph courtesy Thomas Shumaker.*

Redhead pair, Helmet-style low head sleepers, Nathaniel Quillen, Rockwood, Michigan, circa 1880. $15,000. *Collection of George and Miriam Van Walleghem.*

Bufflehead hen, Unknown maker, Holton Lake, Michigan, circa 1930. $750.

Benjamin Schmidt (1884-1968), Centerline, Michigan, in his workshop circa 1950. *Photograph courtesy Thomas Shumaker.*

Henry "Bedgeon" Sampier (1856-1939), Pearl Beach, Michigan, St. Clair flat school carver was a contemporary of noted Michigan carver Chris Smith. *Photograph courtesy of Thomas Shumaker.*

Benjamin Schmidt, Centerline, Michigan, posing with an array of his decoys, circa 1960. *Photograph courtesy Shirley, Joe and Dean Dashner.*

Mallard drake, Benjamin Schmidt, hollow, bottom board, cedar, circa 1935. $4,000.

Pintail pair, Benjamin Schmidt, Detroit, Michigan, circa 1935. $15,000.
Collection of Keith J. Snider. Photograph Joseph Engers.

Black duck, Benjamin Schmidt, Centerline, Michigan, circa 1935. $2,500.
Collection of James R. and Diane Cook.

Green-winged teal drake, Benjamin Schmidt, solid cedar, circa 1935. $5,000.

Pintail pair, Benjamin Schmidt, solid cedar, circa 1940. $10,000.

Wood duck pair, Benjamin Schmidt, Detroit, Michigan, circa 1935. $25,000.
Collection of Keith J. Snider. Photograph Joseph Engers.

Hooded merganser pair, Benjamin Schmidt, Detroit, Michigan, circa 1935. $15,000. *Collection of Keith J. Snider. Photograph Joseph Engers.*

Old squaw pair, Benjamin Schmidt, Detroit, Michigan, circa 1930. $15,000. *Collection of Keith J. Snider. Photograph Joseph Engers.*

Canvasback drake, Benjamin Schmidt, solid cedar, circa 1940. $1,500.

Canada goose, Benjamin J. Schmidt, hollow cedar model, circa 1940. $7,000.
Collection of James R. and Diane Cook.

Blue goose, Benjamin Schmidt, hollow bottom board, cedar, circa 1940. $4,000.

Bluebill drake, Thomas Schroeder (1886-1976), Detroit, Michigan, solid cedar, "box bottom" style which had metal box to hold anchor weight and line so lines wouldn't tangle in the boat, circa 1930. $4,000.

Thomas Schroeder as he appear on cover of *Detroit News Pictorial Magazine*, 1949.

Canvasback pair, Thomas Schroeder, Detroit, Michigan, circa 1950. $7,000. *Photograph Rodney Hartzell. Collection of Tim Godard.*

Pintail pair, National Decoy Contest winning pair, Thomas Schroeder, Detroit, Michigan, circa 1950. $7,000, pair. *Photograph Rodney Hartzell. Collection of Tim Godard.*

Canvasback, Thomas Schroeder, Detroit, Michigan pair, 'box bottom' style, circa 1938. $4,000. *Photograph Rodney Hartzell. Collection of Tim Godard.*

Redhead pair, Thomas Schroeder, Detroit, Michigan, "box bottom' style, circa 1938. $8,000. *Photograph Rodney Hartzell. Collection of Tim Godard.*

Bluebill pair, Thomas Schroeder, Detroit, Michigan, 'Hydrodynamic Skirt' bottom style, circa 1950. $4,000. *Photograph Rodney Hartzell. Collection of Tim Godard.*

Redhead drake, Thomas Schroeder, Detroit, Michigan, 'Hydrodynamic Skirt' bottom style, circa 1950. $3,000. *Photograph Rodney Hartzell. Collection of Tim Godard.*

Brant, Thomas Schroeder, Detroit, Michigan, "Hydrodynamic Skirt" bottom style, circa 1950. $4,000. *Photograph Rodney Hartzell. Collection of Tim Godard.*

Canvasback drake, decorative flying, Thomas Schroeder, Detroit, Michigan, circa 1950. $5000. *Photograph Joe Engers. Collection of Tim Godard.*

Ivory-bill woodpecker, Thomas Schroeder, Detroit, Michigan, circa 1950. $2,500. *Photograph Rodney Hartzell. Collection of Tim Godard.*

Goldeneye drake, John Schweikart (1870-1954), Detroit River, Michigan, oversized, circa 1920. $10,000. *Collection of George and Miriam Van Walleghem.*

Bluebill hen, John Schweikart, Detroit, Michigan, circa 1920. $8,000. *Collection of George and Miriam Van Walleghem.*

Canvasback drake, John Schweikart, Detroit, Michigan, circa 1920. $15,000.
Collection of George and Miriam Van Walleghem.

Canvasback hen, John Schweikart, Detroit, Michigan, circa 1920. $15,000.
Collection of George and Miriam Van Walleghem.

Canvasback hen, John Schweikart, Detroit, Michigan, circa 1920. $10,000.
Collection of George and Miriam Van Walleghem.

Goldeneye hen, John Schweikart, Detroit, Michigan, circa 1920. $15,000.
Collection of George and Miriam Van Walleghem.

Coot, John Schweikart, Detroit, Michigan, circa 1920. $7,000. *Collection of George and Miriam Van Walleghem.*

Widgeon drake, "Mr. X," George Sibley (1861-1938), Chicago, Illinois. Although Sibley designed his decoys while he lived in Illinois, the Sibley Decoy was actually manufactured at his family's lumber mills in Whitehall, Michigan. Sibley was a founding member of the Hennepin Shooting Club, circa 1890. Duck calls, Charles Grubbs, Kankakee, Illinois, custom made for George Sibley, circa 1890. Decoy, $4,000; duck calls, $5,000, each.

J. A. SIBLEY. GEO. M. SIBLEY.

SIBLEY & CO.,

WHITEHALL,

MICHIGAN.

MANUFACTURERS OF THE SIBLEY DECOY.

Business card, Sibley & Company, Whitehall, Michigan, Manufacturers of The Sibley Decoy, circa 1890.

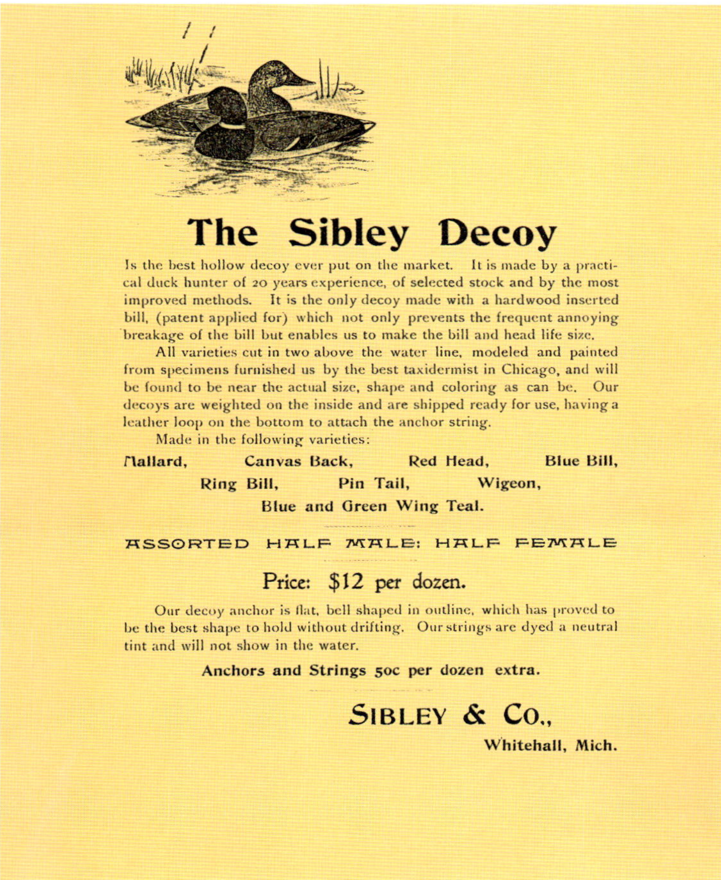

The Sibley Decoy

Is the best hollow decoy ever put on the market. It is made by a practical duck hunter of 20 years experience, of selected stock and by the most improved methods. It is the only decoy made with a hardwood inserted bill, (patent applied for) which not only prevents the frequent annoying breakage of the bill but enables us to make the bill and head life size.

All varieties cut in two above the water line, modeled and painted from specimens furnished us by the best taxidermist in Chicago, and will be found to be near the actual size, shape and coloring as can be. Our decoys are weighted on the inside and are shipped ready for use, having a leather loop on the bottom to attach the anchor string.

Made in the following varieties:

Mallard, Canvas Back, Red Head, Blue Bill, Ring Bill, Pin Tail, Wigeon, Blue and Green Wing Teal.

ASSORTED HALF MALE: HALF FEMALE

Price: $12 per dozen.

Our decoy anchor is flat, bell shaped in outline, which has proved to be the best shape to hold without drifting. Our strings are dyed a neutral tint and will not show in the water.

Anchors and Strings 50c per dozen extra.

SIBLEY & CO.,
Whitehall, Mich.

Flyer, *The Sibley Decoy*. This flyer, uncovered by a collector, circa 1990, solved the mystery of the "Mr. X" decoy. Joseph B. French had labeled George Sibley decoys as the "Mr. X" decoy in an article on unknown Illinois River decoys in the *Decoy Collectors Guide* circa 1966. Sibley, a confirmed bachelor, married at 41 and moved to Denver, Colorado, in 1901 taking most of the existing Sibley decoys with him. Thus collectors only found a handful in the Midwest.

Blue bill hen, "Mr. X," George Sibley, circa 1890. $2,000.

Mallard drake, "Mr. X," George Sibley, circa 1890: Hennepin Shooting Club sign, Hennepin, Illinois, circa 1885. Decoy;. $3,000.

Redhead hen, Walter S. Struebing, Marine City, Michigan, hollow cedar, circa 1940. $1,000. *Collection of George and Miriam Van Walleghem.*

Canvasback hen, Walter Struebing, Marine City, Michigan, hollow bottom board construction. $1,500. *Collection of George and Miriam Van Walleghem.*

Redhead drake, Walter Struebing, Marine City, Michigan, circa 1940. $1,000. *Collection of George and Miriam Van Walleghem.*

Canvasback drake, Walter Struebing, Marine City, Michigan, hollow, bottom board construction. $1,500. *Collection of George and Miriam Van Walleghem.*

Redhead drake, Charles Unger, Detroit, Michigan, circa 1880. $2,500. *Collection of James R. and Diane Cook.*

Duck call, carved head with open bill form barrel of tongue-pincher style duck call, unknown maker, found Lansing, Michigan, circa 1920. $3,500.

Canvasback drake, unknown maker, St.Clair Flats School, hollow, bottom board, pine, circa 1900. $2,000. *Collection of George and Miriam Van Walleghem.*

Wood duck hen, stick-up field decoy, unknown maker St.Clair Flats School, Michigan, circa 1920. $5,000. *Collection of George and Miriam Van Walleghem.*

Redhead, hollow, unknown Michigan maker. $500. *Collection of George and Miriam Van Walleghem.*

Below:
Goldeneye pair, unknown maker, St.Clair Flats School, Michigan, circa 1910. $7,000.

Redhead drake, unknown Michigan maker, St.Clair Flats School, circa 1900. $2,000.

Goldeneye drake, preener, solid cedar, unknown maker, Upper Peninsula, Michigan, circa 1930. $750.

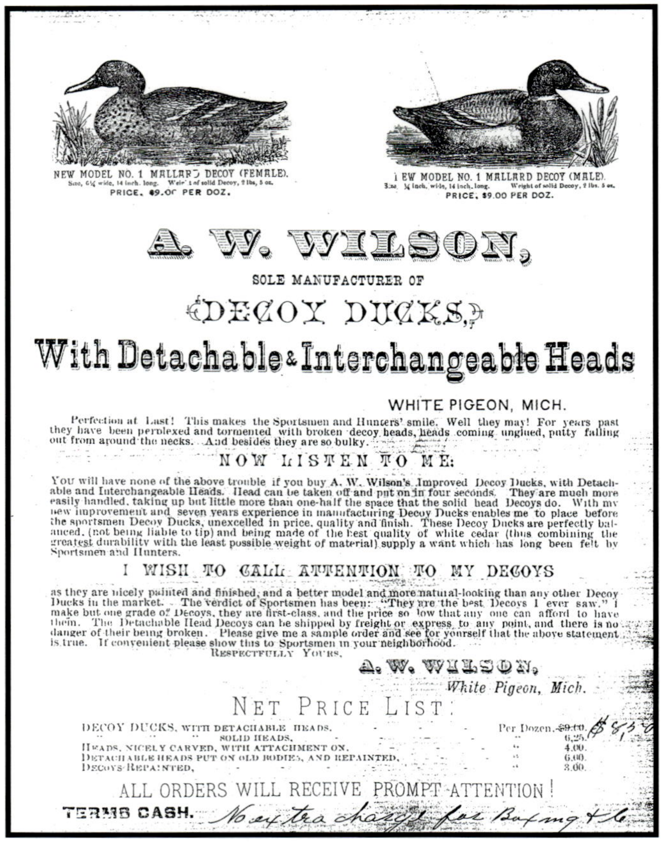

NEW MODEL NO. 1 MALLARD DECOY (FEMALE).
Size, 6¼ wide, 14 inch. long. Weight of solid Decoy, 2 lbs, 5 oz.
PRICE, $9.00 PER DOZ.

NEW MODEL NO. 1 MALLARD DECOY (MALE).
Size ¼ inch. wide, 14 inch. long. Weight of solid Decoy, 2 lbs. 5 oz.
PRICE, $9.00 PER DOZ.

A. W. WILSON,

SOLE MANUFACTURER OF

DECOY DUCKS,

With Detachable & Interchangeable Heads

WHITE PIGEON, MICH.

Perfection at Last! This makes the Sportsmen and Hunters' smile. Well they may! For years past they have been perplexed and tormented with broken decoy heads, heads coming unglued, putty falling out from around the necks. And besides they are so bulky.

NOW LISTEN TO ME:

You will have none of the above trouble if you buy A. W. Wilson's Improved Decoy Ducks, with Detachable and Interchangeable Heads. Head can be taken off and put on in four seconds. They are much more easily handled, taking up but little more than one-half the space that the solid head Decoys do. With my new improvement and seven years experience in manufacturing Decoy Ducks enables me to place before the sportsmen Decoy Ducks, unexcelled in price, quality and finish. These Decoy Ducks are perfectly balanced, (not being liable to tip) and being made of the best quality of white cedar (thus combining the greatest durability with the least possible weight of material) supply a want which has long been felt by Sportsmen and Hunters.

I WISH TO CALL ATTENTION TO MY DECOYS

as they are nicely painted and finished, and a better model and more natural-looking than any other Decoy Ducks in the market. The verdict of Sportsmen has been: "They are the best Decoys I ever saw." I make but one grade of Decoys, they are first-class, and the price so low that any one can afford to have them. The Detachable Head Decoys can be shipped by freight or express to any point, and there is no danger of their being broken. Please give me a sample order and see for yourself that the above statement is true. If convenient please show this to Sportsmen in your neighborhood.

RESPECTFULLY YOURS,

A. W. WILSON,
White Pigeon, Mich.

NET PRICE LIST:

DECOY DUCKS, WITH DETACHABLE HEADS,	Per Dozen,	~~$9.00.~~
" " SOLID HEADS,	"	6.25.
HEADS, NICELY CARVED, WITH ATTACHMENT ON,	"	4.00.
DETACHABLE HEADS PUT ON OLD BODIES, AND REPAINTED,	"	6.00.
DECOYS REPAINTED,	"	3.00.

ALL ORDERS WILL RECEIVE PROMPT ATTENTION!

TERMS CASH.

Flyer & letterhead, A.W. Wilson, White Pigeon, Michigan, manufacturer of duck decoys, and duck and turkey calls. To date the Wilson decoy has not been identified, but the illustrations bear a strong resemblance to the J.N. Dodge Decoy Company decoys. This letter dated 1885 and accompanying flyer describe a decoy with detachable head available in mallards and bluebills which design was based on seven years of decoy making experience, dating the first Wilson decoys at 1878.

Canvasback drake, unknown maker St.Clair Flats School, Bobtail style, circa 1920. $1000. *Collection of George and Miriam Van Walleghem.*

Bear Creek Ice King Decoy, Top: northern pike, 7", wooden, metal tail; bottom: sucker, 7", wooden, wooden tail; K & E Company, Hasting, Michigan, circa 1940. $500 each.

Frog, 6", Judd Blain, Midland, Michigan, circa 1960. $500. *Collection of George and Miriam VanWalleghem.*

Trout, 5 1/2" early example, Kenneth Bruning, Rogers City, Michigan, circa 1940. $2,500. *Collection of George and Miriam VanWalleghem.*

Brook trout, 11", Kenneth Bruning (1919-1974), Rogers City, Michigan, circa 1940. $5,000.

Rainbow trout, 16 1/2", Kenneth Bruning, Rogers City, Michigan, circa 1950. $5,000. *Collection of George and Miriam VanWalleghem.*

Trout, 21 1/2", Mark Bruning, Rogers City, Michigan, circa 1980. $500. *Collection of George and Miriam VanWalleghem.*

Sucker, 18", Alton "Chub" Buchman, Mount Clemens, Michigan, circa 1980. $500. *Collection of George and Miriam VanWalleghem.*

Bottom: brook trout, 12 1/2", $4,500. Top: rainbow trout, 7 1/2", $2,000. Kenneth Bruning, Rogers City, Michigan, circa 1950. *Collection of George and Miriam VanWalleghem.*

Black shiner, 10" Abraham Dehate, Mount Clemens, Michigan, circa 1930. $2,000. *Collection of George and Miriam VanWalleghem.*

Trout, 8 1/2", Isaac Goulette, New Baltimore, Michigan, circa 1930. $2,000. *Collection of George and Miriam VanWalleghem.*

Trout 5 1/2" – 7", John Eddy, Cheboygan, Michigan, circa 1970. $500 each. *Collection of George and Miriam VanWalleghem.*

Trout, 10 1/4", Isaac Goueltte, New Baltimore, Michigan, circa 1950. $4,000. *Collection of George and Miriam VanWalleghem.*

Top: blue herring, 9 1/2", $1,000. Bottom: blue herring, 4 3/4", $500. Isaac Goueltte, New Baltimore, Michigan, circa 1930.

Perch, 3 3/4" - 8 1/2", Isaac Goueltte, New Baltimore, Michigan, circa 1930. $750 each. Collection of George and Miriam VanWalleghem.

Minnows, 4" - 5 1/2", Isaac Goueltte, New Baltimore, Michigan, circa 1930. $750. *Collection of George and Miriam VanWalleghem.*

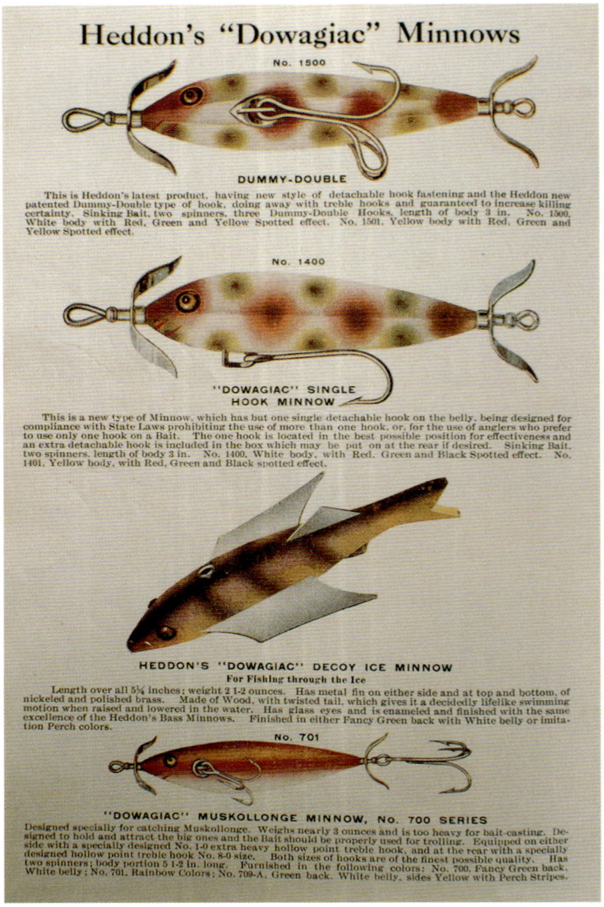

Heddon's "Dowagiac" Minnows

No. 1500

DUMMY-DOUBLE

This is Heddon's latest product, having new style of detachable hook fastening and the Heddon new patented Dummy-Double type of hook, doing away with treble hooks and guaranteed to increase killing certainty. Sinking Bait, two spinners, three Dummy-Double Hooks, length of body 3 in. No. 1500, White body with Red, Green and Yellow Spotted effect. No. 1501, Yellow body with Red, Green and Yellow Spotted effect.

No. 1400

"DOWAGIAC" SINGLE HOOK MINNOW

This is a new type of Minnow, which has but one single detachable hook on the belly, being designed for compliance with State Laws prohibiting the use of more than one hook, or, for the use of anglers who prefer to use only one hook on a Bait. The one hook is located in the best possible position for effectiveness and an extra detachable hook is included in the box which may be put on at the rear if desired. Sinking Bait, two spinners, length of body 3 in. No. 1400, White body, with Red, Green and Black Spotted effect. No. 1401, Yellow body, with Red, Green and Black spotted effect.

HEDDON'S "DOWAGIAC" DECOY ICE MINNOW

For Fishing through the Ice

Length over all 5¼ inches; weight 2 1-2 ounces. Has metal fin on either side and at top and bottom, of nickeled and polished brass. Made of Wood, with twisted tail, which gives it a decidedly lifelike swimming motion when raised and lowered in the water. Has glass eyes and is enameled and finished with the same excellence of the Heddon's Bass Minnows. Finished in either Fancy Green back with White belly or imitation Perch colors.

No. 701

"DOWAGIAC" MUSKOLLONGE MINNOW, No. 700 SERIES

Designed specially for catching Muskollonge. Weighs nearly 3 ounces and is too heavy for bait-casting. Designed to hold and attract the big ones and the Bait should be properly used for trolling. Equipped on either side with a specially designed No. 1-0 extra heavy hollow point treble hook, and at the rear with a specially designed hollow point treble hook No. 8-0 size. Both sizes of hooks are of the finest possible quality. Has two spinners; body portion 5 1-2 in. long. Furnished in the following colors: No. 700, Fancy Green back, White belly; No. 701, Rainbow Colors; No. 709-A, Green back, White belly, sides Yellow with Perch Stripes.

Color insert from 1913 H.H. Michaelson Sporting Goods Catalog, New York, New York, illustrating the Heddon "Dowagiac Decoy Ice Minnow." This wooden tail model is the earliest style of the "Bat-Wing" decoy, which gets its nickname from the shape of its single side fin.

Ice Minnow, 5 1/4", "Bat-Wing," wooden tail James Heddon & Sons Company, Dowagiac, Michigan. $4,000. *Photograph courtesy Frank. R Baron.*

Ice Minnow #400, 4 3/8", tiger musky color pattern, rare color, original box. James Heddon & Sons Company, Dowagiac, Michigan, circa 1923. $3,000. *Collection of Geroge Rader. Photograph Arlan Carter.*

Ice Minnow #400, 4 3/8", James Heddon & Sons Company, Dowagiac, Michigan. Assorted common color patterns, circa 1923. $2,000 each. *Collection of George Rader. Photograph Arlan Carter.*

Ice Minnow #400, 4 3/8", James Heddon & Sons Company, Dowagiac, Michigan. Assorted rare color patterns, circa 1923. $2,000 each. *Collection of George Rader. Photograph Arlan Carter.*

Ice Minnow #400, 4 3/8", James Heddon & Sons Company, Dowagiac, Michigan. Assorted rare color patterns, circa 1923. $2,000 each. *Collection of George Rader. Photograph Arlan Carter.*

Ice Minnows, 6 3/4", rare uncataloged musky-sized Ice Minnow, James Heddon & Sons Company, Dowagiac, Michigan. $3,000 each. *Collection of George Rader. Photograph Arlan Carter.*

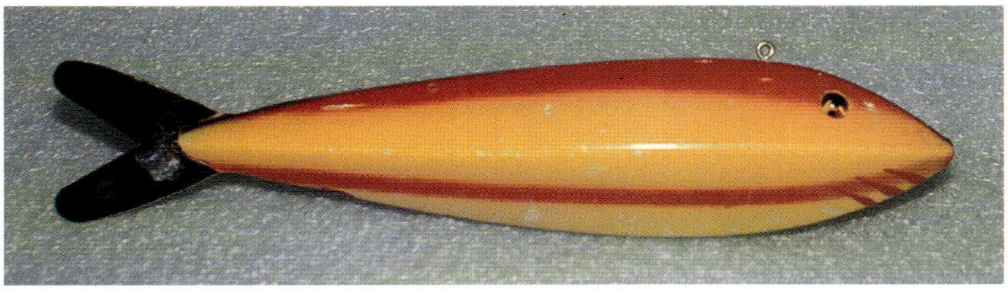

Prototype decoy, 8", uncataloged, made from a large muskellunge lure body, probably the #700 series lure. $5,000.

Perch, Ice Spook, #450, 5", James Heddon & Sons, Dowagiac. In 1930, Heddon announced a new line of 'Spook' baits made of transparent plastic called "Heddylin" with life-like finishes. The Ice Spook had silhouetted body mounted onto an oversized lead belly weight stamped "HEDDON ICE SPOOK." $1,000.

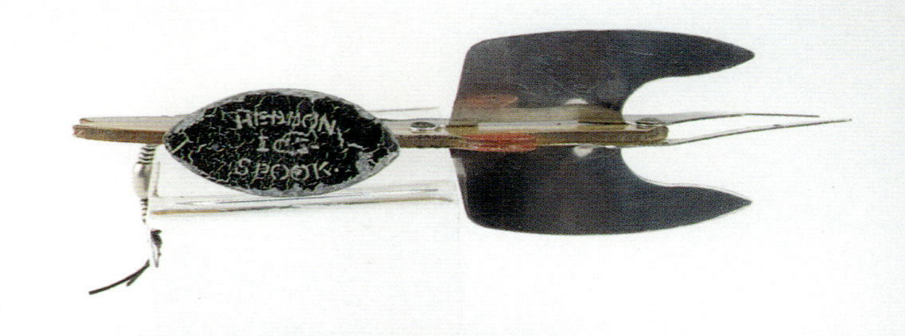

Green Crackle-back. Top: bat-wing Ice Minnow, 4 1/4"; bottom: bat-wing Ice Minnow, 5"; James Heddon & Sons, Dowagiac, circa 1918. $3,000 each.

Perch, 5", Russell Hurlburt, Newberry, Michigan, circa 1930. $500. *Collection of Ron and Kathy Fritz. Photograph Ron Fritz.*

Bass, 6", Russell Hurlburt (1899-1975), Newberry, Michigan sold his decoy out of his barbershop during the 1930s or 1940s. $500. *Collection of Ron and Kathy Frit., Photograph Ron Fritz.*

Bass, 14 1/2", Hans Janner Sr. (1880-1963), Mount Clemens, Michigan, black walnut and brass fins, circa 1930. $12,000. *Collection of George and Miriam VanWalleghem.*

Trout, 11 1/2", Hans Janner Sr., Mount Clemens, circa 1920. $12,000. *Collection of George and Miriam Van Walleghem.*

Above and left:
Trout/walleye, 18", unusual double-sided decoy. Metal and carve fins, Hans Janner Sr., Mount Clemens, Michigan, circa 1920. $10,000. *Collection of George and Miriam VanWalleghem.*

Bass, 13", Hans Janner Sr., Mount Clemens, circa 1920. $4,500. *Collection of George and Miriam Van Walleghem.*

Bluegill, 9 3/4", Hans Janner Sr., Mount Clemens, circa 1920. $7,000. *Collection of George and Miriam VanWalleghem.*

Rock bass, 12", Hans Janner Sr., Mount Clemens, circa 1920. $10,000. *Collection of George and Miriam VanWalleghem.*

Bass, 12", Hans Janner Sr., Mount Clemens, circa 1920. $7,000. *Collection George and Miriam VanWalleghem.*

Bass, 12", Hans Janner Sr., Mount Clemens, circa 1920. $5,000. *Collection of George and Miriam VanWalleghem.*

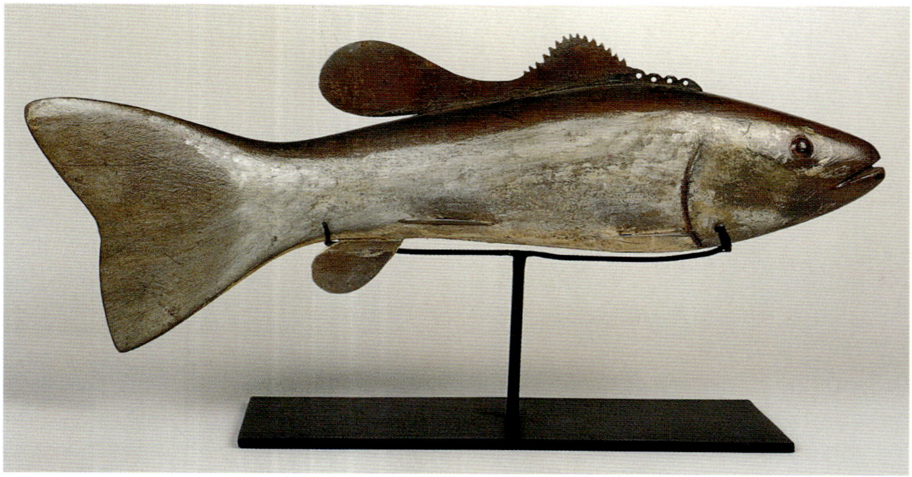

Walleye, 16", Hans Janner, Sr., Mount Clemens, circa 1920. $8,000. *Collection of George and Miriam VanWalleghem.*

Northern pike, 6", Victor Johnson (1885-1959), Ludington, Michigan, circa 1920. $750. *Collection of Ron and Kathy Fritz. Photograph Ron Fritz.*

Mouse, 4 1/2", Victor Johnson, Ludington, Michigan, circa 1920. $600.
Collection of Ron and Kathy Fritz. Photograph Ron Fritz.

Perch, 9 1/2", Edward F. "One-Arm" Kellie, Monroe Michigan, circa 1940, $750. James Rosin, Lake St. Clair, Michigan, circa 1930. $4,000.

Sucker, 9", hollow, Charles Kellman, Detroit, Michigan, circa 1930. $4,000. *Collection of George and Miriam VanWalleghem.*

"Green" fish, 9 1/2", Charles Kellman, Detroit, Michigan, circa 1930. Decoys that were used in deep waters were often finished with this glowing green color because most colors on different species appear simply green in deeper water. $4,000. *Collection of George and Miriam VanWalleghem.*

Sucker, 10", hollow, Charles Kellman, Detroit, Michigan, circa 1930. $4,000. *Collection of George and Miriam VanWalleghem.*

Brook trout, 7 1/2", Marvin Mason, Tower, Michigan, circa 1950. $1000. *Collection of George and Miriam VanWalleghem.*

Northern pike, frog paint pattern, 8", Earl Myers (1902-1992), Rogers City, Michigan, circa 1940. $2,000. *Collection of Ron and Kathy Fritz. Photograph Ron Fritz.*

Minnow, 4", Earl Myers, Rogers City, Michigan, circa 1940. $1,000. *Collection of Ron and Kathy Fritz. Photograph Ron Fritz.*

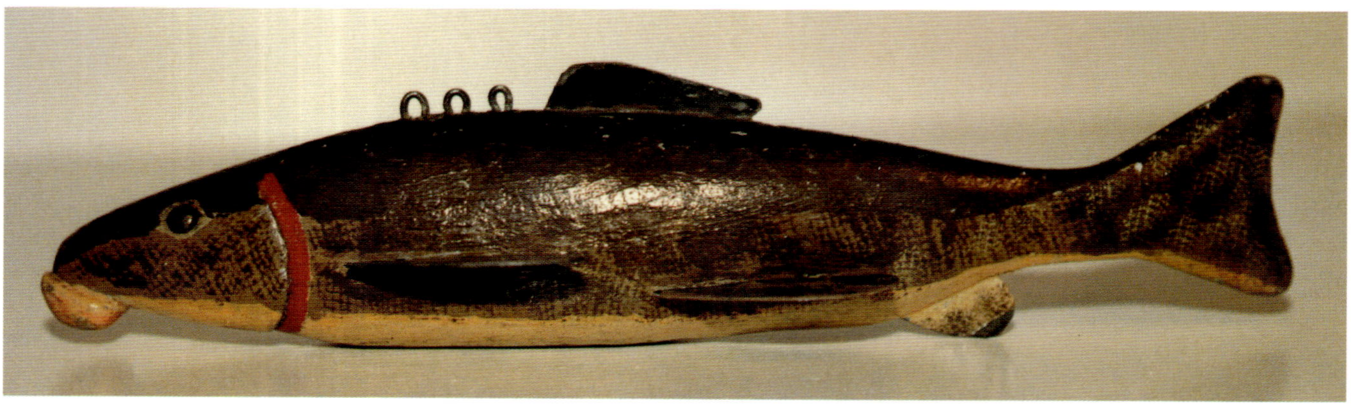

Sucker, 9", Earl Myers, Rogers City, Michigan, circa 1940. $500. *Collection of Ron and Kathy Fritz. Photograph Ron Fritz.*

Trout, 6", James Nelson, Cadillac, Michigan, Cadillac School, early example, circa 1930. $1,500. *Collection of Ron and Kathy Fritz. Photograph Ron Fritz.*

Trout, 7", James Nelson, Cadillac, Michigan, Cadillac School, circa 1940. $1,500. *Collection of Ron and Kathy Fritz. Photograph Ron Fritz.*

Trout, 7", James Nelson, Cadillac, Michigan, Cadillac School, circa 1940. $1,500. *Collection of Ron and Kathy Fritz. Photograph Ron Fritz.*

Dace, 7 1/4", wooden tail, original box, Paw Paw/Moonlight Bait Company, Paw Paw, Michigan, circa 1920. $1,000.

Ice spearing decoys, metal tail. Top: 5"; bottom: 7"; Paw Paw/Moonlight Bait Company, Paw Paw, Michigan, circa 1920. $500 each.

Ice spearing decoys, metal tail. Top: 5"; bottom: 7"; Paw Paw/Moonlight Bait Company, Paw Paw, Michigan, circa 1920. $500 each.

Ice spearing decoys, wooden tail. Top: 5"; bottom: 7"; Paw Paw/Moonlight Bait Company, Paw Paw, Michigan, circa 1920. $400 each.

Perch, 12 1/2", Horace 'Bart' Perkins, New Baltimore, Michigan, circa 1900-1920. $4,000. *Collection of George and Miriam VanWalleghem.*

Trout, 10", Horace "Bart" Perkins, New Baltimore, Michigan, circa 1900. $3,000. *Collection of George and Miriam VanWalleghem.*

Perch, 11", Horace "Bart" Perkins, New Baltimore, Michigan, circa 1900-1920. $4,000. *Collection of George and Miriam VanWalleghem.*

Perch, 8 1/2", Horace "Bart" Perkins, New Baltimore, Michigan, circa 1900. $2,000. *Collection of George and Miriam VanWalleghem.*

White fish, 7 1/2", Horace "Bart" Perkins, New Baltimore, Michigan, circa 1900. $2,000. *Collection of George and Miriam VanWalleghem.*

Trout, 9". Oscar Peterson (1887-1951), Cadillac, Michigan was a prolific folk artist who is believed to have carved fish decoys as early as 1905. He is considered the founder of the Cadillac School of fish decoys. $2,000.

Northern pike, Oscar Peterson, Cacillac, Michigan. Usual straight body, Peterson normally carved a curved into the body of his decoys, circa 1923. $1,500.

Northern pike, 7 1/2", Oscar Peterson, Cadillac, Michigan, circa 1940. $2,000.

Top: northern pike, 8"; bottom: bass, 7"; Oscar Peterson, Cadillac, Michigan, circa 1920. $2,000 each.

Top: northern pike, 7"; middle: walleye, 7"; bottom: northern pike, 7"; Oscar Peterson, Cadillac, Michigan, circa 1920. $1,000 each.

Northern pike, 8", Oscar Peterson, Cadillac, Michigan, circa 1920. $2,000. *Collection of Ron and Kathy Fritz. Photograph Ron Fritz.*

Top: perch, 7", $1500; bottom: trout, 7", $1000. Oscar Peterson, Cadillac, Michigan, circa 1940. *Collection of George and Miriam VanWalleghem.*

Perch, 6 1/2", Oscar Peterson, Cadillac, Michigan, circa 1920. $2,000. *Collection of Ron and Kathy Fritz. Photograph Ron Fritz.*

Perch, 6 3/4", Oscar Peterson, Cadillac, Michigan, circa 1920. $2,000. *Collection of Ron and Kathy Fritz. Photograph Ron Fritz.*

Walleye, 9", Oscar Peterson, Cadillac, Michigan, circa 1920. $2,000. *Collection of Ron and Kathy Fritz. Photograph Ron Fritz.*

Decorative plaque, bluegill, relief carving on walnut, polychrome, Oscar Peterson, Cadillac, Michigan, circa 1920. $7,500.

Decorative plaque, northern pike, Oscar Peterson, Cadillac, Michigan, relief carving from one piece of wood. Polychrome, 29" x 11" circa 1930. $30,000. *Collection of David Fischer. Photograph Alan Haid.*

Northern pike, decorative carving, "in-the-round," 29", Oscar Peterson, Cadillac, Michigan, circa 1925. $40,000. *Collection of Alan and Elaine Haid. Photograph Alan Haid.*

Northern pike, decorative carving, "in-the-round," 48", Oscar Peterson, Cadillac, Michigan, circa 1925. $50,000. *Collection of Alan and Elaine Haid. Photograph Alan Haid.*

Decorative plaque, cardinal, 14" x 8", Oscar Peterson, Cadillac, Michigan, circa 1920. $7,000. *Collection of Ron and Kathy Fritz. Photograph Ron Fritz.*

Top: walleye, 11", Robert Pierce, Mount Clemens, circa 1935, $1500. Middle: trout, 11", curved wooden tail, unknown Mount Clemens maker, circa 1930, $750. Bottom: walleye, 8 3/4", attributed Thomas Schroeder, Detroit, Michigan, circa 1930, $1,000.

Decorative plaque, blue jay, 14" x 8", Oscar Peterson, Cadillac, Michigan, circa 1920. $7,000. *Collection of Ron and Kathy Fritz. Photograph Ron Fritz.*

Minnow, 7 1/2", Jesse Ramey, Cadillac Michigan, Cadillac School, circa 1940. $2,000. *Collection of Ron and Kathy Fritz. Photograph Ron Fritz.*

Perch, 6 1/2", Jesse Ramey, Cadillac Michigan, Cadillac School, circa 1940. $1,500. *Collection of Ron and Kathy Fritz. Photograph Ron Fritz.*

Ice spearing decoy, 7", Jay B. Rhodes, Kalamazoo, Michigan. Two-piece hollow, cast aluminum body, patented 1917. Extremely rare, circa 1919. $5,000. *Photograph courtesy of Frank R. Baron.*

Walleye, 12", James Rosin, Lake St. Clair, Michigan, circa 1930. $4,000. *Collection of George and Miriam VanWalleghem.*

Bluegill, 10 1/2", James Rosin, Lake St. Clair, Michigan, circa 1930. $2,000. *Collection of George and Miriam Van Walleghem.*

Bass, 15", James Rosin, Lake St. Clair, Michigan, circa 1930. $4,000. *Collection of George and Miriam VanWalleghem.*

Top: walleye, 9"; middle: perch, 7 1/2"; bottom: minnow, 6 1/2"; James Rosin, Lake St. Clair, Michigan, circa 1930. $500 each. *Collection of George and Miriam VanWalleghem.*

Trout, 6 1/2", Thomas Schroeder, Detroit, Michigan, circa 1940. $2,500. *Collection of George and Miriam VanWalleghem.*

Display board, variety of Native American fish species, 3 1/2" - 6 1/2". Fish profiles mounted to board, Thomas Schroeder, Detroit, Michigan. Set. $7,000. *Collection of Tim Godard.*

Minnow, Thomas Schroeder, Detroit, Michigan, circa 1940. $1,500. *Collection of George and Miriam VanWalleghem.*

Walleye, 4 1/2", Thomas Schroeder (1885-1979), Detroit, Michigan, circa 1940. $3,000, each.

Sucker, Elman G. "Bud" Stewart (1912-present), Flint, Michigan, circa 1945. Demand became so great for Stewart's handmade baits and fish decoys that, by 1940, he set-up a commercial production with help in the assembly of his baits. Stewart did all of the painting. $1,000.

Minnow, 5 1/2", Charles Sutton (1880-1963), Ludington, Michigan, circa 1920. $2,000. *Collection of Ron and Kathy Fritz. Photograph Ron Fritz.*

Minnow, 6", moveable metal fins, Charles Sutton, Ludington, Michigan, circa 1920. $1,500. *Collection of Ron and Kathy Fritz. Photograph Ron Fritz.*

Minnow 6 1/2", natural finish, wood burned detailing, Charles Sutton, Ludington, Michigan, circa 1920. $1,500. *Collection of Ron and Kathy Fritz. Photograph Ron Fritz.*

Perch, 14", Andrew Trombley (1919-1975), St. Clair Shores, Michigan, circa 1940. $3,000. *Collection of George and Miriam VanWalleghem.*

Muskellunge, 14", Andrew Trombley, St.Clair Shores, Michigan, circa 1940. $2,000. *Collection of George and Miriam VanWalleghem.*

Northern pike, 11 1/2", Andrew Trombley, St.Clair Shores, Michigan, circa 1940. $2,000. *Collection of George and Miriam VanWalleghem.*

Walleye, 11", Andrew Trombley, St.Clair Shores, Michigan, circa 1940. $2,000. *Collection of George and Miriam VanWalleghem.*

Perch, 9 1/4", Andrew Trombley, St.Clair Shores, Michigan, circa 1940. $2,000. *Collection of George and Miriam VanWalleghem.*

Perch, 8 3/4", Andrew Trombley, St.Clair Shores, Michigan, circa 1940. $2,000. *Collection of George and Miriam VanWalleghem.*

Trout, 10", Andrew Trombley, St.Clair Shores, Michigan, circa 1940. $2,000. *Collection of George and Miriam VanWalleghem.*

Blue herring, 11 1/2", unknown Michigan maker, circa 1940. $700.

Top: natural finish wooden decoy, 8 1/4" wood burned detailing, unknown Native American maker, Michigan. Middle: trout, 5 1/2", unknown Michigan maker, circa 1930. Bottom: natural wood finish, 4 1/2", copper fins and tail, unknown Michigan maker, circa 1920. $500 each.

Top: shad, 12", unknown Michigan maker. Bottom: brown trout, 6", unknown Michigan maker, circa 1940. $400 each.

Minnow, 5", unknown Michigan maker, circa 1940. $650. *Collection George and Miriam VanWalleghem.*

Perch, 7 1/2", unknown Michigan maker, circa 1950. $800. *Collection of George and Miriam VanWalleghem.*

Left:
Minnow with jigging stick, 4", bone, unknown Native American maker, Mount Clemens area, Michigan, circa 1930. $500. *Collection of George and Miriam VanWalleghem.*

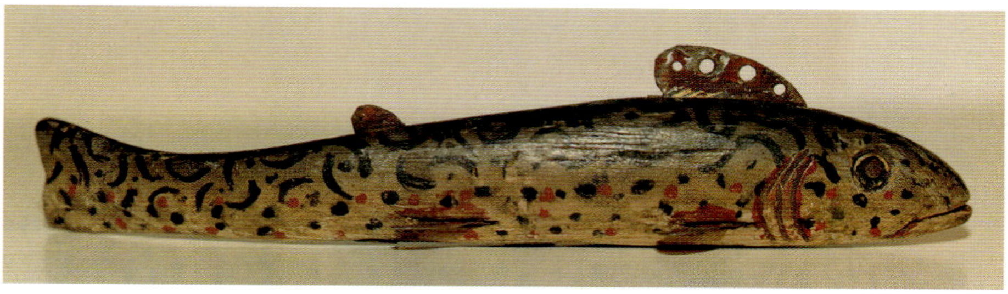

Trout, 7", unknown maker, Cadillac School, Cadillac, Michigan, circa 1940. $1,000. *Collection of Ron and Kathy Fritz. Photograph Ron Fritz.*

Northern pike, 7", unknown maker, Cadillac School, Cadillac, Michigan, circa 1930. $1,000. *Collection of Ron and Kathy Fritz. Photograph Ron Fritz.*

Minnow, 7", Cadillac School, per 1900, Cadillac, Michigan. $850. *Collection of George and Miriam VanWalleghem.*

Minnow, 7 1/4", unknown Native American maker, Marquehe, Michigan. $1,000.

Herring, 6", unknown Michigan maker, circa 1940. $700. *Collection of George and Miriam VanWalleghem.*

Below:
Perch, natural finish, unknown maker, northern Michigan, circa 1930. $500. *Collection of Ron and Kathy Fritz. Photograph Ron Fritz.*

Sucker, 9", unknown Michigan maker, circa 1940. $2,000. *Collection of George and Miriam VanWalleghem.*

Bass, 10", unknown Michigan maker, circa 1940. $1000.

Muskellunge, 16", Daniel Vandenbossche, Mount Clemens, Michigan, circa 1930. $1,500. *Collection of George and Miriam VanWalleghem.*

Detail of Muskellunge.

Bass, 6", Theodore Vandenbossche, Mount Clemens, Michigan, circa 1930. $2,500. *Collection of George and Miriam VanWalleghem.*

TOP: perch, 6 3/4"; bottom: green herring, 8", Albert "Bert" Winnie, Traverse City, Michigan patented the Stumper Dodger fishing lure, circa 1914. $700 each.

Illinois

Located in the center of the Mississippi flyway, Illinois is a major staging area for legions of waterfowl species. The present day Illinois River floodplain was formed when the Wisconsin Glacier covered northern Illinois about 21,000 years ago. Then the ancient Mississippi River entered the valley near Hennepin, Illinois. As this glacier receded, its melt waters cut their way from Lake Michigan to the "great bend" near Hennepin, where the river veers sharply and begins to flow southward instead of toward the west. Here the waters spread out into the valley creating approximately 56,000 acres of lakes, ponds, and sloughs from Utica to Grafton and the Illinois River. In its natural state, a massive prairie that supported remarkable wetlands complemented this river system. These wetlands have names that most waterfowlers can recognize, like the Winnebago Marsh, Kankakee Marsh and the Calumet Marsh. To the west the state is flanked by the present day Mississippi River and the Ohio and Wabash Rivers mark its southeastern borders. Add to this abundance of wetlands and deepwater lakes, the bald cypress-tupelo gum swamps of the state's southern tip where the Sangamon River empties into the Illinois River, and it is no wonder the Illinois has strong waterfowling history.

As the twentieth century approached, the lifestyles of the average Illinoisan was quickly changing. Towns like Chicago, Joliet, and Peoria boomed into industrial centers, which created a new class of businessmen. He was no longer tied to the demands of daily life on the farm, struggling to clear the land and grow crops without the benefits of machinery. His employment afforded him a more structured lifestyle that included more leisure time. As in other Midwestern states, hunting became a sport rather than a necessity. Prior to 1860, there was no need for a sportsman to leave the Chicago area. The city was still little more than a dozen streets setting in the middle of a sea of grass and marsh. As the hunting areas near the industrial cities began to dwindle because of aggressive drainage programs for agriculture and the growth of the cities themselves, the sportsman began to travel into the interior of the state in pursuit of waterfowl. Numerous gunning clubs, like the Hennepin Shooting Club, Swan Lake, Grand Island Club, Senachwine Gun Club, Duck Island Gun Club, and Princeton Game and Fish Club, were formed in central Illinois during the 1880s. They were first established by wealthy visiting hunters in an attempt to preserve and guaranteed their successful waterfowling, and later by locals to keep some good hunting areas out of the control of outsiders. In southern Illinois commercial guiding services offered the hunter day shooting. Some of these guide services evolved into commercial hunting clubs, like the Lakewood Club. With the opening of the Chicago, Milwaukee, St Paul and Pacific Railroad in 1900, the resorts on the Fox Chain-of-lakes rented blinds on Grass Lake and Fox Lake. Just east of Antioch lay the Redwing Slough and Deer Lake, and other privately owned waterfowling hot spots. By the 1940s more than two-thirds of the waterfowl habitat was in private control. The Illinois Conservation Department listed over 700 duck clubs on its 1955 Migratory Bird Kill Report.

Understandably waterfowling began to influence entire communities throughout the state. Hotels rented accommodations. Local hunters served as guides and punters. Women cleaned the game and provided meals. Individual craftsmen produced waterfowling decoys, duck calls, and duck boats for the hunters. The entrepreneurial spirit was strong. One of the earliest known commercial carvers, Robert Elliston, a buggy maker when he moved to the Hennepin area in 1870, was soon building hunting boats and decoys. The quality and volume of artifacts from this region reflect this spirit. Men like Charles Perdew ran cottage industries producing hundreds of decoys, game calls, and hunting boats The classic Illinois River decoy had a hollow, deep V-bottomed body with a two-piece construction designed with a seam that set above the waterline. The most common species were mallards and pintails, which represented the average bag limit. Decoys were painted with bright realistic color so they would show up in the marsh grasses and flooded timbers where most Illinois waterfowling was done. When Parmelee and Loomis documented the decoy carvers of Illinois in *Decoys and Decoy Carvers of Illinois*, several hundred individual makers were listed

Assorted business and membership cards from different Illinois hunting clubs and hunting services.

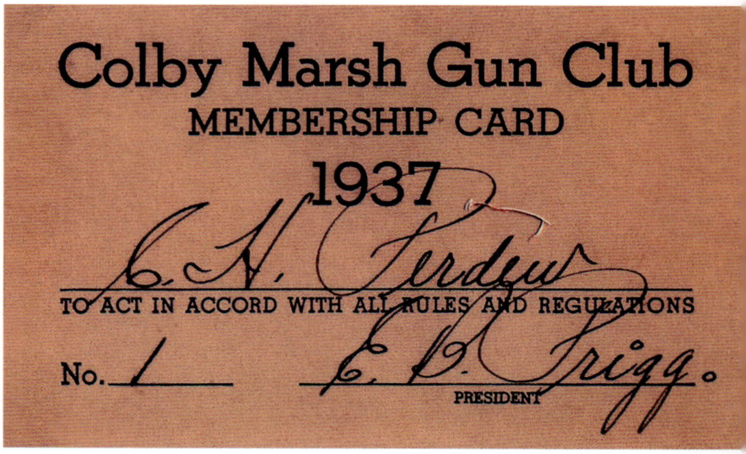

Assorted rulebooks from Illinois hunting clubs.

Another rulebook from an Illinois hunting club.

Fred Forbeck ran his hunting operation off the Hennepin Canal just south of Bureau, Illinois circa 1920-1960. These grounds were formerly managed by the Greenwing Club.

RULES AND REGULATIONS OF FORBECK HUNTING GROUNDS!

All fees payable in advance before leaving clubhouse.
Blinds to be drawn for.
Going to and from blinds, firearms must be unloaded.
Don't leave blinds unless instructed by caretaker.
All hunting to be according to law.
All hunting equipment to be returned to clubhouse.
Hunters to report kill to caretakers.

Not responsible for accidents on premises.

11 *Advertisement for Senachwine Lake Shooting Resort from The American Field, December 1881, p. 24.*

Soon after the Civil War early railroad companies capitalized on the availability of recreational lands along the Illinois River. Lake Senachwine became a popular resort for boaters, fishermen and waterfowlers.

Illinois River Valley duck hunters favored mallard and pintail decoys which are the predominate species bagged in the state. Shallow double-bowed hunting skiffs. Were common here where hunting was done mostly in shallow backwaters and lakes of the Illinois Rivers watershed area.

Pen and Ink drawing. Lou Schifferl, Neehna, Wisconsin, originally used to illustrate *Push*Paddle*Punt- Historic Midwestern Boats* Lou Schifferl, published Decoy Collector's Guide Annual 1966-67. Nee-Pee-Nauk boats were used on North Fox River. A brace fore and aft of the cockpit reinforced its sturdy hull while an ample cockpit with foldaway canvas offered protection from the weather and concealed the hunter. *Courtesy Barbara Sorenson and Lou Schifferl.*

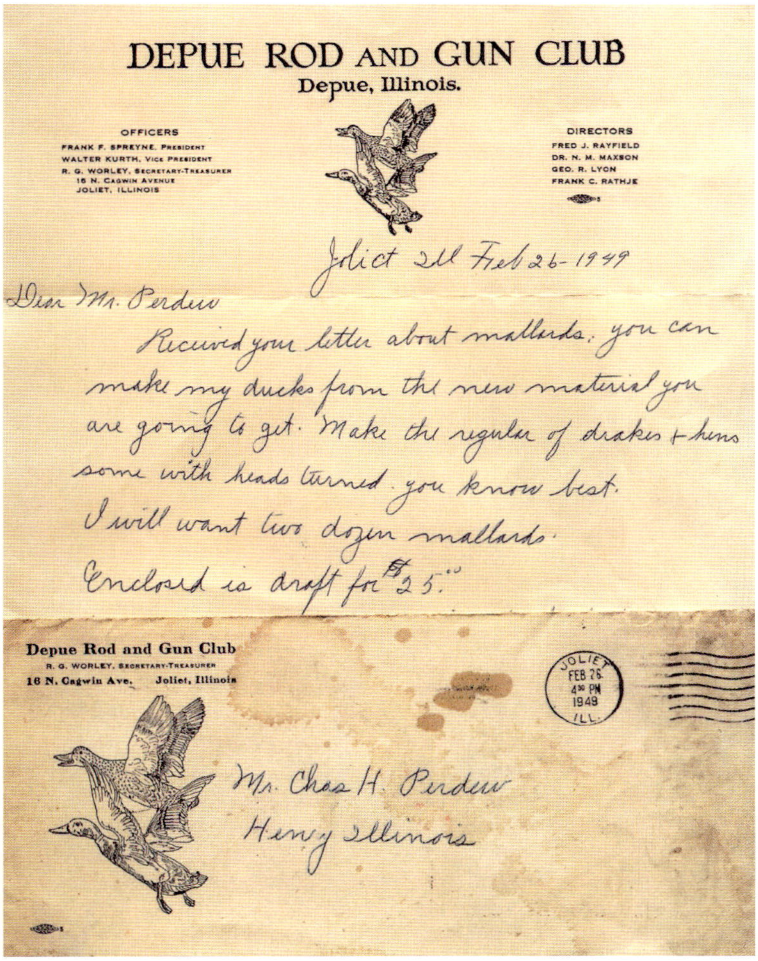

DEPUE ROD AND GUN CLUB
Depue, Illinois.

OFFICERS
FRANK F. SPREYNE, PRESIDENT
WALTER KURTH, VICE PRESIDENT
R. G. WORLEY, SECRETARY-TREASURER
16 N. CAGWIN AVENUE
JOLIET, ILLINOIS

DIRECTORS
FRED J. RAYFIELD
DR. N. M. MAXSON
GEO. R. LYON
FRANK C. RATHJE

Joliet Ill Feb 26-1949

Dear Mr. Perdew

Received your letter about mallards. you can make my ducks from the new material you are going to get. Make the regular of drakes + hens some with heads turned. you know best.
I will want two dozen mallards.
Enclosed is draft for $25.00

Depue Rod and Gun Club
R. G. WORLEY, SECRETARY-TREASURER
16 N. Cagwin Ave. Joliet, Illinois

JOLIET FEB 26 4 PM 1949 ILL.

Mr. Chas H. Perdew
Henry Illinois

Letterhead, Depue Rod and Gun Club, Depue, Illinois, circa 1930.

Letterhead, Senachwine Club Putman, Illinois.

N. E. SIMONSEN, PRESIDENT
2243 ORRINGTON AVE.
EVANSTON

GEORGE C. DAVIS, VICE PRESIDENT
422 MILWAUKEE AVE.

C. P. ZACHER, SEC'Y-TREAS.
1842 E. 79TH STREET

OFFICE OF SECRETARY - TREASURER

Senachwine Club

1842 E. 79TH STREET

PHONE SOUTH SHORE 5050

CHICAGO

DIRECTORS
N. E. SIMONSEN
GEORGE C. DAVIS
C. P. ZACHER
CHAS. E. CARSON
HARRY SEVERSON
A. L. WILCOXSON
GERALD W. PECK

GROUNDS: PUTNAM, ILL.

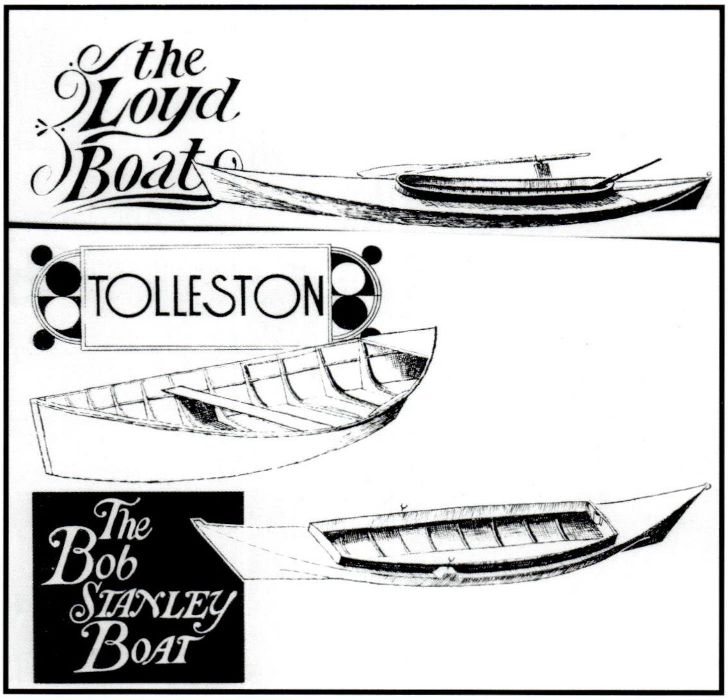

Illinois River duck skiffs: The Loyd, Alex T. Loyd, Calumet Lake; Tolleston boat, Calumet Lake, The Stanley Boat, Robert Stanley, Fox Lake, Illinois. *Courtesy Barbara Sorenson and Lou Schifferl.*

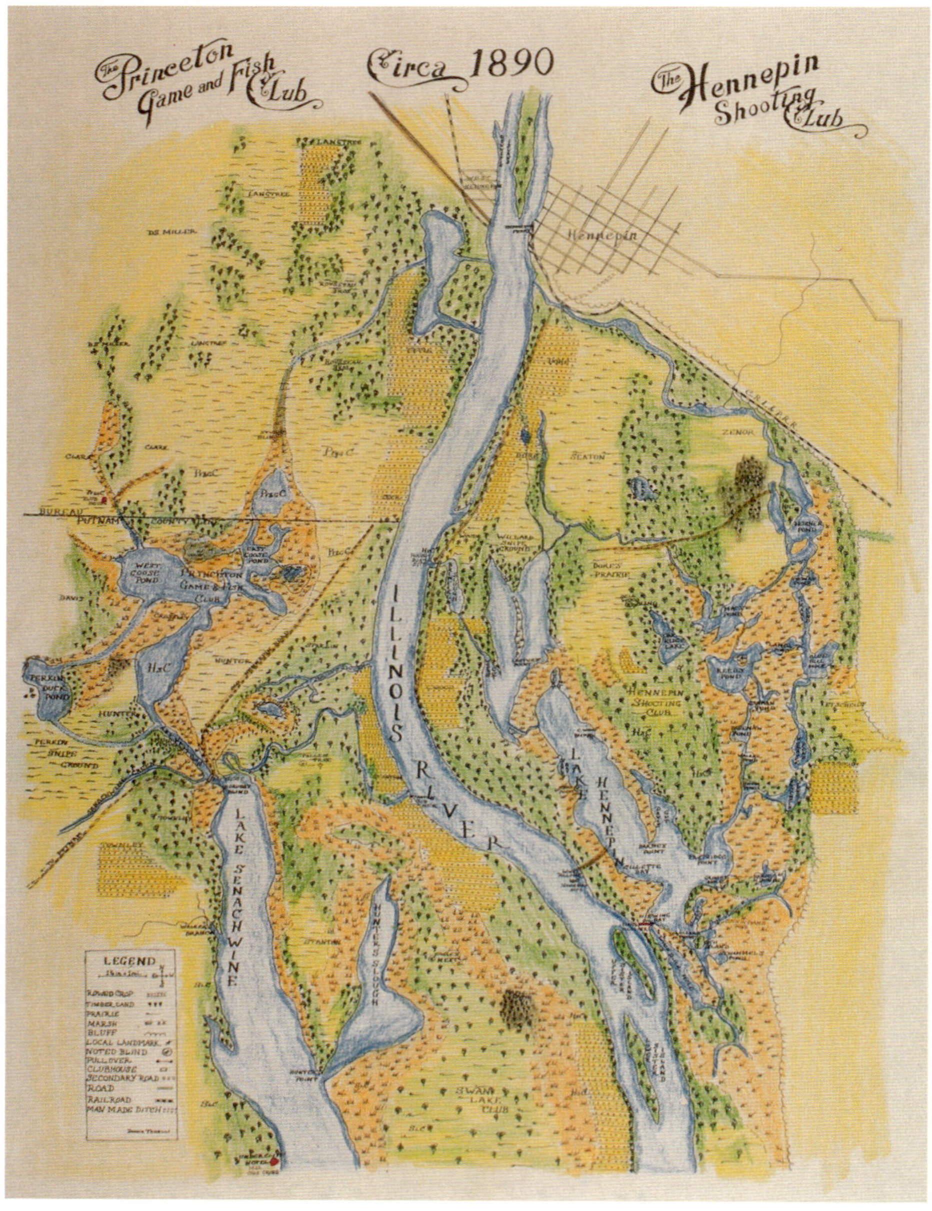

Map of the Hennepin area, circa 1890, Illinois area near "Big Bend" of Illinois River where the Illinois's backwaters created outstanding waterfowl habitat. Some of the earliest and most prestigious hunting clubs were centered here including, Hennepin Shooting Club, Princeton Game and Fish Club, Swan Lake Club, Senachwine Club, and Undercliff Shooting Association.

Hennepin Shooting Club sign was part of the original houseboat that was used as a clubhouse, circa 1880.

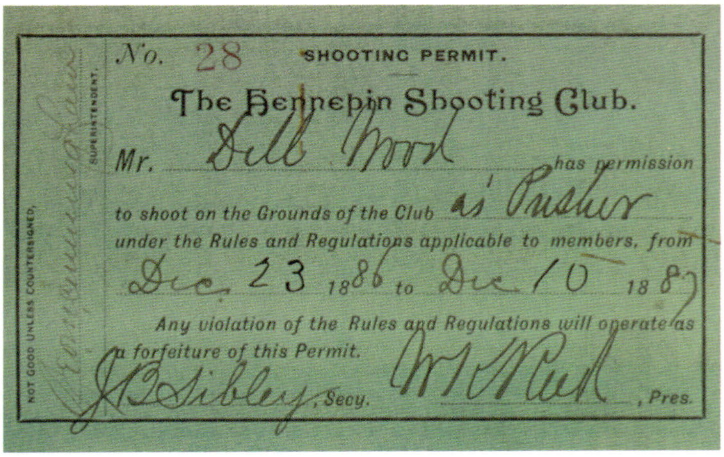

No. 28 SHOOTING PERMIT.

The Hennepin Shooting Club.

Mr. Dell Wood has permission to shoot on the Grounds of the Club as Pusher under the Rules and Regulations applicable to members, from Dec 23 1886 to Dec 10 1887

Any violation of the Rules and Regulations will operate as a forfeiture of this Permit.

J.B. Sibley, Secy. , Pres.

NOT GOOD UNLESS COUNTERSIGNED, SUPERINTENDENT.

Local hunters who worked as guides, A.K.A. pushers, were allowed to accompany a member to assist him on his hunt. The Pusher was responsible for all the preparations; push-poling the hunter's boat, setting out the decoys, retrieving downed ducks and picking up when the hunt was over. This card was issued which identified a non-member as a pusher at Hennepin Shooting Club, dated December 1887.

Hennepin Shooting Club rulebook. Most clubs had extensive rules of conduct that were laid out in handbooks that were distributed to the membership.

Jack Atin, Browning, Illinois captured in a classic "pushers" pose as he maneuvers his boat into the boat hide behind his blind.

No. 6.

CERTIFICATE OF MEMBERSHIP
IN THE
Princeton Game & Fish Club.

This is to certify that Mr. Douglas Moseley has subscribed to the by-laws and paid to the Treasurer the membership fee of twenty-five dollars for one share represented by this certificate, and has complied with all requirements necessary to entitle him to membership in The Princeton Game and Fish Club. This certificate is issued in accordance with the by-laws, and may be transferred or forfeited in manner provided thereby, and is at all times subject to the action of the Club and its rules, regulations and by-laws.

In witness whereof The Princeton Game and Fish Club has caused its seal to be hereto attached and these presents to be subscribed by its President and Secretary at Princeton, Illinois, this 13th day of May A. D. 1892.

Douglas Moseley, President.

George S. Skinner, Secretary.

Princeton Game and Fish Club membership certificate issued to Douglas Moseley founding member in 1892. Many of the early hunting clubs were set-up like small businesses following basic parliamentary procedures. Each member was issued a share much like a stock certificate. Whenever a member left the club, he sold his share usually including his boat and decoys to a prospective member who was then voted on by the membership.

DECOYS

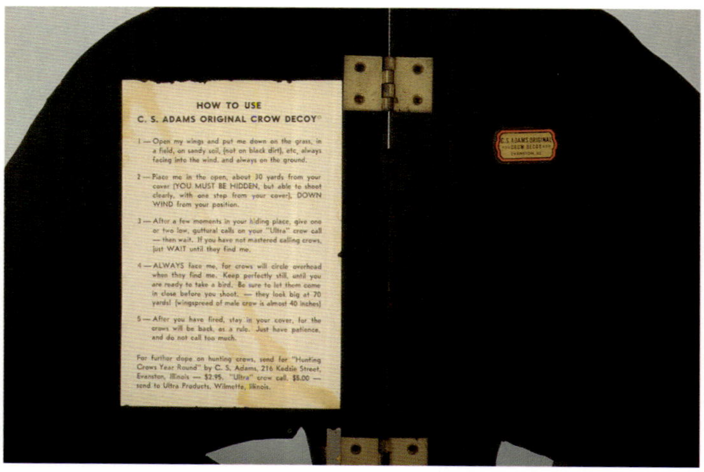

Mallard drake, Oscar F. Alford (1883-1962), Beardstown, Illinois, circa 1920. $3,500. *Collection of Randy and Judy Mayers. Photography Joseph Engers.*

Crow, C.S. Adams, Ultra Products, Evanston, Illinois. The information about this folding silhouette decoy came from a label on the backside, circa 1950. $300. *Collection of Conrad Sundeen.*

Mallard hen, Oscar Alford, Beardstown, Illinois, circa 9120. $3,500. *Collection of Randy and Judy Mayers. Photography Joseph Engers.*

Fred A. Allen (1838-1912), Monmouth, Illinois.

Nickel-plated duck calls, Fred Allen, Monmouth, Illinois, circa 1880. $700 each.

Duck call set, Fred Allen, Monmouth, Illinois, circa 1880, Call set, $2,000; individual calls, $200 each.

Bluebill drake, Fred Allen, Monmouth, Illinois, $2,500. Fred Allen sold his wooden shell duck calls under the name Fred A. Allen Sportsmen's Specialty Company. They were packaged by the half dozen in a burgundy box with a printed end label, circa 1880. Call set (6 in box). $2,000. Allen also produced a nickel-plated brass duck call, circa 1880. $700 each.

Game bird calls, Fred Allen, Monmouth, Illinois, circa 1880, shown with Allen advertising bill, circa 1880. (Left) duck call with raised lip, $250; (center) duck call, $200; (right) crow call, $150.

Redhead drake, Fred Allen, Monmouth, Illinois;. $5,000. *Collection Alan and Elaine Haid. Photograph Alan Haid.*

Mallard pair, Fred Allen, Monmouth, Illinois;. $10,000: *Collection Alan and Elaine Haid. Photograph Alan Haid.*

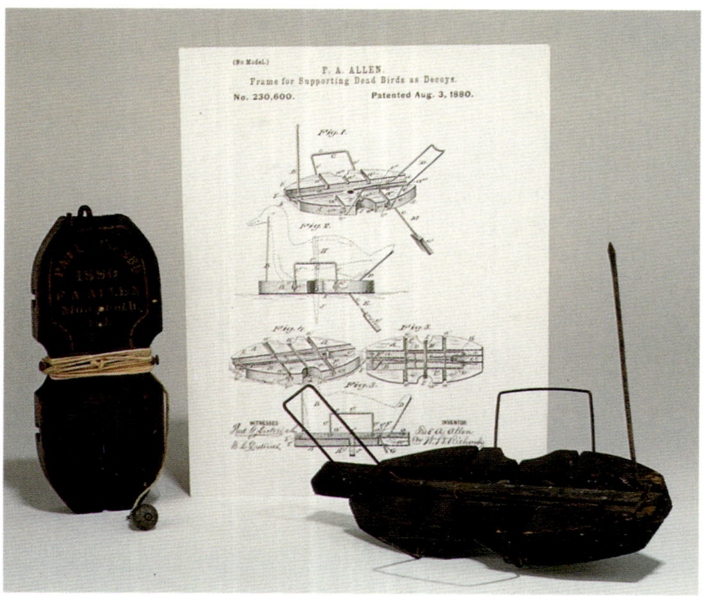

Duck holder designed and manufactured by Fred Allen. Earliest models are unmarked, Later ones are stenciled. These frames were designed to hold a dead duck in a natural position so it could be floated as a decoy, and were marketed in two sizes, circa 1890. $300 each.

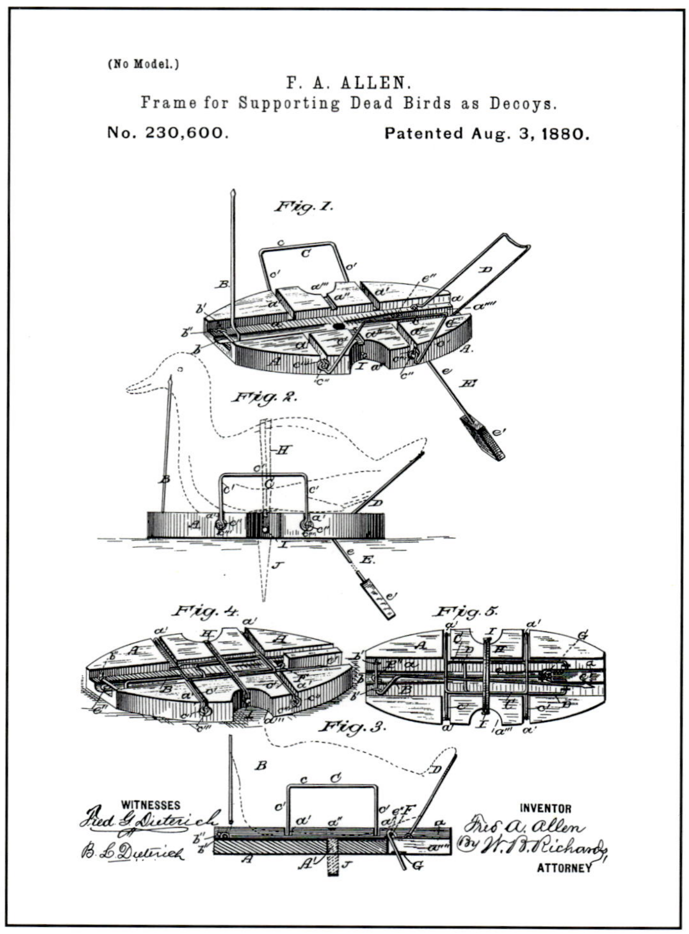

Patent drawing #230,600; duck holder, Fred Allen, Monmouth, Illinois, circa 1880.

Mallard hen, Charles Althoff (1859-1942), Princeton, Illinois, Althoff was also known locally as a talented carver of carousel animals. His association with the young Charles Walker has led some collectors to credit him with instructing Walker in his painting techniques circa 1890. $3,500. *Collection of James R. and Diane Cook.*

Pintail drake, Charles Althoff, Princeton, Illinois, circa 1890. $4,000. *Collection of Alan and Elaine Haid. Photograph Alan Haid.*

Mallard pair, George "Skippy" Barto, Fairmont (Joliet), Illinois, circa 1930. Only known sleeper decoy by Barto. $3,500.

George "Skippy" Barto (1880-1959), Fairmont (Joliet), Illinois, originally from Tiskilwa, Illinois, Barto became a semi-professional baseball player with the Joliet Standards. He returned to the Hennepin area to hunt and learned to carve decoys by emulating the master carvers of this area. Charles and Edna Perdew became his personal friends and taught him their 'tricks of the trade'. Photograph, Art Schuman, outdoor editor for Joliet Herald. Barto's workshop on Grandview Avenue in Fairmont, 1950.

Pintail drake, George "Skippy" Barto, Fairmont (Joliet), Illinois, circa 1940. $2,000.

Duck calls, George "Skippy" Barto, Fairmont (Joliet), Illinois, circa 1940. $1,000 each. *Collection of Robert Christensen.*

Greenhead duck call, Louis "Louie" Bicocchi (1909-1979), LaSalle, Illinois, adjustable duck call in original box, circa 1950. $100.

Mallard pair; canvasback pair (miniature) by Arthur "Artie Bennett" Behemetuik (1919-?), Lockport, Illinois, Longtime friend and hunting companion of "Skippy"Barto, circa.1960. $300 pair.

Duck calls, Richard Burnes (1865-c. 1925), Pekin, Illinois was one of the first makers of hard rubber duck call. Center call was his personal call, circa 1900. $700 each.

Glen "Judge" Cameron (far right) (1882-1958), Chillicothe, Illinois noted Illinois waterfowler and judge, circa 1937.

Mallard hen, Judge Glen Cameron, Peoria, Illinois, circa 1930. $7000. *Collection of James R. and Diane Cook.*

Frank 'Scull Boat' Cassini (1899-1967) Galesburg, Illinois hard at work in his workshop. Note the mourning dove decoys in the foreground, circa 1960. Doves, $1,000 each.

Left:
Mallard drake, Judge Glen Cameron, Peoria, Illinois, circa 1930. $5,000.

Shoveler (spoonbill) pair, Frank Cassini, circa 1930. $50,000. This pair of decoys were the cover birds on *Decoys and Decoy Carvers of Illinois*. *Collection of Diane and James R Cook.*

Mallard pair, Frank Cassini, Galesburg, Illinois, circa 1940. $5,000. *Collection of James R. and Diane Cook.*

Mallard hen, Frank Cassini, Galesburg, Illinois, circa 1940. $3,000. *Collection of James R. and Diane Cook.*

Frank Cassini decorative plaques combined his wood carving skills and talent with flat works. Pairs of flying mallards were showcased on a marsh scene painted in oils on a masonite backboard. The feet are formed from rubber and wire, circa.1940. $2,000 each.

Verne Cheesman, Monmouth, Illinois with one of his pintail drake decoys in his workshop. *Photograph Joseph B. French, circa 1957.*

Mallard pair, Verne Cheesman (1897-1964), painted by Cheesman. Circa1930. $1,500 pair.

Mallard hen, Verne Cheesman, like several decoy carvers in the state, took finished decoy blocks to Edna Perdew to be painted, circa 1940. $700.

Bluebill pair, Verne Cheesman, painted by Edna Perdew, circa 1940. $7,500. *Collection of James R. and Diane Cook.*

Duck calls, William Clifford (1877-1958), River Forest, Illinois, circa 1940. Clifford, a decorative tile setter by trade, applied geometric designs to his decoy call. This was achieved by laminating varying woods and metal together before the call barrel was turned on a woodcutting lathe. $4,000 each *Collection of Robert Christensen.*

Duck calls and laminated display rack, William Clifford's duck calls sold at V.L. & A. (Von Lengerke & Antoine) Sporting Goods, Chicago, Illinois where they were displayed on beautiful laminated stands that Clifford made, circa 1930. Stand, $4,000. *Collection of Robert Christenson.*

Duck calls; William Clifford, Chicago, Illinois, laminated, circa 1940. $4,000 each. *Collection of Gary Rieker.*

Green-winged teal drake by Fred Coleman, (1898-1990) who owned and operated the Coleman Gun Club near Hennepin, Illinois, circa 1925. $3,500.

Coleman Hunting Club Sign hung on the clubhouse until the Donnelly family bought the grounds. These grounds and Coleman Lake have since been donated to the state of Illinois and are still operational as a managed hunting area, circa 1930.

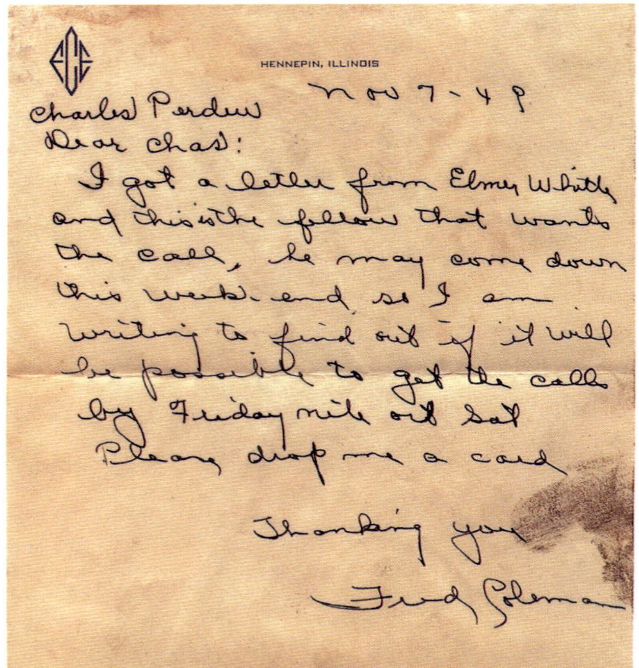

HENNEPIN, ILLINOIS

Nov 7-49

Charles Perdew
Dear Chas:
I got a letter from Elmer White and this is the fellow that wants the call, he may come down this week-end so I am writing to find out if it will be possible to get the calls by Friday nite or Sat
Please drop me a card

Thanking you

Fred Coleman

Letter dated Nov 7, 1949 from Fred Coleman ordering a duck call from Charles Perdew; written on his personal stationery with Coleman Duck Club Logo on envelope.

Francis W. Collins (1925-?), Milan, Illinois. Best known for his miniature bird carvings, he also carved two-dozen wood ducks and teal decoys. He is holding one of his green-winged teal drakes, circa 1968.

Cobbe Corn corn decoys were packaged with eleven ears in an imprinted canvas bag. Manufactured by Beard & Morency Mill Company, Oak Park, Illinois, circa 1935. 11 ears complete set with bag, $2,500. Individual ears. $200.

Walter "Tube" Dawson (1882-1955)[far left] and friends pose after a good early fall hunt outside his workshop. Photograph entitled "Sept 1st '07 / 100 in shade / 51 wood ducks.".

Mallard pair, Duane Corbin, Joliet, Illinois, circa 1940. $3,000.

Illinois River duck calls, circa 1880, Putman County. Left: fancy hand carved duck call with vine and leaf design, George Cunningham (1842-1923), Hennepin, $7,500. Right: large checkered duck call by Delbert S. "Dell" Woods (1860-1933), first Putman County game warden and caretaker of Hennepin Shooting Club, $5,000. Also shown is the rulebook from Hennepin Gun Club, circa 1890, and a shooting pass from Hennepin Shooting Club, circa 1886.

Tube Dawson and Leon Thompson, Thompson fisheries, Hennepin, Illinois, pose with their bag of canvasbacks shot on Lake Senachwine, circa 1930.

Pintail drake, Tube Dawson, circa 1930. Shotgun shell box, Wilson & Wilson Hardware Store, Mason City, Illinois, hand-loaded Challenge shot shells, 12 gauge. Decoy, $1,000; shell box, $1,000. *Collection of Michael and Joan Pierce.*

Oversized mallard pair by Walter 'Tube' Dawson, circa 1920. $3,000.

Tube Dawson's Letterhead: W.H. Dawson, Manufacturer of Boats, Decoys and Duck Calls, Putman, Illinois. Tube had his workshop set up near the railroad tracks in Bureau where he could easily cater to visiting duck hunters as well as local hunters who were in the market for decoys, duck calls, or a new duck boat.

Special-order high head mallard, Tube Dawson. Extra length was added to the necks so the heads could be seen in high marsh grasses on Illinois River backwater ponds, circa 1920. $7,000 *Photograph Gene Kangas. Courtesy Gene and Linda Kangas.*

Fred Destri (1909-1992) Spring Valley, Illinois began to carve decoys during the depression. He had hunted over a rig of Charlie Perdew decoys but burned many of the decoys one winter so he wouldn't have to buy more coal to heat his home. Before he burned the decoys he took patterns off them and thus started his own carving career.

Green-winged teal drakes with sleeper, Fred Destri, circa 1960. $1000 each.

Mallard hen, Fred Destri, circa 1940. $2,000.

Left:
Pair of mallard tip-up decoys, Fred Destri. Tip-up decoys were used to represent feeding ducks, circa 1950. $500.

Right:
Charles Harris Ditto (1865-1935), Keithsburg, Illinois. Although Ditto held the 1908 U.S. Amateur Trapshooting Championship, he is best remembered for his call making. Newspaper clipping, circa 1910.

C. H. DITTO, KEITHSBURG, ILL., WINNER PRELIMINARY HANDICAP.

Duck & goose calls, Charles Ditto, Keithsburg, Illinois. Mississippi River Duck and Goose Call, metal combination call, $2500; hard plastic duck call, $500; New Eureka Duck Call, $500.

Assorted game calls with original order form, Charles Ditto, Keithsburg, Illinois. Far left: special order walnut call made for Ditto's brother-in-law, circa 1890, $1,000. Center front: Eureka Duck Call, Standard No. 1 production call, circa 1910, $200. All-metal nickel-plated combination duck and goose call, extremely rare, circa 1900, $2,500. Hard rubber call, circa 1910, (the patent was sold to P.S. Olt Specialty Company, Pekin, Illinois.), $500.

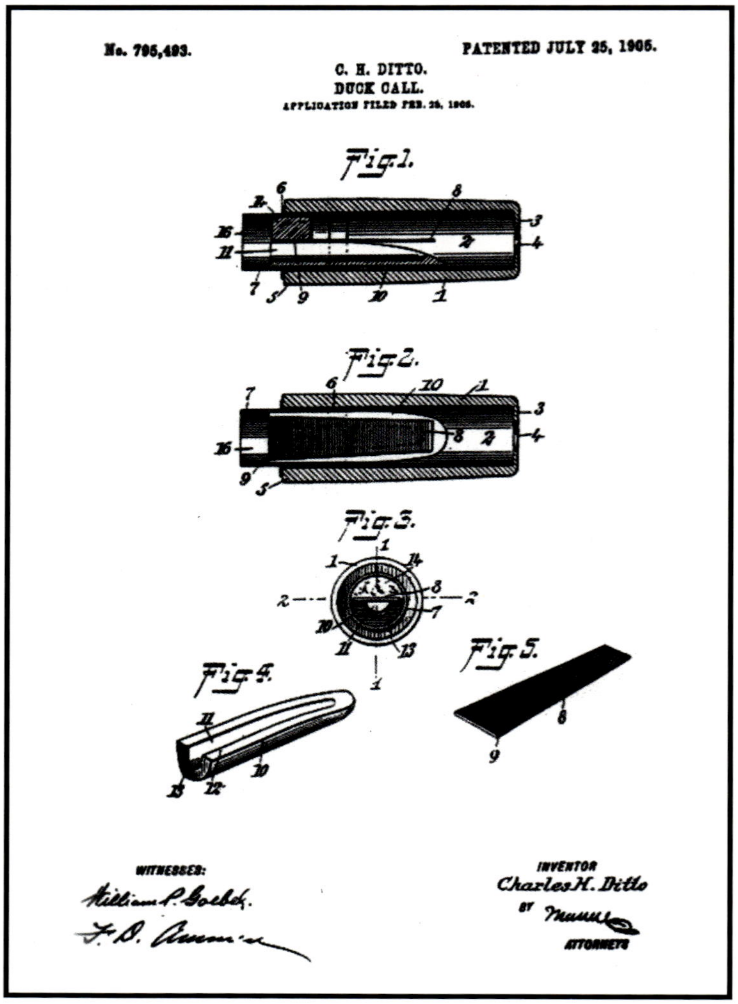

Patent drawing Ditto duck call, patented July 1905.

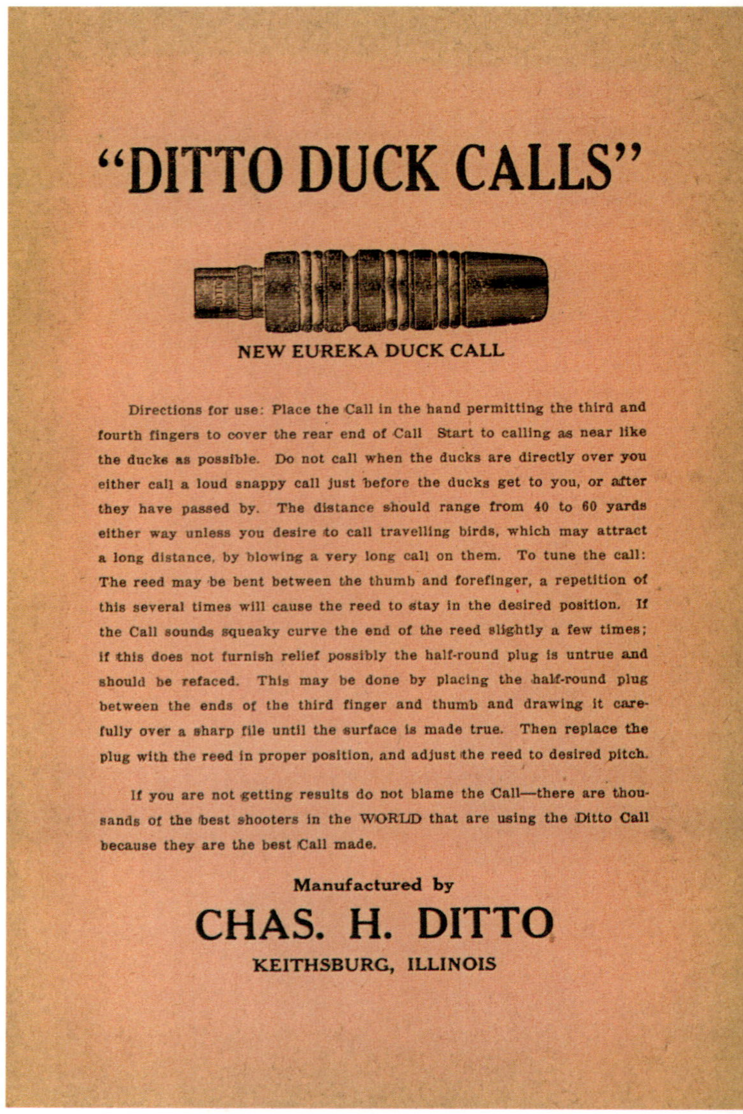

"DITTO DUCK CALLS"

NEW EUREKA DUCK CALL

Directions for use: Place the Call in the hand permitting the third and fourth fingers to cover the rear end of Call Start to calling as near like the ducks as possible. Do not call when the ducks are directly over you either call a loud snappy call just before the ducks get to you, or after they have passed by. The distance should range from 40 to 60 yards either way unless you desire to call travelling birds, which may attract a long distance, by blowing a very long call on them. To tune the call: The reed may be bent between the thumb and forefinger, a repetition of this several times will cause the reed to stay in the desired position. If the Call sounds squeaky curve the end of the reed slightly a few times; if this does not furnish relief possibly the half-round plug is untrue and should be refaced. This may be done by placing the half-round plug between the ends of the third finger and thumb and drawing it carefully over a sharp file until the surface is made true. Then replace the plug with the reed in proper position, and adjust the reed to desired pitch.

If you are not getting results do not blame the Call—there are thousands of the best shooters in the WORLD that are using the Ditto Call because they are the best Call made.

Manufactured by

CHAS. H. DITTO

KEITHSBURG, ILLINOIS

Advertising handbill announcing "New Eureka Duck Call" circa 1910.

Leonard Doren (1895-1963), Pekin, Illinois, in his workshop painting a mallard decoy. Note the owl decoy in the background, circa 1960. *Photograph, Willis Pennington. Courtesy Mrs. Dottie Pennington.*

Duck call, Selectone Duck Call, adjustable duck call, Walter "Wally" Drennen, Depue, Illinois, circa 1940. $200 each.

Owl, Leonard Doren, Pekin, Illinois, circa 1960. Doren owl decoys are often mistaken for owl decoy made for the P.S. Olt Specialty Company by John Hyatt, also from Pekin. The carvers obviously used the same pattern, but Doren carved the wing areas in relief. $2,500.

Drennen's Selectone Duck Calls, Wally Drennen, Depue, Illinois, circa 1950.

Duck calls, Frank "Cotton" Eckard, Putman Illinois, circa 1920. Eckard was caretaker of the prestigious Senachwine Club for most of his life. Senachwine Club rulebook, circa 1920. Duck calls, $750 each.

Robert (1848-1915) and Catherine Elliston (1858-1953) were one of Illinois' premier husband and wife decoy producing teams. Pictured with their family circa 1890, the couple settled in Bureau, Illinois near the hub of duck hunting at the "Big Bend" of the Illinois River. Robert, a buggy maker by trade soon began to produce hunting boats and decoys. Catherine painted all of the decoys and continued to paint decoys after Robert's death for other carvers like Bert Graves. Her influence can be seen in the painting of many classic Illinois River decoys.

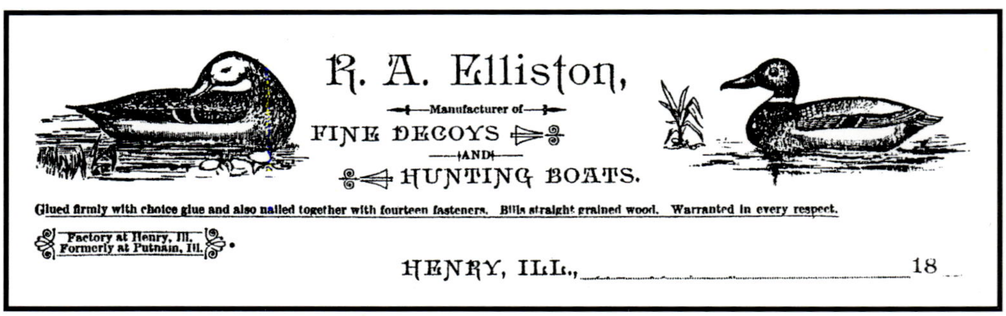

R. A. Elliston,
Manufacturer of
FINE DECOYS
AND
HUNTING BOATS.

Glued firmly with choice glue and also nailed together with fourteen fasteners. Bills straight grained wood. Warranted in every respect.

Factory at Henry, Ill.
Formerly at Putnain, Ill.

HENRY, ILL., ____________ 18__

This recently discovered R. A. Elliston letterhead documents that Elliston had a "decoy factory" in Putman, then in Henry (circa 1880), before he and Catherine settled in Bureau. The later letterhead (shown at right), with Alba Miller's receipt, shows the Bureau address.

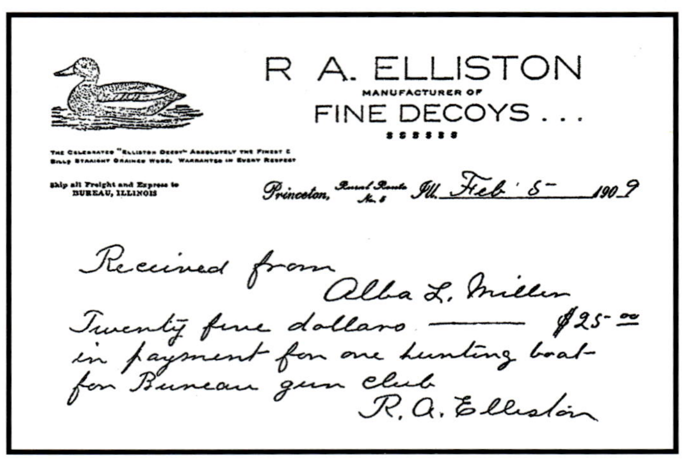

R A. ELLISTON
MANUFACTURER OF
FINE DECOYS . . .

Ship all Freight and Express to
BUREAU, ILLINOIS

Princeton, Rural Route No. 5 Ill. Feb' 5 1909

Received from
Alba L. Miller
Twenty five dollars —— $25.00
in payment for one hunting boat
for Bureau gun club
R. A. Elliston

Mallard pair, Robert and Catherine Elliston, Bureau, Illinois, circa 1890. $8,000.

Black duck sleeper, oversized, Robert and Catherine Elliston, Bureau, Illinois, circa 1880. Only known example in original condition. $50,000. *Collection Alan and Elaine Haid. Photograph Alan Haid.*

Miniature mallard carvings that Robert Elliston carved for a family member, circa 1880. $5,000. Assorted hand tools and head patterns including a hand-forged striker Elliston used to hand stamp his lead keel weights; it reads "THE ELLISTON DECOY.".

Pintail drake, Robert and Catherine Elliston, Bureau, Illinois, circa 1900. $5,000.

Below:
Blue-winged teal drake, Robert and Catherine Elliston, Bureau, Illinois. Extremely rare spring plumage, circa 1890. $30, 000.

Canvasback drake, Robert Elliston, Bureau, Illinois, circa 1885. $15,000. *Collection of James R and Diane Cook.*

Green-winged teal hen, Robert and Catherine Elliston, Bureau, Illinois, circa 1890. $10,000.

Canvasback drake, early deep, round-bottom style, Robert and Catherine Elliston, Bureau, Illinois, circa 1890. $7,500.

Canvasback drake, Robert and Catherine Elliston, Bureau, Illinois, circa 1890. $10,000.

Bluebill drakes, Robert and Catherine Elliston, circa 1890. Earlier deep, round body style. $10,000. Flat body style, $6,000.

Redhead drake, round body style Robert and Catherine Elliston, circa 1880. $15,000.

Coot, extremely rare, one of two known examples, Robert Elliston, Bureau, Illinois, circa 1880. $35,000. *Collection of James R. and Diane Cook.*

Canvasback drake, Jack Eppel, (1899-?), Peoria, Illinois. Eppel carved several dozen mallard and canvasback decoys for his own use using Bert Graves's patterns, circa 1940. $2,500. *Collection of James R. and Diane Cook.*

Duck call, Edward "Doll" Emerick, Rushville, Illinois, circa 1930. $1,000.

Snow goose, Nicholas Englhart (1888-?), Manito, Illinois, Englhart owned and operated a river ferry near Moline, Illinois. He also built hunting boats. Although he wasn't an avid hunter, he did make a few goose decoys for goose shooting along the river sandbars for himself, circa 1940. $5,000. Assorted wooden corn decoys. $500-. $1,000 each.

Canada goose, Nicholas Englhart, Manito, Illinois, circa 1930. $5,000.

Pintail Drake, William "Skinny" Evans, Peru, Illinois was one of several carvers from Peru who hunted the river bottoms in this area and made decoys for their own use, circa 1920. $3,500. *Collection of Diane and James R. Cook.*

Pintail drake, August P. Ewand (1865-1825), Peru, Illinois, circa 1890. $1,000. *Collection of Alan and Elaine Haid.*

Mallard pair, Commodore Model, hard rubber, Flap-O-Matic Company, Chicago, Illinois. Patents numbered #2,747 and 316 were issued to Frank Benedetto, Chicago, Illinois for this mechanical decoy, circa 1950. $200 each.

Mallard drake, papier-mâché model, Flap-O-Matic Company, with original box and instruction sheet, circa 1940. $200.

Goose calls, Fuller Goose Call, David Fuller, Chicago, Illinois, circa 1880. Original Fuller call box, instruction sheet and extra metal reeds. Calls, $200 each.

Mallard pair, Jack Fischer (1913-?), Peoria, Illinois was an associate of Bert Graves. His decoys reflect a strong Graves influence. Fischer designed a special router to hollow out decoy bodies, which was also used by Graves, circa 1960. $750.

Otto Garren (1890-1968) sitting in his Canton, Illinois workshop painting a mallard hen sleeper. Photograph by Joseph B. French, 1952.

Mallard Hen sleeper, Otto Garren, circa 1950.This the actual decoy Garren is holding in Joseph B. French's photograph. $2,000.

Wood duck drake, Otto Garren, Canton, Illinois circa 1940. $5,000. *Collection of James R. and Diane Cook.*

Wood duck drake, Otto Garren, circa 1930. $5,000.

Pintail drake, Otto Garren, circa.1930. $1,000.

Green-winged teal, Otto Garren, circa 1930. $1,500.

Mallard hen, Otto Garren, early example with swing weight, circa 1920. $1,000.

Green-winged teal pair, Otto Garren from Garren's personal hunting rig, circa 1940. $2,500.

Mallard drake, Charles Giesler (1892-1953) and Fred Weber (1862-1953), Peru, Illinois. These two men made decoys together, which they used at the White Timbers Gun Club, west of Peru on the Illinois River, circa 1920. $750. *Collection of William Klein.*

Duck Calls: Glodo family, Jackson County, Illinois, circa 1920-1930 The Glodo call makers included Joseph Victor Jr. (1845-1910), John Nicholas (1847-1907), Albert Henry (1869-1940), William Albert (1873-195), Joseph E. (1889-1977), Walter Albert (1891-1970), and Arzia Emerson (1902-1979). Together they made what is known as the Glodo Style duck call consisting of a one piece stopper with wooden wedge block, flat tone board, and curved metal reed. $4,000 each. *Photograph and collection Robert Christensen.*

George 'Bert' Graves (1887-1956), Peoria, Illinois, pictured with his brother-in-law and hunting companion, George Snider (right), after a day of canvasback shooting on the far west side of Upper Peoria Lake. Here there was once a vast 1000 acre sago pondweed and wild celery bed off the sea wall near Rome, Illinois. Because Graves often hunted canvasbacks, he was one of few Illinois River carvers who produced canvasback decoys on a regular basis, circa 1940.

Mallard drakes, Bert Graves. Large drake is one of twelve known oversized mallards. The smaller drake is an example of a "white-sided" Graves. Catherine Elliston painted this style decoys for Graves when he first started his commercial production using her late husband Robert's pattern. Later "gray-sided" mallards were painted by Graves's sister, Nellie Graves, as were most of the Graves decoys, circa 1920. Oversized drake, $20,000; regular drake;. $7,500.

Mallard pair with sleeper, Bert Graves, Peoria, Illinois. Painted by Catherine Elliston, circa 1940. $30,000. *Collection James & Diane Cook.*

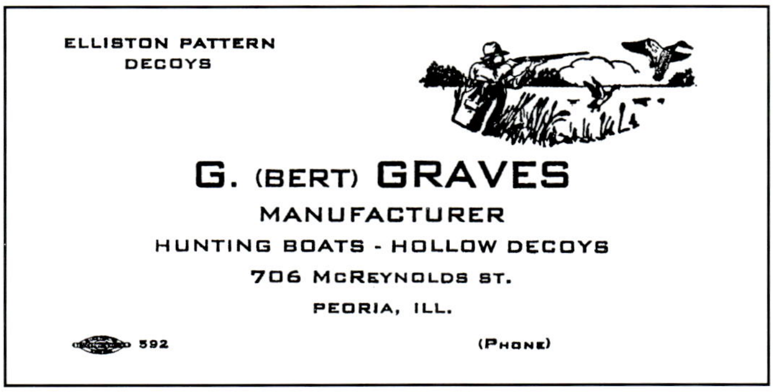

ELLISTON PATTERN
DECOYS

G. (BERT) GRAVES
MANUFACTURER
HUNTING BOATS - HOLLOW DECOYS
706 McREYNOLDS ST.
PEORIA, ILL.

592 (PHONE)

Business card, George Bert Graves, Peoria, Illinois.

Mallard hen, swimmer head style, Bert Graves, Peoria, Illinois, circa 1930. $7,000. *Collection of James R. and Diane Cook.*

Black duck, Bert Graves, Peoria, Illinois, circa 1930. $7,500. *Collection James R. and Diane Cook.*

Mallard pair by G. Bert Graves, Peoria, Illinois. Painted by Catherine Elliston, circa 1920. $12,000.

Charles Grubbs (1848-1933), Senachwine Lake, Chicago, Illinois, Pascagoula, Mississippi, and Houston, Texas, is considered by many to be the father of the Illinois River-style duck call. Photograph, circa 1910.

Pintail pair, Bert Graves, circa 1930. $10,000.

Pintail pair, Bert Graves, Peoria, Illinois, circa 1930. $10,000. *Collection of James and Diane Cook.*

Canvasback pair, Bert Graves, circa 1920. $10,000.

C.W. Grubbs catalog cover, circa 1920.

Business card, C.W. Grubbs established the Hotel Undercliff on the shores of Lake Senachwine, circa 1880, which became a popular resort hotel offering boating, swimming, and fishing. The Undercliff Shooting Association would later use the hotel's facilities for their headquarters.

Duck calls, Charles Grubbs, Kankakee, Illinois. Left to right: Perfection duck call, circa 1870, $2,000; Perfect Duck Call, circa 1890, $1,000; Perfection duck call, circa 1880, $1,000.

Duck call, Charles Grubbs, Kankakee, Illinois, Special order calls for George Sibley, circa 1880. Business card, Sibley Decoy, circa 1900. Duck calls, $5,000 each.

Variations of Grubbs Standard duck call sold by Montgomery Wards, Sears & Roebuck and various Midwest sporting goods distributors, circa 1880. $500 each.

Pintail drake, August Haas (1890-1962), Peru, Illinois, painted by Charles Althoff (Princeton, Illinois), circa 1910. $15,000.

Canvasback drake by Harold Haertel, Dundee, Illinois, circa 1969. $8,000.

Harold Haertel (1904-1996), Dundee, Illinois was one of the few master decoy carvers who was able to make the transition from classic working hunting decoys to contemporary floating sculptural decoys. His birds are highly collectible, with gentle flowing forms textured entirely with paint creating subtle natural waterfowl decoys in realistic poses. The decoy display in his den was a blend of his contemporary carvings and top quality vintage decoys. He was active in both fields.

Redhead drake, only known example, Harold Haertel, Dundee, Illinois, circa 1967. $10,000.

Below:
Gadwall pair, Harold Haertel, Dundee, Illinois, circa 1970. $25,000.
Collection of Barbara Sorenson.

Ringbill pair, with sleeper hen. Harold Haertel only carved a handful sleeper style decoys, circa 1950. $10,000.

Miniature Canada goose, Harold Haertel's miniature decoys are extremely rare. Most were made for a complete set of waterfowl Harold carved over the years for his wife, circa 1970. $3,000.

Horned grebe, Harold Haertel, extremely rare sleeper style decoy, circa 1972. $5,000.

Pied-bill grebe, Harold Haertel, circa 1969. $2,000.

Pintail hen with brood of ducklings, Harold Haertel, circa 1968. $5,000. *Photograph by Kent Butcher, 1995.*

Standing wood duck drake, Virgil Hodge, Plainfield, Illinois, circa 1960. $1,000.

Mallard pair, oversized models, Henry Holmes, circa 1900. $8,000.

Mallard pair, Hiram "Hy" Holtz (1886-1968), Peoria, Illinois was an expert trap shooter and waterfowler. Since he carved decoys for his own use, he made several dozen mallard and canvasback decoys. Holtz signed and dated the inside of the body of his hollow decoys and the initials H.H. are stamped on his anchor weights, circa 1930. $10,000.

Pintail drakes. Henry Holmes (1870-1940), Bureau, Illinois was one many locals who took advantage of the influx of visiting duck hunters. He set up a cottage industry producing hand crafted hunting decoys. Painted with heavy oils, utilizing classic wet-on-wet and comb graining techniques, his decoys rate among the finest made in the state. Part of Douglas Moseley rig, a founding member of the Princeton Game & Fish Club, Princeton, Illinois, circa 1900. $3,000 each.

Canvasback drake, John "Hy" Holtz, Peoria, Illinois, circa 1930. $7,500. *Collection of James R. and Diane Cook.*

Left:
Owl, John Hyatt. During the 1940s Hyatt was commission by P.S. Olt sporting Goods Company to make 100 wooden owl decoys which would be sold in a crow hunting set including the Hyatt owl decoy. A box of P.S. Olt silhouette paper crow decoys and a Olt crow call. $2,500.

Right:
Pheasant, life-sized. John Hyatt, circa 1930. $3,000.

Cardinal pair, John Hyatt, circa 1930. $4,000.

Left:
Great gray owl, John Hyatt. Commissioned by the owner of the Owl Tavern Inn Neehna, Wisconsin, circa 1930. $10,000.

Right:
Quail decorative, John Hyatt, circa 1930. $1,000.

Bluebill drake Louis Kelly (1878-c.1958), Peoria, Illinois ran a boat rental at Kelly Beach in Peoria. His decoys exhibit a strong influence of the Lacon, Illinois carvers, Stephen Lane and William Shaw. The initials " L.P.K." are stamped on the underside of the decoy's tail, circa 1930. $2,000.

Roy Kamm (1902-?) Lacon, Illinois exhibits the typical Lacon style decoy, captured on film by Joseph B French in his workshop. He is holding decoys he had used during his market-hunting days on the Illinois River in the early 1900s. Photograph, circa 1960. *Courtesy Joseph B. French.*

Mallard hen, Louis Kelly, Peoria, Illinois, circa 1930. $7,000. *Collection of James R. and Diane Cook.*

Mallard pair, Edward Keller (1888-1963), Bartonville, Illinois took great pride in the decoys he made mostly for his own use, even to the extent of putting each decoy into a cloth bag to protect it when it wasn't in the water, circa 1930. $4,000.

Pintail drake, Louis Kelly (1878-1958), Peoria, Illinois, circa 1930. $5,000.

Mallard drake, Louis Kelly, Peoria, Illinois, circa 1930. $5,000.

Mallard pair, George Kessler (1868-1955), Pekin, Illinois. Decoy carving started as a hobby for Kessler but soon became a commercial venture that produced hundreds of working decoy and miniature carving in three varying sizes, circa 1940. $3,000.

Mallard drake, sleeper, Leopold Koehler, Peru, Illinois, circa 1930. $1,000. *Collection of Randy and Judy Mayers. Photography Joseph Engers.*

Mallard drake. Leopold "Dody" Koehler (1871-1944), Peru, Illinois was the patriarch of the Koehler family, which included his sons George and Arthur who also carved decoys and built double-bowed duck skiffs. The Koehler men hunted at the Peru Gun Club and Wing Shooters Club, circa 1930. $750. *Collection of Fritz and Lori Neuschel.*

Pintail drake, Leopold Koehler, Peru, Illinois, circa 1930. $750. *Collection of Randy and Judy Mayers. Photography Joseph Engers.*

Miniature mallard pair. George Koehler sold his miniature decoys through the gift shop on Starved Rock Lodge, an Illinois landmark near Utica, Illinois, circa 1940. $800. *Collection of Fritz and Lori Neuschel.*

George "Jim" Koehler, Peru, Illinois in his basement workshop, 1969. *Photograph courtesy Fritz and Lori Neuschel.*

Ad for Mascot Duck Call, Multi-Novelty Company, Chicago, Illinois.

Mascot duck call, August R. Kuhlemeier, Mutli-Novelty Company, Chicago, Illinois, patented October 27, 1903. Advertising sale bill, Mascot duck call. Duck call, $2,500.

Mallard pair: drake (original paint); hen (repaint). Brink B. Lane, circa 1925: drake, $4,000; hen, $2000. *Photograph and collection Gary Lane Meister.*

Widgeon drake, Brink B. Lane, circa 1905. $10,000. *Photograph and collection Gary Lane Meister.*

Mallard hen, Brink B. Lane, circa 1945. $4,000. *Photograph and collection Gary Lane Meister.*

Pintail drake, Stephen R. Lane, circa 1890. $5,000.

Mallard pair. Stephen Randolph Lane (1842-1900), Lacon, Illinois, one of the earliest documented Illinois decoy carvers is considered by most collectors to be the "father" of the Lacon style decoy. A carpenter and an avid waterfowling market hunter, Lane produced a fine decoy, which he often marked with the letter "S" on the underside of the bill. Circa 1885. $4,000 each. *Photograph and collection Gary Lane Meister.*

Duck call with original carrying cloth bag and instruction pamphlet, Tru-tone Duck Call, Lawrence Casper Larson, Sr., Oak Park, Illinois, circa 1940. $200.

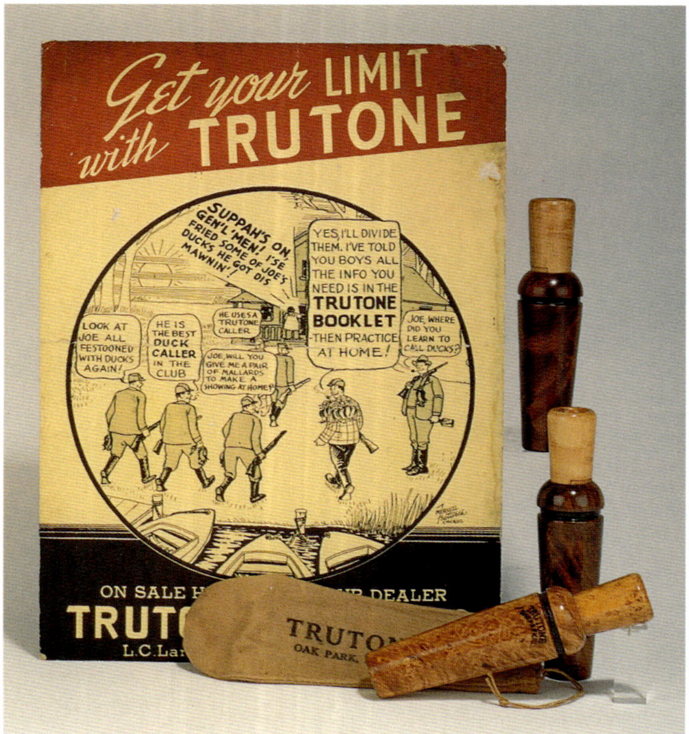

Tru-tone duck calls, Lawrence Casper Larson, Sr. (1888-1947), Oak Park, Illinois. Top right: Blue Ribbon Call, burl walnut, circa 1930, $800. Bottom right: Blue Ribbon Call, burl walnut, circa 1930, $800. Foreground: special order Blue Ribbon Call, curly maple with carrying bag, circa 1935, $1,000. Background: original store counter display board, $750. *Collection of Gary Rieker.*

Duck calls, Tru-tone, Lawrence C. Larson. Left: standard duck call, walnut barrel, maple stopper, $75. Middle: Blue Ribbon Call, burl walnut barrel, maple stopper, $800. Right: Red Ribbon Call, walnut barrel, maple stopper, $200. *Photograph and collection Robert Christensen.*

Crow call with only known original Tru-tone call box, Lawrence Casper Larson, Sr., Oak Park, Illinois, circa 1930. $500 with box.

Three icons of decoy carving tradition: C. Haddon Perdew (left), Harold Haertel (center), and Virgil Lashbrook (right), circa 1970.

Mallard drake and canvasback pair miniatures, Virgil Lashbrook, Pekin, Illinois, circa 1960. $150 each.

Duck calls. Left: laminated wooden barrel with decorative German silver bands, fluted end, circa 1920, $1500. Right: red cedar call decorated with small etched duck filled with light wood fillings on barrel, German silver bands, fluted end, circa 1920; Val Leonard, Bureau, Illinois, $1500. *Photograph and Collection Robert Christensen.*

Mallard drake, Cline McAlpin, circa 1940. $1,000.

Mallard drake, Cline McAlpin, Chicago, Illinois, circa 1940. $1,000. *Collection of Randy and Judy Mayers. Photography Joseph Engers.*

Cline McAlpin (1919-1969), Chicago, Illinois shows off his latest batch of pintail and blue-winged teal decoys. McAlpin learned to carve decoys from the master carver Charles Perdew in 1945. A Chicago policeman, his carving career produced approximately 1000 decoys. It was ended when he died tragically in a work-related accident in his squad car. Note the pair of mallards and two canvasback drakes off to one side.

Mallard hen, sleeper, Cline McAlpin, circa 1940. $2,500. *Collection of Randy and Judy Mayers. Photography Joseph Engers.*

Blue-winged teal drake and hen sleeper, Cline McAlpin, Chicago, Illinois, circa 1965. $1,500 pair. *Collection of Randy and Judy Mayers. Photography Joseph Engers.*

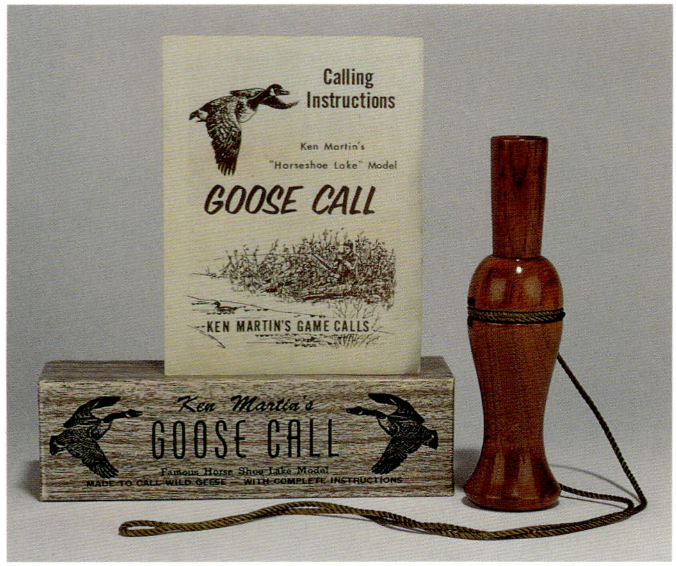

Goose call, Ken Martin (1922-present), Lemont, Illinois, Horseshoe Lake Model, circa 1950. $200.

Pintail drake, Cline McAlpin, Chicago, Illinois, circa 1965. $1,000. *Collection of Randy and Judy Mayers. Photography Joseph Engers.*

Redhead drake, only known example in original paint, Douglas Moseley (1860-1924) Princeton, Illinois. A founding member of the prestigious Princeton Game & Fish Club, Moseley carved a single hunting rig for his own use painted by Henry Holmes, circa 1890. $5,000.

Mallard pair, Douglas Moseley, circa 1890. $5,000.

Canvasbacks, Douglas Moseley, circa 1890. $3,000 each.

Pintail drake, circa 1920. John Fred Mott Sr. (1866-1934), Pekin, Illinois, lived the life of a market hunter. $1,000.

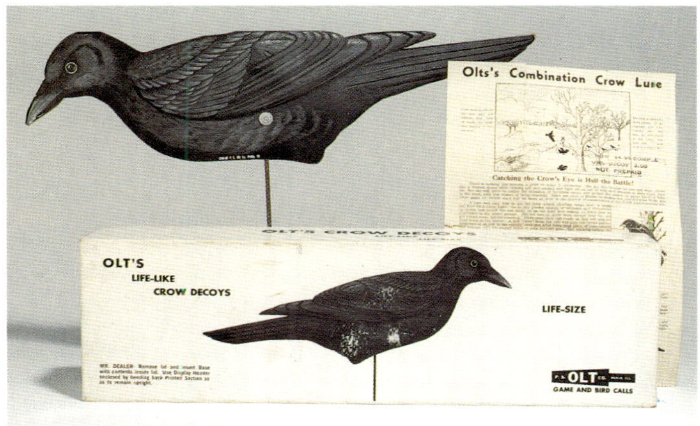

Crow decoys, P.S. Olt Sports Products Company, Pekin, Illinois. Constructed of heavy weight paper, these decoys were fold-over silhouettes with a metal wire leg that folded into the body for storage. A dozen decoys were packaged in an imprinted display box, circa 1950. $125 per dozen with box.

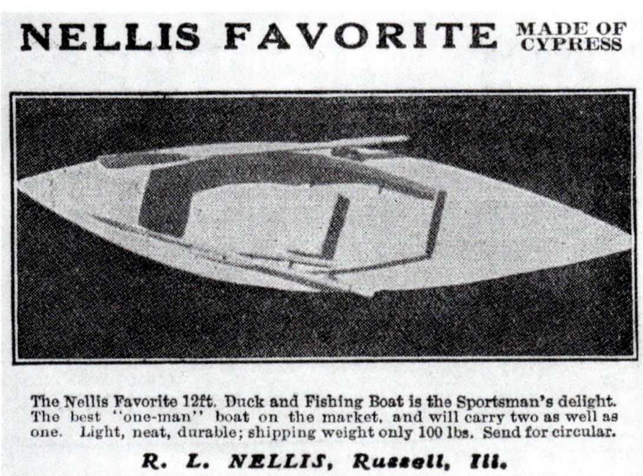

NELLIS FAVORITE MADE OF CYPRESS

The Nellis Favorite 12ft. Duck and Fishing Boat is the Sportsman's delight. The best "one-man" boat on the market, and will carry two as well as one. Light, neat, durable; shipping weight only 100 lbs. Send for circular.

R. L. NELLIS, Russell, Ill.

Left: Advertisement, duck boat by R.L. Nellis, Russel, Illinois, circa 1915.

Right: Dove decoys, P.S. Olt Sports Products Company, Pekin, Illinois. Constructed of heavy weight paper these decoys were fold-over silhouettes with counter-balance weight that allow decoys to be set on telephone wires. A dozen decoys were packaged in an imprinted display box, circa 1950. $125 per dozen with box.

Olts's Combination Crow Lure

Crow shooting affords the same sport and difficult shots from all angles that game bird shooting in season does.

The crow is the duck's worst enemy. If we eliminate all the "thinks" about this pest, we will arrive at the simple true fact that "a good crow is a dead crow."

NOW $4.95 COMPLE
OWL DECOY 3.00
NOT PREPAID

Catching the Crow's Eye is Half the Battle!

There is nothing like proving a point to make it convincing. We say this because an owl will draw crows like a magnet draws steel. Crows will mill around and fight off an owl as long as it remains in their sight, then too, the owl will serve to center the attention of incoming crows and permit the hunter to move about a little in the blind, with less chance of being detected. Since the crow is known to destroy our insectivorous birds and other game we should start war on them at once in the interest of conservation of our North American bird life.

A sure and easy way to get the crow within shooting range now, is using the New Olt's Crow Lure. Go to any gooded section or secluded spot frequented by crows, and mount the owl decoy on an old dead tree, stump, or fence post as illustrated in the above picture. Set out two or more crow decoys near by, and get behind some natural covering. Have your crow call ready as this will add the final touch to the layout. A few "caws" from the call will give the crows perfect assurance of an owl in the vicinity, until you arise from your place of concealment and respond with the snappy tunes of your favorite gun. The warning telling the crows to depart in a hurry or remain forever as only fate will tell.

The Owl Decoy, 15 inches in height, is made of the light but durable Balsa wood, hand carved, full size and shape, weighing but 16 ounces, and artistically hand painted in natural true-to-life colors. The Crow Decoys are made of durable wood-pulp, full in size, true-to-life in shape and color, weighing only 10 ounces apiece.

There are some owl decoys on the market today that have either movable wings, or a head that turns with the pulling of a cord. To use these motions in attracting the crow's attention is entirely unnecessary. Did you ever notice an owl sitting in a nearby tree through the continuous flapping of its wings, or the turning of its head from side to side? No, but you probably have however, noticed an owl sitting perfectly still in a tree, many times, and through no movements of its own. So it is with the crow for a crow's eyesight is considered about five times as keen as the human eye. The crow's sharp eyes will only too often spot the movement of the pull cord, and away they will go. All that is necessary is the owl's presence to keep them interested.

It has been our aim to design decoys such as would warrant your trying them. You may be able to buy Crow Luring outfits at less, but always remember — **There is hardly anything in the world today that some man cannot make a little poorer and sell a little cheaper and the people who consider price only, are this man's lawful prey.**

Proper consideration of the influences of good decoys must convince the thoughtful sportsman that these are inseparable from the scientific hunting of the crow. Therefore, a good Crow Luring outfit will bear as important a relation to crow shooting as the well trained setter or pointer does to quail shooting. You can hunt quail without a dog, and you can shoot crows without using decoys. But when you do, you miss the essence of sport.

OLT'S GENUINE COMBINATION CROW LURE consists of the following: 1 Owl, 2 Crow Decoys, and 1 Olt's hard rubber crow call. Price $5.85 Prepaid. Sold Separately — Owl Decoy $4.00, Crow Decoys, 85c each; or $9.00 per dozen. Genuine Olt's Hard Rubber Crow Call, $1.00. All prices postpaid.

Not Sold Through the Trade — Order Today

PHILIP S. OLT — Manufacturer — Pekin, Ill.

Advertising flyer for Combination Crow Lure, which included wooden owl decoy by John Hyatt, Pekin, Illinois, silhouette crow decoys, and hard rubber crow call.

Mallard drake, store display for Feather-Lite Decoys, tenite molded plastic decoys, P.S. Olt Specialties Company, Pekin, Illinois, circa 1950. $100.

Duck Calls, P.S. Olt Specialty Company, Pekin, Illinois, circa 1905-1930. D-2 adjustable duck call, $200; brass banded duck call, $1,000.

Duck calls, Salesman's display set, D-2 series, P.S. Olt Specialty Company, Pekin, Illinois, circa 1920. $5,000.

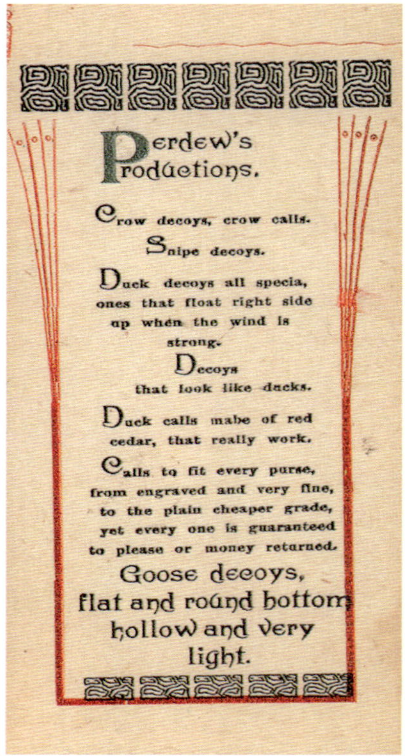

Perdew's Productions.

Crow decoys, crow calls.

Snipe decoys.

Duck decoys all specia, ones that float right side up when the wind is strong.

Decoys that look like ducks.

Duck calls mabe of red cedar, that really work.

Calls to fit every purse, from engraved and very fine, to the plain cheaper grade, yet every one is guaranteed to please or money returned.

Goose decoys, flat and round bottom hollow and very light.

Advertising card, Perdew Productions used by Charles Perdew to promote his hunting decoy. These rare early cards, circa 1900, not only offered duck and crow decoys and calls but also snipe and goose decoys.

Charles (1882-1963) and Edna Perdew (1882-1974) in their yard. Photograph, Joseph B. French, circa 1957.

RETURN IN 5 DAYS TO
CHAS. H. PERDEW & CO.
HENRY · ILL.

Mr. Joseph French
3418 Gratiot
St Louis 3.
Mo.

Dupont advertising envelope imprinted with Chas. Perdew return address. Note the addressee was Joseph French, an early decoy collector who became a personal friend of Charlie and Edna, circa 1950.

Charles Perdew surrounded with his varied creations: carved cheek model hen and drake mallards with raised carved wings, Miniatures, standing with and without out-stretched wings. *Photograph courtesy Steve Hutton, Perdew Museum.*

Chas H. Perdew.
Game Calls and decoys
HENRY, ILL.

Charles Perdew letterhead, circa 1940.

Mallard hen, "sleepy-eyed" model; carved wings, carved cheeks, Charles Perdew, painted by Edna, circa 1930. "Saci" Sacarro hunting rig. $50,000.

Detail of "sleepy-eyed" mallard hen.

Mallard drake, carved wing. Carved and painted by Charles Perdew, circa 1930. Rig-mate to "sleepy-eyed" mallard hen from "Saci" Sacarro Rig. $20,000.

Mallard pair, Charles Perdew, painted by Edna, circa 1937. $20,000.

Mallard drake, Charles Perdew, painted by Edna, circa 1930. $7,500.

Mallard hen, Charles Perdew, painted by Charles and Edna, circa 1930. $7,000.

Mallard drake, three-piece body construction. Charles Perdew, painted by Edna, circa 1915. Blatchford Cartridges shot shell box, Blatchford Cartridge Works, Chicago, Illinois 12 gauge, circa 1900. Mallard, $7,000; shell box, $2,000.

Mallard drake, carved wing style, carved and painted by Charles Perdew, circa 1935. $7,500.

Mallard drake, Charles Perdew, painted by Charles, circa 1945. $5,000.

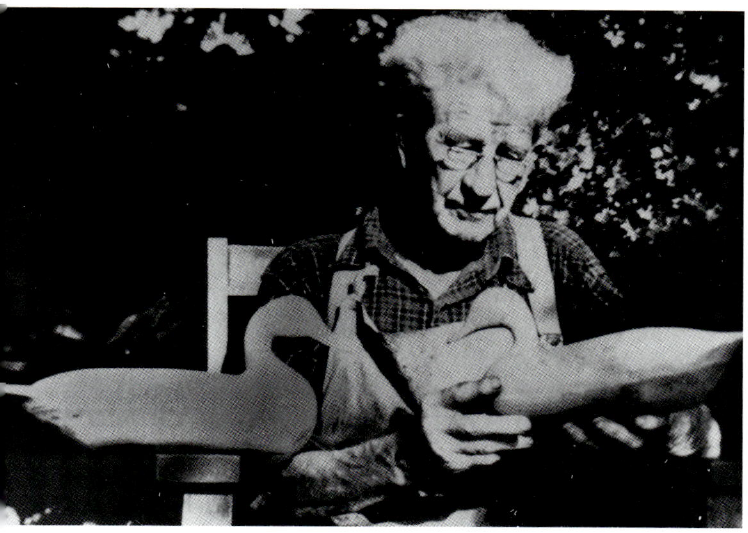

Charles Perdew carved decoys until his death in 1963. As he got older, the heads of his decoy got smaller and the necks thinner. This is a good way to date Perdew decoy. Although Edna outlived Charles by over ten years, she was unable to paint decoys by the 1950s because of poor health. *Photograph courtesy of Steve Hutton, Perdew Museum.*

Mallard hen, Charles Perdew. An entire rig of Charles Perdew hunting decoys, painted by Edna and branded "G.K. Schmidt," was found stored in a bank vault in 1965. Apparently Mr. Schmidt ordered a pair with a sleeper of each species of duck that frequents the Illinois River Valley. The "G K Schmidt" rig consisted of some of the finest examples of Charles and Edna Perdew's hunting decoys and super minty Mason Decoy Company mallards, circa 1920. $10,000.

Mallard hen, sleeper, carved and painted by Charles Perdew, circa 1945. $10,000.

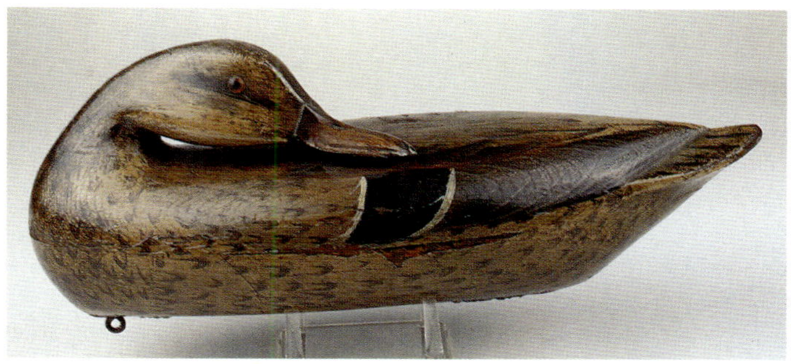

Mallard hen, sleeper, Charles Perdew, painted by Edna, circa 1937. $15,000.

Mallard drake, preener, only known example, carved and painted by Charles Perdew, circa 1935. $15,000.

Charles Perdew whittling a decoy head surrounded by decoys in varying stages of completion, circa 1950.

Mallard hen, carved cheek style, Charles Perdew, painted by Charles, circa 1940. This style decoy was a favorite of William Mackey, decoy historian, and was featured in his classic decoy book, *American Bird Decoy*. $5,000.

Mallard hen, swimmer style, Charles Perdew, Painted by Charles, circa 1940. Branded "J.N.Z," This decoy was part of the John Ziggly rig. Ziggly was a well-known architect from Peoria, Illinois. $5,000.

Black duck, Charles Perdew, painted by Edna Perdew, circa 1920. $10,000. *Collection of Alan and Elaine Haid. Photography Alan Haid.*

Pintail hen, Charles Perdew, painted by Charles, circa 1940. $7,000.

Pintail drake, Charles Perdew, painted by Edna, circa 1920. This particular decoy was purchased by William Pratt to be used as a model at the decoy department of Pratt Manufacturing, Inc. Joliet, Illinois. $15,000.

Canvasback drake, Charles Perdew, painted by Edna, circa 1920s. $15,000.

Pintail hen, sleeper, Charles Perdew, painted by Edna, circa 1920. $50,000.

Pintail drake, Charles Perdew, painted by Edna Perdew, G.K. Schmidt Rig, circa 1928. $20,000. *Collection of James R. and Diane Cook.*

Pintail drake, Charles Perdew, painted by Charles, circa 1948. $5,000.

Green-winged teal drake, sleeper, Charles Perdew, painted by Edna. One of two known examples, circa 1920. $40,000. *Collection of James R. and Diane Cook.*

Below:
Special order set of fancy carved duck calls made for the Postulka family, Granville, Illinois, includes a smaller call designed for a woman and personalized to Sandra who hunted with her father, Joseph J., and brother, Joseph A. Charles Perdew, circa 1952. $5,000 each. Watercolor, Charlie Perdew's "Fancy Duck Call," Edna Perdew, "EHP 1944". 6" x 4". $1,000.

Blue-winged teal drake, Charles Perdew, painted by Edna, Perdew, circa 1945. $7,000. *Collection of James R. and Diane Cook.*

Green-winged teal drake. This is known as a "Weeks Rig teal" because it was part of one dozen teal decoys which were originally owned by Robert Weeks (Bureau), noted Illinois River decoy carver in his own right and avid waterfowler. It was unusual to have a special rig of green-winged teal decoys because these birds will decoy to almost any common puddle duck decoy spread, but these were a gift to Weeks since he especially loved to hunt teal. $7,500.

Fancy carved duck calls, Charles Perdew. Each has a carved "crown" stoppers and large script initials which are considered Perdew's top of the line calls. Most were made during the depression when Perdew had less business and more time, circa 1925-30. $10,000 each.

Match set of Perdew duck calls made for Stanley H. Drake, Constantine, Michigan. Drake was a nationally renown duck caller during the 1930-40s. He hunted on Sawmill Lake near Henry, Illinois. All calls have initials, S.H.D., inscribed by Perdew. Left: St. Frances River (V.L. & A.) duck call, walnut, circa 1925, $2,500. Center: one of three known fancy duck calls with only two flying mallards separated by a teardrop panel, amber mouthpiece, circa 1925, $10,000. Right: special order duck call, three teardrop panels, unusual black mouthpiece, 1925, $4,000.

Matched set of duck calls made for Chet Caswell (C.J.C.) who hunted Rice Pond near Chillicothe, Illinois, circa 1935. Left: fancy carved duck call with initials carved into a raised banner, $8,000. Right: St. Frances River walnut duck call with initials "C.J.C.," $4,000. Mr. Caswell had the finest rig of Bert Graves decoys ever used on the Illinois river.

Matched set of fancy carved duck and crow calls, Charles Perdew, made for John L. Peer, circa 1953. Crow call, $15,000; duck call, $10,000.

Matched set of fancy carved duck and crow call, Charles Perdew, made for Robert E. McFarland, Chicago, Illinois. One of three known fancy carved duck and crow call sets by Charles Perdew, circa 1935. Crow call, $10,000, duck call, $8,000.

St. Francis River duck calls, Charles Perdew, walnut checkered call with three panels. Three variations shown: Perdew would leave a rectangular space in the center of one checkered teardrop where the owners initials or initials "V.L. & A" would be inscribed, circa 1930. $2,000 each.

V. L. & A. St Frances River duck calls, Charles Perdew, circa 1930. The V.L. & A poster announces a duck calling competition, 1935. Calls, $2,000 each.

V.L.&A was one of Perdew's major outlets. As early as 1906 Perdew sent sample decoys to V.L.&A. for consideration. Their response requested "quantity lots of, say gross at a time".

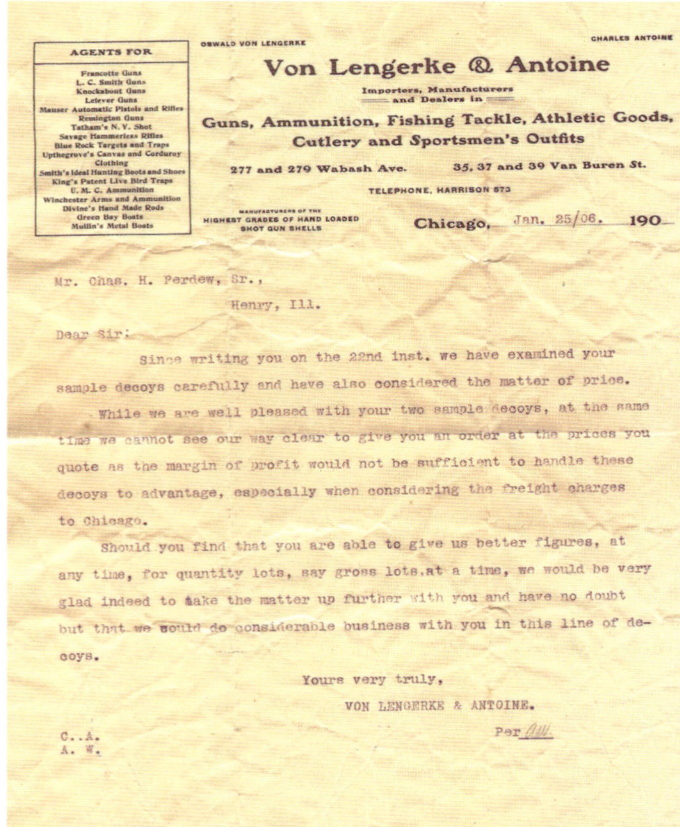

AGENTS FOR
Francotte Guns
L. C. Smith Guns
Knockabout Guns
Lefever Guns
Mauser Automatic Pistols and Rifles
Remington Guns
Tatham's N. Y. Shot
Savage Hammerless Rifles
Blue Rock Targets and Traps
Upthegrove's Canvas and Corduroy Clothing
Smith's Ideal Hunting Boots and Shoes
King's Patent Live Bird Traps
U. M. C. Ammunition
Winchester Arms and Ammunition
Divine's Hand Made Rods
Green Bay Boats
Mullin's Metal Boats

OSWALD VON LENGERKE CHARLES ANTOINE

Von Lengerke & Antoine

Importers, Manufacturers and Dealers in

Guns, Ammunition, Fishing Tackle, Athletic Goods, Cutlery and Sportsmen's Outfits

277 and 279 Wabash Ave. 35, 37 and 39 Van Buren St.

TELEPHONE, HARRISON 573

MANUFACTURERS OF THE HIGHEST GRADES OF HAND LOADED SHOT GUN SHELLS

Chicago, Jan. 25/06. 190

Mr. Chas. H. Perdew, Sr.,
Henry, Ill.

Dear Sir:

Since writing you on the 22nd inst. we have examined your sample decoys carefully and have also considered the matter of price.

While we are well pleased with your two sample decoys, at the same time we cannot see our way clear to give you an order at the prices you quote as the margin of profit would not be sufficient to handle these decoys to advantage, especially when considering the freight charges to Chicago.

Should you find that you are able to give us better figures, at any time, for quantity lots, say gross lots at a time, we would be very glad indeed to take the matter up further with you and have no doubt but that we would do considerable business with you in this line of decoys.

Yours very truly,
VON LENGERKE & ANTOINE.
Per AW.

C..A.
A. W.

V.L.& A. St Frances River duck call in original box imprinted "V.L. &A, Chicago, Illinois," Charles Perdew. $4,000.

Variations of St. Francis River (V.L. & A.) calls, Charles Perdew, circa 1925-45. Left: special order call with decorative German silver band; center: call with no checkering and single tear drop panel; right: teardrop panel not carved in relief. Special order call, $3,000; other calls, $2,500 each.

Rare three-banded red cedar duck calls, Charles Perdew, stamped "Chas Perdew, Henry, ILL Nov 1909." Also shown are an early business card and an envelope with duck call illustration. Calls, $1,500 each.

Early rare red cedar duck calls, Charles Perdew, stamped "Manufactured by Chas. Perdew." Dupont advertising envelope imprinted Perdew address, circa pre-1930. Calls, $1500 each; envelope, $75.

St. Francis River (V.L. & A) duck call, special order call with black mouthpiece and silver band, circa 1925, $2,500. Business card for call's owner, Leon "Buster" Thompson, Henry, Illinois, renowned Illinois guide and commercial fisherman who once owned 1000 acres on Lake Senachwine and Sawmill Lake. Thompson at one time had as many as 1000 Charles Perdew and Tube Dawson decoys.

Early rare red cedar duck calls, which don't have the decorative grooves usually found on call stoppers made by Charles Perdew, circa pre-1925. Unusual early business card that advertises Perdew goose and snipe decoys. Calls, $1000 each.

Regular red cedar duck calls, three German silver bands, and decorative rings on stoppers, stamped "Chas Perdew, Henry, ILL." Charles Perdew, circa 1930-40. $1,500 each.

Crow decoy, mechanical moveable wings and bill, Charles Perdew, painted by Charles. One of two known examples of mechanical crow decoys, which are superb examples of Perdew's mastery of mechanical devices. The gears, which move the wings in a flapping motion and cause the mouth to open and expose a tongue, are totally encased in the decoy's wooden body, circa 1940. Fancy carved crow calls, Charles Perdew, painted by Charles. Throughout his carving career, Perdew accepted commissions to create fancy personalize duck and crow calls. These calls would have relief scenes and the owner's initials. A reoccurring theme on Perdew's fancy crow calls was crows in a tree near a nest of eggs illustrating the crow's practice of stealing eggs from another bird's nest. Shown here are two exceptionally fine calls with large script lettering, circa 1935. Crow decoy, $20,000; crow calls. $10,000 each.

Crow decoy. Perdew's earliest known style of crow decoy has a hollow body and sleek lines. A photograph of this style crow was used as a letterhead on 1909 Perdew stationary: fancy carved crow call, circa 1930, Charles Perdew, painted by Charles. The backside of this call has typical tree with crows but added to the scene is a hunter hiding against the tree with his gun in one hand and a string that operated the owl decoy shown here. Perdew is known to have made one mechanical owl decoy, which flapped its wings, turned its head, and emitted a rasping sound at the pull of a string. Crow, $4,000; call with owl decoy and hunter, $20,000; fancy crow call with tree and crow alone, $10,000.

Side view of slide mechanical crow decoy.

Fancy carved crow call, Charles Perdew, Henry, Illinois, circa 1930. $20,000.

"Baby" crow calls, Charles Perdew, circa 1920. Perdew made two versions of his red cedar crow call. These shorter "baby" crow calls were supposed to sound like a helpless baby crow in distress. Calls, $750 each.

Fancy crow call with tree and crows, circa 1930. Red cedar crow call, stamped "Chas Perdew, Henry, ILL Nov 1909," circa 1950. Crow calling instruction sheet, Charles Perdew, Henry, Illinois. Fancy crow call, $10,000; red cedar crow call, $300.

Variations of fancy carved crow calls, Charles Perdew; each call has a slightly different scene and personalized initials, circa 1920. $10,000 each.

Variously sized red cedar crow calls, Charles Perdew. Generally speaking, the smaller the call, the earlier it was made. Copy of 1907 advertisement for Perdew crow calls.

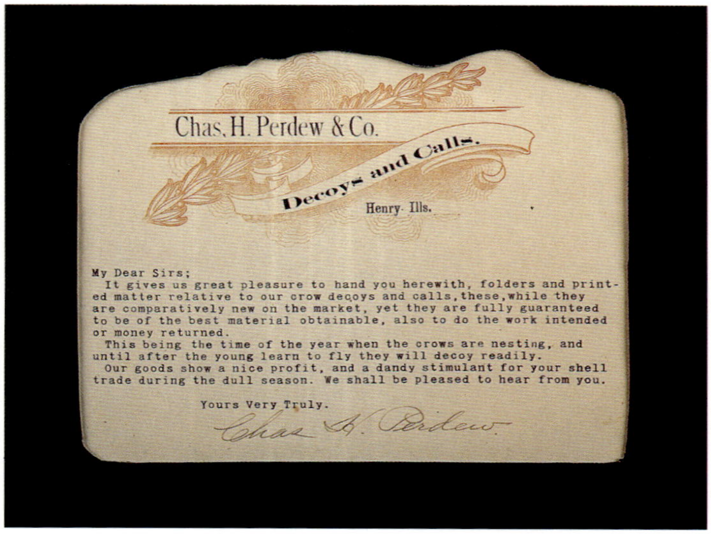

Chas. H. Perdew & Co.
Decoys and Calls.
Henry- Ills.

My Dear Sirs;
It gives us great pleasure to hand you herewith, folders and printed matter relative to our crow decoys and calls, these, while they are comparatively new on the market, yet they are fully guaranteed to be of the best material obtainable, also to do the work intended or money returned.
This being the time of the year when the crows are nesting, and until after the young learn to fly they will decoy readily.
Our goods show a nice profit, and a dandy stimulant for your shell trade during the dull season. We shall be pleased to hear from you.

Yours Very Truly.
Chas H. Perdew

Advertising bill crow call, Charles Perdew, Henry, Illinois, circa 1920.

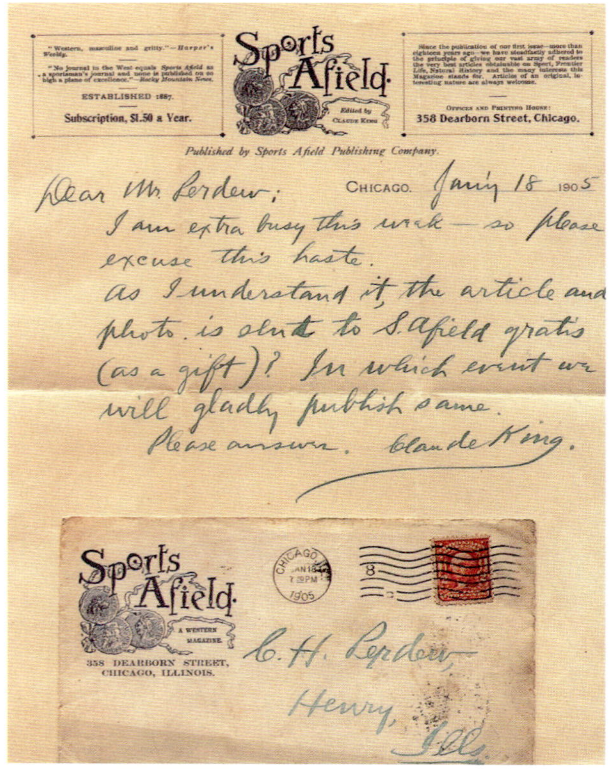

Sports Afield
ESTABLISHED 1887.
Subscription, $1.50 a Year.
358 Dearborn Street, Chicago.
Published by Sports Afield Publishing Company.

CHICAGO. Jany 18 1905

Dear Mr. Perdew;
I am extra busy this week — so please excuse this haste.
as I understand it, the article and photo. is sent to S. afield gratis (as a gift)? In which event we will gladly publish same.
Please answer. Claude King.

Sports Afield
A WESTERN MAGAZINE.
358 DEARBORN STREET, CHICAGO, ILLINOIS.
C. H. Perdew
Henry, Ills.

Price $9.00 per doz.
75 cts. each.

"OUR CROW DECOY"

Every one who is interested in shooting should try our crow decoys, shooting every month in the year, no bag limit; "One trial will convince you." Our decoys are extremely lifelike, are full life size! Each decoy has two sharp metal feet to stick into grorund, or fence, to enable one to place them out readily.
All of our decoys have the best glass eyes that the market affords, they being true to color, making them appear "VERY" lifelike indeed.

Try these
during the close season on game and be convinced; And at the same time you are protecting the game birds by shooting the crows, for the greatest destroyer of our quail is the crow.
Mfg.. and for sale by,
Chas H. Perdew & Co.
Henry, Ills.
A nice profit for the dealer.

Advertising card Perdew used to promote his classic crow decoy, circa 1920.

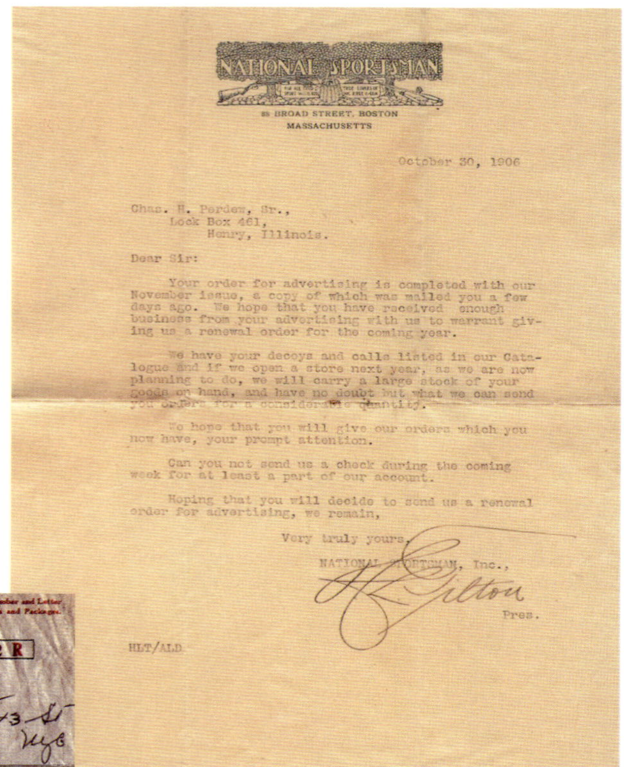

NATIONAL SPORTSMAN
88 BROAD STREET, BOSTON
MASSACHUSETTS

October 30, 1906

Chas. H. Perdew, Sr.,
Lock Box 461,
Henry, Illinois.

Dear Sir:

Your order for advertising is completed with our November issue, a copy of which was mailed you a few days ago. We hope that you have received enough business from your advertising with us to warrant giving us a renewal order for the coming year.

We have your decoys and calls listed in our Catalogue and if we open a store next year, as we are now planning to do, we will carry a large stock of your goods on hand, and have no doubt but what we can send you orders for a considerable quantity.

We hope that you will give our orders which you now have, your prompt attention.

Can you not send us a check during the coming week for at least a part of our account.

Hoping that you will decide to send us a renewal order for advertising, we remain,

Very truly yours,
NATIONAL SPORTSMAN, Inc.,
H L Tilton
Pres.

HLT/ALD

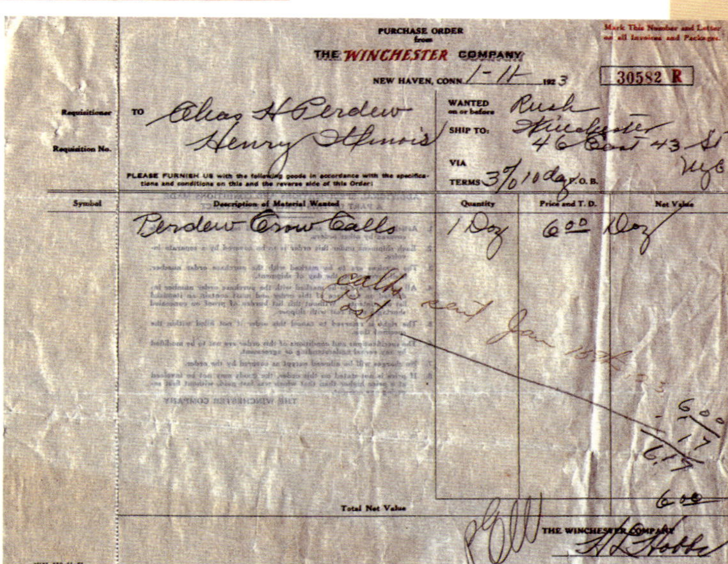

PURCHASE ORDER
from
THE WINCHESTER COMPANY
NEW HAVEN, CONN. 1-11 1923
30582 R
Mark This Number and Letter on all Invoices and Packages.

TO Chas H Perdew
Henry Illinois
WANTED on or before Rush
SHIP TO: Winchester 46 East 43 St NYC
TERMS 3/10 days F.O.B.

Symbol	Description of Material Wanted	Quantity	Price and T.D.	Net Value
	Perdew Crow Calls	1 Doz	6.00	Doz

Total Net Value 6.00
THE WINCHESTER COMPANY
H L Hobbs

Above and left:
During 1905 and 1906 Perdew ran an aggressive ad campaign including ads in national sporting magazines, National Sportsman, Sports Afield, and American Field to promote his crow calls. As a result, he was inundated with orders for his crow calls, which sold for 75 cents each. Perdew crow calls can be found in almost every state.

Crow decoys, flocked. Fancy crow call, Charles Perdew, painted by Charles, circa 1940. Perdew softened the glare of the black paint on his crows by flocking them. Crow, $2500 each; call, $10,000.

Crow decoy, carved wing, only known examples, Charles Perdew, painted by Charles, circa 1940. $7,500.

Like many creative personalities, Perdew's talents were not limited to carving hunting decoys and game calls. He also dabbled in poetry.

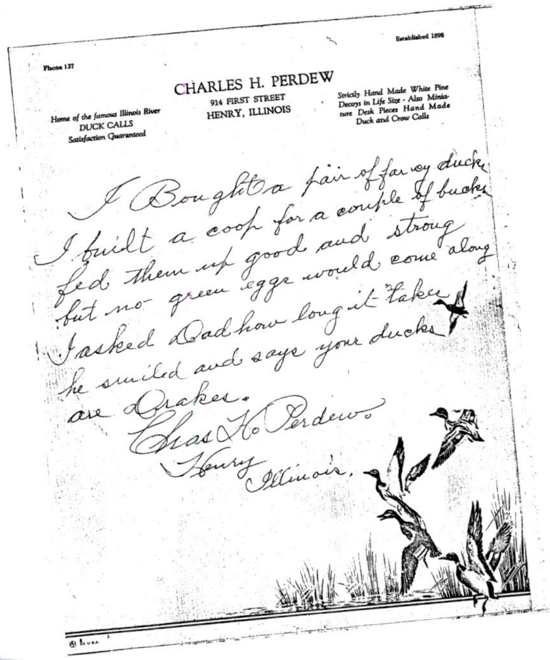

Phone 137

Established 1898

CHARLES H. PERDEW
914 FIRST STREET
HENRY, ILLINOIS

Home of the famous Illinois River
DUCK CALLS
Satisfaction Guaranteed

Strictly Hand Made White Pine Decoys in Life Size - Also Miniature Desk Pieces Hand Made Duck and Crow Calls

I Bought a pair of fancy ducks
I built a coop for a couple of bucks
fed them up good and strong
but no green eggs would come along
I asked Dad how long it takes
he smiled and says your ducks
are Drakes.
Chas. H. Perdew.
Henry Illinois.

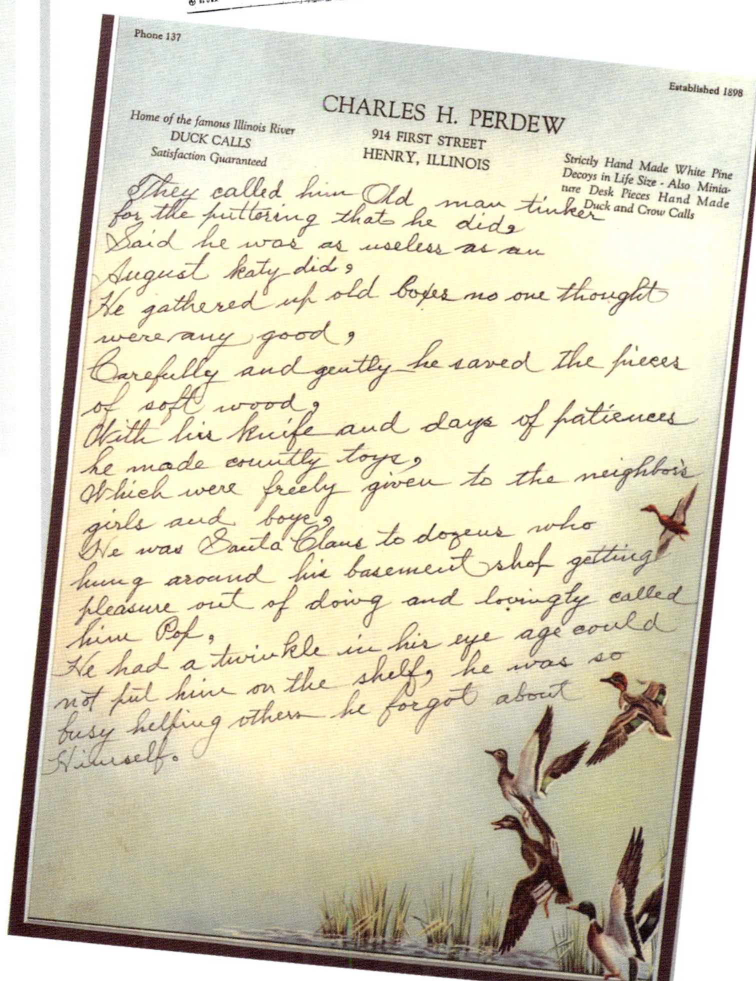

Phone 137

Established 1898

CHARLES H. PERDEW
914 FIRST STREET
HENRY, ILLINOIS

Home of the famous Illinois River
DUCK CALLS
Satisfaction Guaranteed

Strictly Hand Made White Pine Decoys in Life Size - Also Miniature Desk Pieces Hand Made Duck and Crow Calls

They called him Old man tinker
for the puttering that he did.
Said he was as useless as an
August katy did,
He gathered up old boxes no one thought
were any good,
Carefully and gently he saved the pieces
of soft wood,
With his knife and days of patiences
he made country toys,
Which were freely given to the neighbor's
girls and boys,
He was Santa Claus to dozens who
hung around his basement shop getting
pleasure out of doing and lovingly called
him Pop,
He had a twinkle in his eye age could
not put him on the shelf, he was so
busy helping others he forgot about
Himself.

Mallard pair, miniature 1/2 size, Charles Perdew, painted by Charles, circa 1948. $7,500.

Mallard pair, miniatures, 1/4 sized, Charles Perdew, painted by Edna, circa 1946. $7,500. *Collection of James R. and Diane Cook.*

Mallard drake, miniature 1/3 size, Charles Perdew, painted by Charles, circa 1950. $2,500.

Miniature mallards, 1/4 size, Charles Perdew, painted Charles Perdew, circa 1930. $4,000.

Blue-winged teal, flying diorama, Charles Perdew, painted by Charles, circa 1950. $7000. *Collection of Dan Combs.*

Robins, full-sized pair, Charles Perdew, painted by Edna. Perdew's carvings were not limited to hunting decoys. True folk artists, the Perdews created a variety of polychromes and natural finish carvings from the delightful "God of Mirth" figures to these wonderful pair of robins. This male robin seems to have his head cocked to one side listening, circa 1935. $25,000. *Collection of David Galliher. Photograph courtesy of Gene and Linda Kangas.*

Wood duck drake, Charles Perdew, painted by Charles, carved wing decoy mounted on carved burl base, 1/4 size, circa 1940. $3,000.

Cardinal, female songbird, Charles Perdew, painted by Charles, circa 1940. $7,500.

Wood duck drake, Charles Perdew, painted by Charles, standing miniature, 1/4 size, mounted on burl base, circa 1940. $2,000.

Mallard pair, Charles Perdew, painted by Edna, miniature 1/3 size, carved berry branch on base, polychrome, circa 1930. $4,000.

Mallard drake, Charles Perdew, painted by Charles, standing with outstretched wings, 1/4 size miniature, mounted on burl base, circa 1950. $2,500.

Right:
Mallard drake, Charles Perdew, painted by Charles, standing with raised wing tips, 1/4 size miniature, mounted on burl base, circa 1950. $1,500.

Oil painting, Edna Perdew, circa 1930. $3,000.

Pheasant pair, 1/4 size miniature, flying cock and standing hen mounted on walnut burl. Charles Perdew painted by Charles, Henry, Illinois, circa 1950. $750 each.

Redheaded woodpecker, Charles Perdew, painted by Charles, miniature 1/4 size, circa 1950. $1,000.

Duck and pheasant lapel pins, Charles Perdew, painted by Charles, Perdew had a special fondness for the ladies and often presented ladies who visited with their husbands a piece of jewelry he had whittled, circa 1940. $750 each

Duck calls, C. Haddon Perdew (1910-1998), Henry, Illinois, circa 1970. Left to right: St. Frances River Style red cedar duck call, $1,000; St. Frances River Style hedge duck call with decorative German silver bands and initials, $1,000; Illinois River coco bola duck call, $800; classic red cedar Illinois River duck call, $500. *Collection of Gary Rieker.*

St Frances River Style red cedar duck calls, Haddon Perdew, Henry, Illinois, circa 1970. $700. *Photograph and collection Robert Christensen.*

Left:
Charles Haddon Perdew (1910- 1998), Henry, Illinois. Although his main interest was gun repair, Haddon continued the Perdew carving tradition using his father's pattern to produce hunting style decoys and miniatures for the mantle. In his later years Haddon gained recognition among the duck call collectors for his call making. Because he made so few calls in comparison to his father, Haddon's common cedar duck and crow calls often bring more than Charles's, circa 1995.

Left: classic red cedar Illinois River duck call, circa 1970, $500. Middle: miniature red cedar duck call, Haddon Perdew, Henry, Illinois, circa 1970, $800. Right: Illinois River duck call, coco bola duck call, circa 1970, $800. *Photograph and collection Robert Christensen.*

Mallards, drakes, Haddon Perdew, Henry, Illinois, circa 1990. $1,000 each.

Mallard miniature pair, cast lead paperweights, Haddon Perdew, $200: rare spring mallard call, red cedar, Haddon Perdew, circa 1970, $700.

Haddon Perdew with miniature mallard drake, circa 1990. $1,500.

Mallard drake, Mario Piolotti (1900-1964) and Henry Piolotti (1901-1961), Spring Valley, Illinois. The Piolotti brothers carved a large hunting rig for their personal use including regular and oversized mallards that are characterized by spectacular realistic paint, circa 1940. $3,000.

Miniature mallard pair, 1/2 size, with brass tag etched "C. Haddon Perdew, 1983, #19" and #20. $3,000.

Mallard pair, Chris Powers (1902-1958), Peru, Illinois, was prompted to carve a rig of hunting decoy when his son became interested in duck hunting. Unhappy with the quality of their hunting blocks, he pull out his late father's violin-making tools and learned the basics of decoy carving from his co-worker at the Westclox plant, Hector Whittington, circa 1950. $3,000. *Collection Alan and Elaine Haid. Photograph Alan Haid.*

Mallard pair, flying miniatures in diorama, Chris Powers, circa 1950. $1,000 pair.

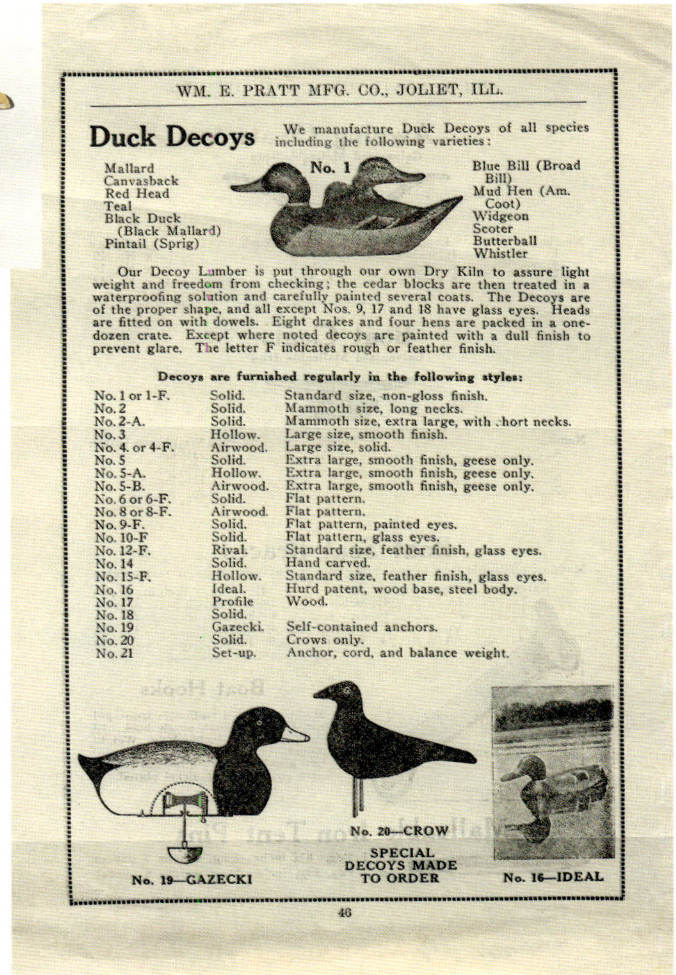

WM. E. PRATT MFG. CO., JOLIET, ILL.

Duck Decoys We manufacture Duck Decoys of all species including the following varieties:

Mallard
Canvasback
Red Head
Teal
Black Duck (Black Mallard)
Pintail (Sprig)

No. 1

Blue Bill (Broad Bill)
Mud Hen (Am. Coot)
Widgeon
Scoter
Butterball
Whistler

Our Decoy Lumber is put through our own Dry Kiln to assure light weight and freedom from checking; the cedar blocks are then treated in a waterproofing solution and carefully painted several coats. The Decoys are of the proper shape, and all except Nos. 9, 17 and 18 have glass eyes. Heads are fitted on with dowels. Eight drakes and four hens are packed in a one-dozen crate. Except where noted decoys are painted with a dull finish to prevent glare. The letter F indicates rough or feather finish.

Decoys are furnished regularly in the following styles:

No. 1 or 1-F.	Solid.	Standard size, non-gloss finish.
No. 2	Solid.	Mammoth size, long necks.
No. 2-A.	Solid.	Mammoth size, extra large, with short necks.
No. 3	Hollow.	Large size, smooth finish.
No. 4. or 4-F.	Airwood.	Large size, solid.
No. 5	Solid.	Extra large, smooth finish, geese only.
No. 5-A.	Hollow.	Extra large, smooth finish, geese only.
No. 5-B.	Airwood.	Extra large, smooth finish, geese only.
No. 6 or 6-F.	Solid.	Flat pattern.
No. 8 or 8-F.	Airwood.	Flat pattern.
No. 9-F.	Solid.	Flat pattern, painted eyes.
No. 10-F	Solid.	Flat pattern, glass eyes.
No. 12-F.	Rival.	Standard size, feather finish, glass eyes.
No. 14	Solid.	Hand carved.
No. 15-F.	Hollow.	Standard size, feather finish, glass eyes.
No. 16	Ideal.	Hurd patent, wood base, steel body.
No. 17	Profile	Wood.
No. 18	Solid.	
No. 19	Gazecki.	Self-contained anchors.
No. 20	Solid.	Crows only.
No. 21	Set-up.	Anchor, cord, and balance weight.

No. 19—GAZECKI

No. 20—CROW

SPECIAL DECOYS MADE TO ORDER

No. 16—IDEAL

46

Original page from 1936 Wm E Pratt Manufacturing Company catalog.

Catalog, Wm. E. Pratt Manufacturing Company established 1893, Joliet, Illinois. William Pratt (1870-1936), an avid waterfowler became a shareholder in Senachwine Club, Hennepin, Illinois, circa 1920. Not long afterwards his company, which manufactured malleable iron products, introduced a line of duck hunting products including decoys, live decoy harnesses and hobbles, duck calls and assorted boat oars and oar locks. After Pratt died in 1936 the decoy department was sold to the Animal Trap Company of Pascagoula, Mississippi.

Crows, Wm. E. Pratt Manufacturing Company, Joliet, Illinois, circa 1920. $1,500 each.

WM. E. PRATT MFG. CO., CHICAGO, ILL.

Duck Decoys

We manufacture Duck Decoys of all species including the following varieties:

Mallard	Black Duck (Black Mallard)	Wigeon
Canvasback	Pintail (Sprig)	Scoter
Red Head	Blue Bill (Broad Bill)	Butterball
Teal	Mud Hen (Am. Coot)	Whistler

Our Decoy Lumber is put through our own Dry Kiln to assure light weight and freedom from checking; the decoy blocks are then treated in a water proofing solution and then carefully painted several coats. The Decoys are of the proper shape, painted in natural colors, with dull finish to prevent glare, and all have glass eyes. To reduce the chance of heads breaking off, decoys have the heads fitted on with dowels. Eight drakes and four hens are packed in a one dozen crate. Special Decoys made to order. Decoys are furnished regularly in the following styles:

No. 1.	Solid.	Standard size, smooth with non-gloss paint.
No. 1-F.	Solid.	Standard size, feather or rough finish.
No. 2.	Solid.	Mammoth size, about twice regular size, smooth finish.
No. 3.	Hollow.	Smooth Finish, large size, hollow.
No. 3-F.	Hollow.	Feather Finish, large size, hollow.
No. 4.	Airwood.	Large size, but lighter than cork, smooth finish.
No. 4-F.	Airwood.	Large size, with Feather Finish.
No. 5.	Hollow.	Extra Large, Smooth Finish, Hollow, Geese only.

Decoy Heads

Heads only, painted and with glass eyes, can be furnished for any species.

Glass Eyes

Glass Eyes, finished in natural colors, red, brown, straw, yellow. In ordering state species desired.

Profile Decoy Geese

No. 1 made from Sheet Steel, painted by hand in natural colors. Neck and feet can be folded into body of decoy.

No. 2 same as No. 1, but with hinged wings.

Perfect Duck Calls

Made of Black Walnut or Red Cedar with German Silver tongue. Imitates ducks perfectly. 6¼ inches long. Packed one dozen in a box.

Page from Wm E Pratt Manufacturing Company's hunting supply catalog.

Goldeneye drake, Wm. E. Pratt Manufacturing Company, Joliet, Illinois, circa 1920. $750.

Redhead pair, hollow top grade, Wm. E. Pratt Manufacturing Company, Joliet, Illinois, circa 1920. $500 pair.

Canada goose, rare example, Profile Decoy Goose No.1, folding silhouette field decoy, metal, Wm. E Pratt Manufacturing Company, Joliet, Illinois, circa 1920. $400.

Advertisement for Ideal Decoy, *Field & Stream,* August, 1928. The Ideal Decoy was patented (1923 #1,447,474) design by Leigh G. Hurd, Klamath Falls, Oregon. Stamped Wm E. Pratt Manufacturing Company, this decoy was offered in the Pratt 1936 catalog. Whether this was a joint operation or if Pratt purchased the patent is unknown.

Mallard pair, Perdew pattern, Wm. E. Pratt Manufacturing Company, Joliet, Illinois. The late Walter Stewart, manager of the Pratt decoy painting department recalled in an interview with the late Willis Pennington, decoy collector, when Mr. Pratt returned from a hunting trip with two decoys by Charlie Perdew, a mallard drake and a pintail drake. He brought the decoys to Stewart and instructed him to copy them for a new decoy line, circa 1925. Shot shell box, Ideal, 12 ga., Hibbard Spencer & Barlett Company, Chicago, Illinois, circa 1920. Decoys, $1,500 pair; shell box, $500. *Collection of William Klein.*

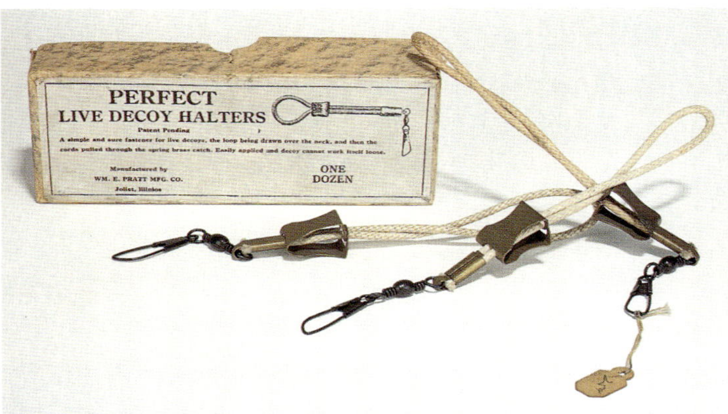

Wm. E. Pratt Manufacturing Company, Perfect Live Decoy Halters, box, circa 1930. Halters, $100 each; box, $250.

Mallard drake, Wm. E. Pratt Manufacturing Company, Ideal (Hurd Decoy) Grade. Decoy was formed metal body with wooden bottom board and head, circa 1930. $350.

Otto H. Questch (1865-1949). Chicago, Illinois.

Right:
Duck calling instruction booklet, Otto Questch, copyrighted 1941. $50.

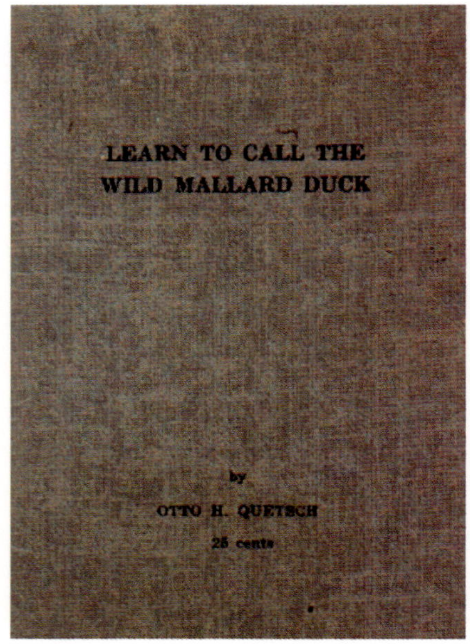

Canada goose, Otto Questch (1865-1949), Chicago, Illinois. Questch inserted a small valve into his hollow decoy bodies behind the head to equalize the temperature and pressure in hopes of reducing body splits and leakage in his decoys. $2,000.

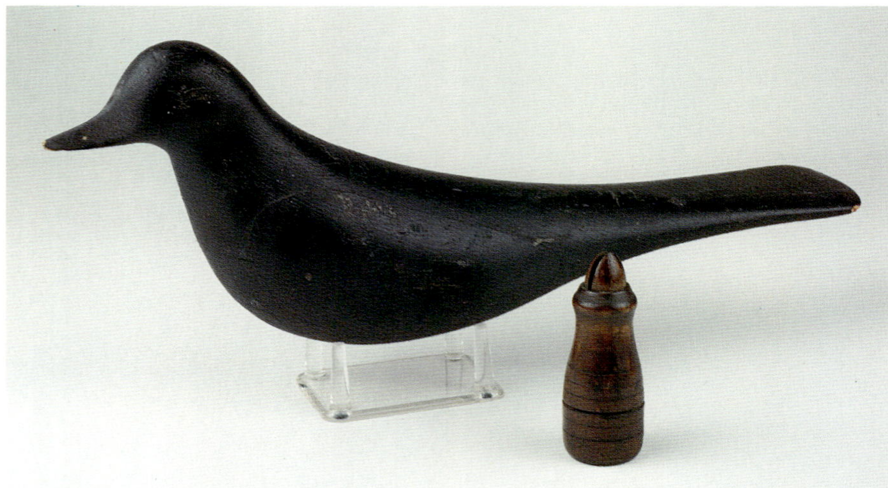

Crow decoy and crow call, Charles Quimby (1875-1940), Spring Valley, Illinois. c.1930. Crow, $2,500 call, $1,000.

Duck call; crow call, Charles Quimby; rulebook, West End Gun Club, Turner Lake (Mud Lake), Putman County, Illinois, circa 1940. Duck call, $1,500; crow call, $1,000.

Miscellaneous songbirds by Stanley Racic, LaSalle, Illinois, circa 1920. $500 each.

Edward Rafter (right), Spring Valley, Illinois, and Richard Hall (center) with friend outside. Princeton Game & Fish Clubhouse after a good day of Timber Mallard shooting, c. 1925.

Advertisement, Hill's Handy Halter, commonly known as Eddie Rafter's live decoy holder, circa 1925.

At the far right is Rafter's live decoy halters on its original metal forming jig, circa 1930. Center: Cook's Live Decoy Holder, Chicago, Illinois with anchor: Princeton Game and Fish Club letter informing membership of rules for using live decoys. Left: Samuel Humane Live Duck Fastener, jointed metal collar with anchor: Rafter halter, $100; Cook's holder, $75; Samuel's fastener, $100, circa 1920.

Rafter/Hill Live Decoy Holder This unique live decoy holder was fashioned out of a single piece of copper wire using a metal jig designed by Edward Rafter. Once fastened around a live duck's neck an anchored string was attached to the swiveled halter allowing the duck to swim among the decoy spread. The original patent was issued to his partner Richard Hill, Spring Valley, Illinois who marketed the live decoy holder, circa 1920.

Duck call, Ervin Redshaw, Granville, Illinois, circa 1935: business card, "Leon Buster" Thompson, commercial fisherman and waterfowler, Putman, Illinois, circa 1930. Duck call, $500.

Ervin Redshaw, Granville, Illinois looks up from his task of preparing his rig of Charlie Perdew and Al Ries Tru-Duk decoys for the upcoming season. *Photograph by John Redshaw.*

Rice Lake duck calls were produced by Arnold Hegele and Harold Davis, Canton, Illinois, circa 1940, in original box. $200.

Mallard pair, $400, pintail drake, $500. Tux-Dux Wood Products Company, Long Grove, Illinois, designed and marketed by Al Ries, circa 1940.

Wood duck pair, Alfred E. Ries, painted by R.G. Rodell. Tru-Dux Wood Products Company. Special order wood duck decoy rig was made for Louis Barkhausen, well known Illinois sportsman and conservationist, to use at his hunting club in Central Illinois. Ries made less then 18 wood duck decoys. $1,500 each.

Flyer, Tru-Dux Wood Products Company, "The 'Litewate' Champion of Decoydom." Distributor, Alfred Ries, circa 1940.

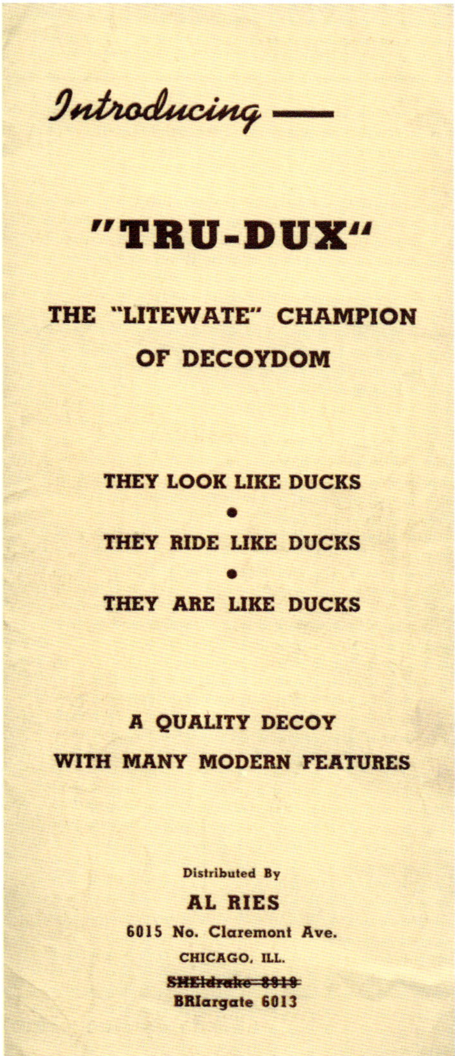

Advertisement, J. W. Reynolds Decoy Company, circa 1915.

Pintail Drake, Herman F. Rietgraf (1888-1959), Peru, Illinois, circa 1920. $750. *Collection of Randy and Judy Mayers. Photography Joseph Engers.*

THE MECHANICAL

"FLAPPER" DUCK DECOY

FLAPS ITS WINGS

WINGS OPEN

CORD

CORD

WINGS CLOSED

(Patented)

Here, Mr. Sportsman, is a decoy that the ducks spot a long distance away, because it is the MOST attractive on the market today.

Try it out among your regular artificial decoys. You will be amazed at its wonderful alluring qualities.

By simply pulling a cord from your blind you can make this decoy FLAP ITS WINGS and ripple the water around it in a manner very similar to the actions of a live duck. This lively movement gives the "Flapper" decoy unusual ability to coax many shy old birds, within shooting range, that would otherwise pass up your whole layout.

Really, the "Flapper" resembles the wild duck so closely in color, shape and action that it is taking the place of live decoy. Before the ban on live decoys, the "Flapper" proved to be an advantage even when used among them. Because the live ducks did not always show action at exactly the proper time to be most effective. While this decoy never failed to flap its wings the instant the cord was pulled.

The "Flapper" Duck Decoy is a mighty good lure for marsh, lake, pond or river shooting. In fact, it is practical for all shallow water duck shooting, where a stake can be used to place the decoy out. You will notice the illustration shows a plate extending beyond the front end of the decoy. Through a hole in this plate a screw eye can be fastened into the top of a stake to hold the decoy in position. The operating cord is then extended from the lure to your blind and the "Flapper" is ready for use.

The body of the "Flapper" Decoy is made of canvas, with other steel wire fixtures and it has a wooden bottom. It is artistically colored to show many of the fine feathery effects of the real duck and is life-like in shape. The decoy can be opened or folded in a "jiffy" by means of a wire loop extending under the tail. It is light in weight, very durable and is made to resemble both the DRAKE AND THE HEN MALLARD.

So, for better duck shooting use this remarkable decoy. Or, for additional attraction get a pair of the "Flappers," both hen and drake. You'll find them the MOST alluring decoys you ever used. Each decoy is packed in a carton, ready for use, with cord, instructions, etc. **Price per pair $6.85**

Price Each....................$3.50
When only one decoy is ordered, we reserve the right to ship either the hen or drake.

FOLDED

OPEN

(Patented)

"Veri-Good" Canvas Duck Decoys

These decoys have a great number of desirable features. They will move about with the slightest breeze . . . are compact . . . light in weight and can be opened or folded in a jiffy. They also have a REAL NATURAL FEATHERY effect obtained by our coloring process. All these points of merit combined with the true-to-life shape and general construction of the lures makes them very practical decoys in every respect.

The "Veri-Goods" open up and fold by means of a wire loop which extends under the tail of the decoys as shown in the illustration. They are made to closely resemble the MALLARD specie—6 drakes and 6 hens to the dozen and are packed in a fibre box, size 7x13x18 inches. Weight 14 pounds per dozen, with cords and anchors complete.

Price per Dozen...............$13.30

J. W. Reynolds Decoy Company catalog description "the mechanical 'Flapper' duck decoy" and "Veri-Good" canvas duck decoys.

Mallard hen, Flapper Model, flapping wing design, J.W. Reynolds Decoy Company, Chicago, Illinois, circa 1900. $500.

Mallard drake, Veri-Good Model, folding canvas decoy J.W. Reynolds Decoy Company: Reynolds Combination duck call, J.W. Reynolds Folding Illinois River Decoy Company, Chicago, Illinois, circa 1920. Decoy, $300; call, $1,500.

Advertisement for Veri-Good Model duck decoy, J. W. Reynolds Decoy Company, circa 1915.

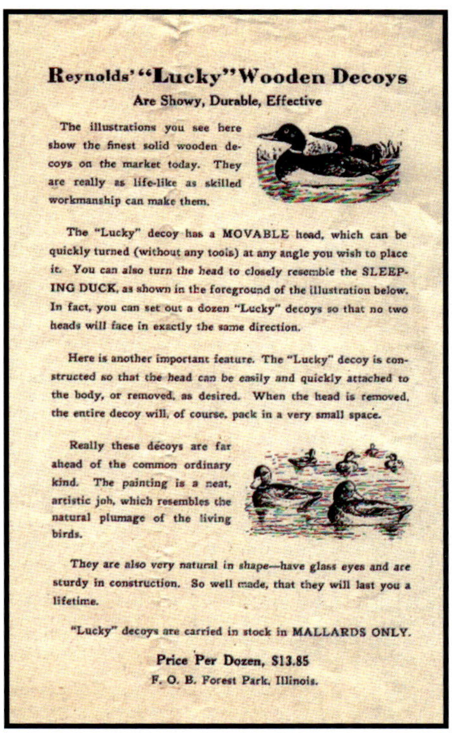

Reynolds' "Lucky" Wooden Decoys

Are Showy, Durable, Effective

The illustrations you see here show the finest solid wooden decoys on the market today. They are really as life-like as skilled workmanship can make them.

The "Lucky" decoy has a MOVABLE head, which can be quickly turned (without any tools) at any angle you wish to place it. You can also turn the head to closely resemble the SLEEPING DUCK, as shown in the foreground of the illustration below. In fact, you can set out a dozen "Lucky" decoys so that no two heads will face in exactly the same direction.

Here is another important feature. The "Lucky" decoy is constructed so that the head can be easily and quickly attached to the body, or removed, as desired. When the head is removed, the entire decoy will, of course, pack in a very small space.

Really these décoys are far ahead of the common ordinary kind. The painting is a neat, artistic joh, which resembles the natural plumage of the living birds.

They are also very natural in shape—have glass eyes and are sturdy in construction. So well made, that they will last you a lifetime.

"Lucky" decoys are carried in stock in MALLARDS ONLY.

Price Per Dozen, $13.85

F. O. B. Forest Park, Illinois.

J. W. Reynolds catalog description "Lucky" wooden decoy.

Pintail hen, Lucky Model, finest known example, J.W. Reynolds Decoy Company: Reynolds duck call, J.W. Reynolds Decoy Company, Chicago, Illinois, circa 1920. Decoy, $750; call, $2,000.

A NECESSARY PART OF EVERY SPORTSMAN'S KIT.

Easy to Blow. 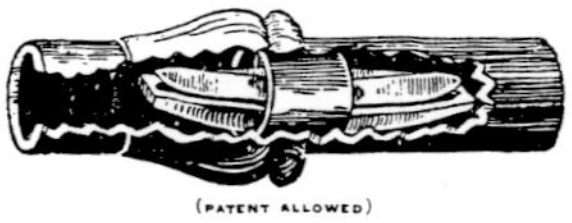 The Best Yet.

The Reynolds' Double Duck Call

TWO DUCK CALLS COMBINED IN ONE.

THE sportsman of the present day much needs to be well equipped if he wishes to be successful in his quest for game. When duck hunting a prime necessity is a call. The call illustrated herewith is claimed to be the best, because it is the most simple in construction and consequently the least likely to get out of order. The parts of this device are made **double ended,** so that the call may be sounded by blowing into either end. The parts are all fitted together sufficiently snug to hold them in place, but any one of them can be moved to vary the notes desired and produce any effect from raw muffled notes up to very piercing notes—thus one end can be tuned to call Mallards, Teal, etc., the other end tuned exclusively for Wood Duck, Blue Bills, etc.

Within the moisture-proof outer sections of the call is a metal tube containing a bronze bill (or channel), a cork plug and a bronze composition reed (or tongue), and every part of the device is guaranteed not to shrink, swell, crack or corrode, and keep a natural tune at all times, imitative to the duck species.

The outside of the call is made in two sections of different shapes so that either end can be quickly distinguished when the occasion for its use arises.

TO TAKE THE CALL APART

Remove one outside section, then hold the channel and reed between the thumb and forefinger, pull same from the metal tube. Then remove the tube from other section.

TO TUNE THE CALLER

Place the channel in the metal tube with the reed in position over the channel, also place the cork plug on the reed inside of the metal tube. Put the metal tube within the outer sections.

The reed (or tongue) may be bent more at one end than at the other. This produces **many sounds** imitative to the duck variety. The reed should be handled with care. Do not twist or kink the same. The cork plug may be pushed toward either end of the metal tube and thus vary the length of the respective ends of the reed, consequently varying the vibration and sound produced by each end.

These calls are tuned when they leave the factory, but may be tuned differently to suit the sportsman, if he so desires.

WHEN CALLING DUCKS

Hold the caller on one end, between the thumb and forefinger. Try different ways, open and close the fingers and with little practice any sportsman will soon be able to call ducks successfully.

One of the sections of the outer case is provided with a groove that a cord may be tied to the same and one end of the cord to the buttonhole of the sportsman's coat.

These calls are made with hard rubber outside sections and also wood outside sections. Both are double-ended calls.

Price, Hard Rubber Call .... $1.00 each
" Wood Call .... .75 "

J. W. REYNOLDS,

anufacturer of Hunting Specialties. 68 S. Morgan St., CHICAGO, U. S. A.

Reynolds' "True Tone" Crow Caller

It's New and the Most Alluring

If you want a caller that is a REAL CROW CHARMER give this one a trial. With it you can imitate the crows to perfection. You'll be amazed how the natural sound of this call will draw the birds within shooting range. In fact, this caller is quite different than the old style call. There is absolutely nothing to get out of order. You won't have any trouble with the reed sticking or becoming bent. It is HIGH in quality, but LOW in cost.

The "True Tone" Crow Call is made of the best materials and it is tuned and tested with the utmost care before it leaves the factory, so that it will actually SOUND LIKE A CROW. It is really a very practical caller in every respect and it's inexpensive, too.

Price 80c each

Reynolds' "True Tone" Duck Caller

MODEL 1938

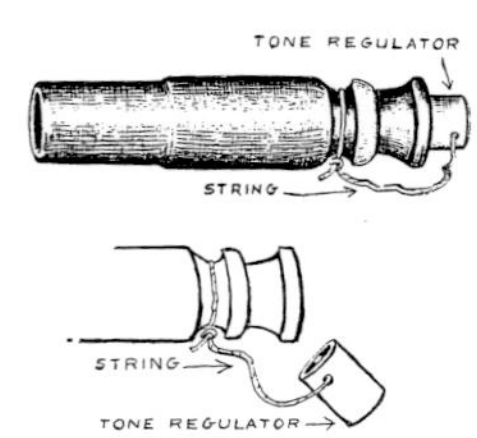

A duck call, to be of any value whatever, must like its companion agent of trickery, the decoy duck, be as nearly a life-like imitation as it is possible to devise. It must be constructed to imitate the different calls of the various species of ducks and this necessitates a wide range of sound, from the Mallard's rasping quack to the soft fluttering call of the Blue Bill. With the "True Tone" caller you will always be able to call the different ducks within shooting range repeatedly.

The "True Tone" duck call is made of high grade moisture-proof materials. Easy to blow and very durable.

This call is also equipped with our new removable TONE REGULATOR. When the caller is used without the regulator the little device swings free, as shown in the outline drawing. However, for a further variety of sound imitative to the duck species, just slip the regulator into the end of the caller. Then you'll have a loud, properly tuned caller when you wish to use it on birds at a great distance from you.

So, give this remarkable caller a trial and convince yourself that it is far better than any you have ever used.

Price $1.00 each

Advertisement for J.W. Reynolds game calls: Reynolds' True-Tone Duck Caller, Model 1938; Reynolds' True-Tone Crow Caller; Reynolds' Double Duck Call, available in wood and hard rubber.

Flyer, Reynolds "Flapper" owl decoy, stuffed canvas decoy with moveable wings; Reynolds' Canvas Crow, J.W. Reynolds Decoy Company, Chicago, Illinois.

This Is the Original Mechanical

"Flapper" Owl Decoy

It Flaps Its Wings

This Illustration Shows Our Owl with the Wings Open and Closed.

Crow shooting is becoming more popular every day because it's a mighty good sport with either shotgun or rifle. It also helps to protect young song and game birds, which often fall prey to the crows.

Many hunters now use the "Flapper" Owl Decoy to lure the crows within gun range, for it has many attractive features.

The "Flapper" is very natural in color and closely resembles a large Great Horned Owl. It can be easily set out for use onto the top of a pole, stump, dead snag, or the projecting limb of a tree. Note illustration. By pulling a cord, which is attached to the decoy and extended to your blind, you can make the owl FLAP ITS WINGS and move its body. This performance will attract the crows' attention immediately.

The "Flapper" Owl Decoy is 20 inches in length, and it is made of canvas with a steel wire leg and other wire parts. The body of the decoy is EASILY stuffed by the sportsman with straw, excelsior, paper or cotton. It will then have the natural shape and curves of the living bird. Full instructions for use with each decoy.

Price $4.50 Each

WARNING! Be sure that you get the ORIGINAL Reynolds Canvas Owl and Crow decoys. Guard against imitations.

Reynolds' Canvas Crow Decoys

These crow decoys when used in conjunction with our "Flapper" Owl or even alone, make irresistible lures. They are FULL SHAPED, natural appearing decoys when stuffed with excelsior, straw or paper as described for filling our owl. You can set them up on the ground or on the top of wheat shocks, corn shocks, dead snags, etc.

Full instructions for use packed with the decoys.

Price $7.60 per Dozen. Half Dozen $4.00.

You Can Fool The Crows

BY USING OUR

Perfect Crow Luring Outfit

We all know that crows are very watchful and are always on their guard against danger. Therefore, to get real good shooting you will find it pays to be well equipped with lures that are the ultimate in LURING POWER.

The Perfect Crow Luring Outfit rates extremely high in this respect. You can so completely attract the crows' attention with this outfit that the birds seem to forget their habit of being cautious and they fly within gun range repeatedly. It is really the most perfect set of lures ever offered the crow shooters.

The use of this set of lures has got any other way of shooting crows "skinned a mile" for alluring the crafty fellows from great distances. It's the best trick in years. All you have to do is to set out the decoys, properly conceal yourself and at the first sight of the crows use your crow caller. When the birds respond to your calling flap the wings of the owl decoy. Then as they dart down, pop 'em off. It is done just as easily as it is said.

Remember, that this outfit is VERY LIGHT in weight, easy to carry about and extremely durable. Also don't forget that every item included in the set is EXACTLY as represented in this circular.

PLAY SAFE! Buy the genuine Perfect Crow Luring Outfit. No substitute can equal it. Order now at this low price.

HERE IS OUR SPECIAL OFFER!

Perfect Crow Luring Outfit

THE SET INCLUDES

- ONE MECHANICAL "FLAPPER" OWL DECOY.
- THREE REGULAR REYNOLDS CROW DECOYS.
- ONE REYNOLDS TRUE TONE CROW CALLER.

Price $6.65 complete, with cord, wire line holder and instructions for use.

J. W. REYNOLDS DECOY FACTORY

Manufacturers of Decoys Since 1904

113 Marengo Avenue **Forest Park, Illinois**

HOW TO STUFF THE DECOYS

All our Crow Decoys, also the "Flapper" Owl, are stuffed in the same manner and it is easily done in a few minutes.

Through the opening at the bottom of the decoy, fill the cloth body with excelsior, straw, cotton or paper. However, excelsior is the best if you can obtain same. Always be sure to press the material into the decoy to THOROUGHLY EXPAND THE BODY. When the decoy is stuffed lap one edge of the opening over the other and pin together.

To make the owl decoy compact for carrying, fold the wings to the body and wind a few feet of the operating cord around the decoy.

J. W. REYNOLDS DECOY FACTORY
FOREST PARK, ILLINOIS

— HOW TO USE THE —

"FLAPPER" OWL DECOY

TO LURE HAWKS AND CROWS

This owl decoy can be used with good results when it is placed out in an open spot, where it will show up from a distance, and when the gunner is well concealed in a good blind. Along a hedge fence or at the edge of a strip of timber is an excellent place to build your blind.

Stuff the decoy at home before leaving for the shoot. Fill the body with straw, paper, hay or any other suitable material, pressing the filling into the decoy to properly expand the body. Select your shooting spot and fasten the "Flapper," by means of the screw eye, onto the top of a fence post, stake, the projecting limb of a tree, or a dead snag. Run the operating cord to the inside of the blind. Put a small stick in the ground, inside of the blind, to slip the wire cord holder over, thus holding the wings closed when desired.

About 15 yards from the blind is the proper distance to stake out the "Flapper" and we furnish with each decoy 15 yards of cord for working the wings. The cord is dark in color so that it will not be noticed by the crows.

Flap the wings of the decoy, by a series of short jerks on the cord, at the first sight of the crows, slowing up the wing movement as the crows near you. A rapid motion of the wings is not necessary. Just work them enough so that the decoy will appear alive.

Additional attraction is afforded by setting some of our crow decoys on the ground near the owl decoy, or on a nearby fence or post. If necessary small holes in the fence can be made with a nail, to receive the legs of the decoys.

To make the "Flapper" compact for carrying, fold the wings to the body and wind a few feet of the operating cord around the decoy.

J. W. REYNOLDS DECOY FACTORY
113 Marengo Avenue
FOREST PARK, - - - - ILLINOIS

Above and right:
Owl, stuffed canvas decoy with moveable wings, "Flapper Decoy" with original papers and stand, J.W. Reynolds Decoy Company, Chicago, Illinois, circa 1920. $500 set.

Illinois River Folding
DECOYS
Have many advantages.
Price, in carry box, dozen, ... $4 50
1 Cord and Anchor for Each Group of 3 Decoys.
The Quickest Set Out & Taken Up. Write for cir.
J.W.Reynolds, 68 S.Morgan St.,Chicago

Advertisement for "Illinois River Folding" decoys, J. W. Reynolds Decoy Company.

Illinois River Folding Wooden Decoy Ducks

(Patented)

If you want the best in PROFILE DECOYS, here they are.

These decoys can be picked up or placed out THREE AT A TIME. They fold up very compactly, are light in weight, easy to carry and a marvel in luring ducks.

Illinois River Folding Decoys are painted in natural colors on both sides and are attached to a wooden float in groups of three. The float is in three pieces and joined at one end with a three plate hinge. When extended the float forms a large Y and a bird floats at each extremity of the Y. THE FLOAT SINKS BELOW THE SURFACE OF THE WATER, PRESENTING JUST THE DECOYS.

When placed out they show up from any angle. Only one cord and anchor is needed for each group of three decoys. They are made of wood to imitate the following species.

MALLARDS, WIDGEONS, PINTAILS, BLACK DUCKS, CANVAS BACKS, BLUE BILLS, RED HEADS, GOLDEN EYES, AND WHISTLERS—eight drakes and four hens to the dozen.

Four floats take one dozen of the decoys, which are packed, complete with cords and anchors, in a strong fibre box, size 6x7x21 inches. Weight, 10 pounds.

Price per Dozen...............$7.60

Canada Geese Decoys
For Land Shooting

Our Profile Geese Decoys are used for field shooting, on sandbars and in shallow water. They are made of wood and fold up compact as shown. The decoys represent full sized geese in side view and may be set up with the head and neck in different positions to resemble a flock feeding. They will lure the old honkers to perfection. Packed in a strong fibre box. Weight about 14 pounds.

Price per Dozen...............$14.50
Half Dozen 7.50

Automatic Canvas Decoy Ducks

Our automatic decoys have become favorites of many sportsmen. Thousands of them have been used in all parts of the country and they are still popular on account of their simplicity of construction, light weight and their self distending feature.

The Automatic Canvas Decoys are made in MALLARDS ONLY. To open or fold the decoy, there is no adjustment, nothing necessary but the simple use of the anchor cord in the regular manner. The decoy automatically expands by means of a spring when the anchor cord is unwound, such cord being wound around the device holds same in folded position. They will float if punctured by stray shot pellets.

These decoys are packed 6 drakes and 6 hens per dozen, complete with cords and anchors, in a neat fibre box, size 7x12x18 inches. Weight complete about 14 pounds.

Price per Dozen........................$12.70

(Patented)

Right:
J. W. Reynolds Decoy Company catalog description "Illinois River Folding" decoys, which were offered in sets of green-winged teal, mallards, redheads, canvasbacks and bluebills.

Canvasbacks, Illinois River Folding Model, J.W. Reynolds Decoy Company, Chicago, Illinois, circa 1920. Set of three. $250.

Below:
Canada goose, rare example, folding silhouette, field decoy, wooden, J.W. Reynolds Decoy Company, Chicago, Illinois, circa 1920. $300.

Bluebill, Illinois River Folding Model, J.W. Reynolds Decoy Company, Chicago, Illinois, circa 1920. Set of three. $250.

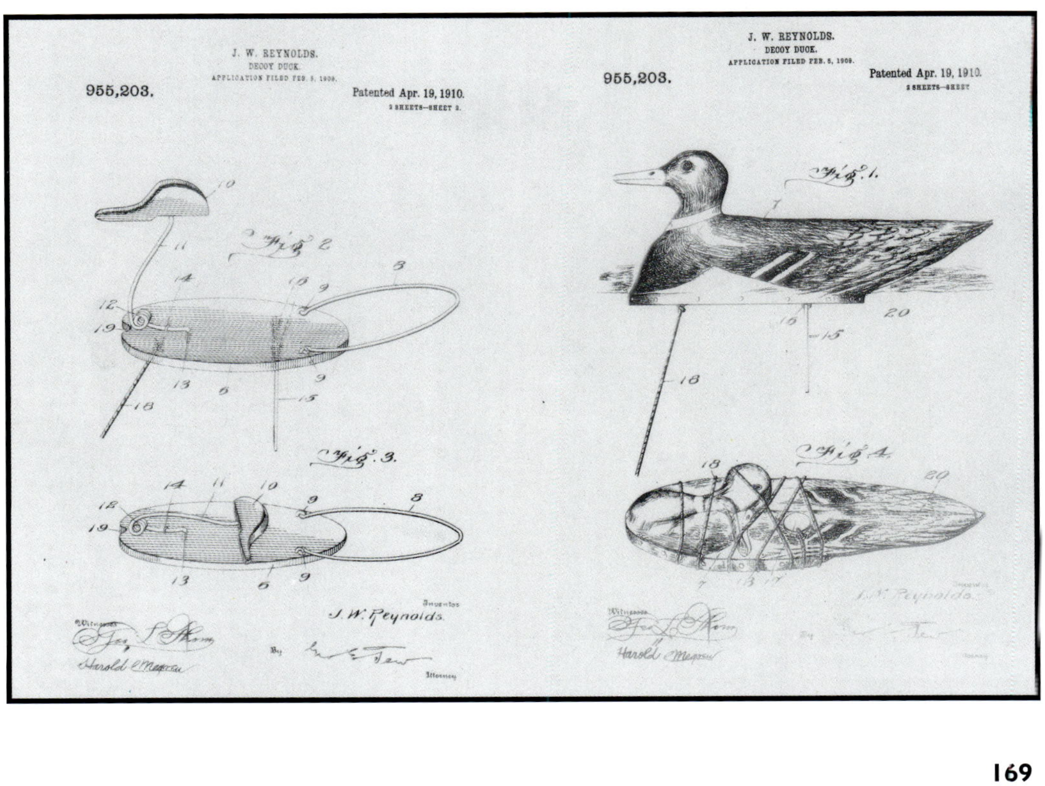

Copyright drawings for Veri-Good Model, folding canvas decoy J.W. Reynolds Decoy Company: Reynolds.

Shoveler pair, rare example, Rose Folding Decoy Company, Chicago, Illinois, circa 1900. $1,500. *Collection of William Rigsbee.*

Bluebill drake, black duck, Rose Folding Decoy Company, Chicago, Illinois, circa 1900. $250 each.

Stenciling on bottom of Rose Folding Decoy.

Advertisement Rose Folding Decoy Company, Chicago, Illinois, circa 1905.

Photo of unknown hunter posing in front of hunting shack on Rice Pond near Henry, Illinois. Note stack of Henry Ruggles decoys in foreground, circa 1900.

Rice Lake Preserve, Chillicothe, Illinois, stationery, circa 1945.

Canvasback drake, Henry W. Ruggles, Henry, Illinois, circa 1880. Large checkered duck call with German silver band, Dell Woods (1860-1933), caretaker at Hennepin Shooting Club and first Putman County game warden, circa 1880. Decoy, $3000; call, $5,000.

Mallard drake, unknown Henry, Illinois maker. Possibly very early Charles Perdew, c.1880. Fancy hand-carved duck call with leaf and vine design, George Cunningham (1842-1923), Hennepin, Illinois, personal call, circa 1870. Decoy, $4,000; call, $7,500.

John "Newt" Rule (1870-1949), Beardstown, Illinois (right) stands outside his clubhouse where he ran duck hunting day-shoots. Rule made his livelihood doing what he loved best hunting and fishing.

Mallard hen, Henry W. Ruggles, Henry, Illinois, circa 1880. $4,000.

John "Newt" Rule supplemented his income by operating a shooting gallery during the summer months. This photograph was taken at Henry, Illinois 1908.

Hunting club literature, John "Newt" Rule (1870-1049), Beardstown, Illinois, circa 1920.

Pintail drake, John "Newt" Rule, Beardstown, Illinois, circa 1940. $2,000.

Mallard pair, John "Newt" Rule, Beardstown, Illinois, circa 1940. $3,000.

Corn decoys, John "Newt" Rule (1870-1049), Beardstown, Illinois, circa 1930. $1,000 each.

Corn decoys, Unknown maker, Havana, Illinois, circa 1930. $400 each.

Charles Schoenheider, Sr. (1854-1944), Peoria, Illinois. Professional carpenter who supplemented his income by market hunting.

Corn decoys were created in an attempt to replace real corn cobs, which were commonly used for baiting prior to legislation which outlaw all baiting in Illinois, circa 1933.

Below:
Canada geese, Charles Schoenheider, Schoenheider is best known for his unique standing decoys that were mounted on a single cast iron foot. This dozen goose decoys were commissioned by the Daniel Voohees, Jr. When Voohees quibbled about Schoenheider's asking price of $100 for the dozen, Schoenheider put the decoys away. After his death, his son, Charles, Jr., kept them in the rafters of his garage where they remained until collectors discovered them during the 1960s. Collectors bought up the dozen, one or two at a time at $100-$150 each. Photograph, circa 1919.

Left:
Duck call, Oliver Ruppert, Peru, Illinois, walnut, stamped "Manufactured by Oliver Ruppert," circa 1920. $1,000.

Canada goose, standing ice decoy, Charles Schoenheider, circa 1900. $75,000. *Collection Alan and Elaine Haid, photograph Alan Haid.*

Mallard drake, standing ice duck. Charles Schoenheider, Sr., Peoria, Illinois, circa 1900. $75,000. *Collection of James R. and Diane Cook.*

Pintail pair, standing ice decoys, Charles Schoenheider, circa 1900. $100,000. *Collection James R. and Diane Cook.*

Blue-winged teal drake, Charles Schoenheider, Sr., one of two known examples, circa 1900. $35,000.

Detail of the pintail drake.

Canvasback drake, Charles Schoenheider, Sr., circa 1900. $3,000

Mallard pair, Charles Schoenheider, Sr., circa 1900. $12,000.

SATURDAY, OCTOBER 29, 1966

Peoria Journal Star

The Weekender

7 DAY TV PREVIEW
ENTERTAINMENT
FEATURES

Peoria Journal Star—Rochester Institute Of Technology Spectacolor Experiment 167

Charles Schoenheider, Jr., was featured in the Peoria Journal Star's Weekender Magazine, October 29, 1966, carrying on his family's tradition of decoy carving using his father's decoy patterns.

Blue-winged teal drake, Charles Schoenheider, Jr., circa 1950. $500. *Collection of Randy Nelson.*

Blue-winged teal drake, William Thomas "Billy" Shaw (1849-1927), Lacon, Illinois, circa 1890. $5,000.

Mallard hen, standing ice duck, Charles Schoenheider, Jr., circa 1950. $2,000.

Mallard hen, William "Billy" Shaw, Lacon, Illinois, painted by Edna Perdew Henry, Illinois, circa 1890. $3,000.

Mallard drake, Charles Shelstrom (1856-1932), Princeton, Illinois, circa 1890. $4,000.

Mallard hen, Charles Sheldon, Tiskilwa, Illinois, circa 1880. $3,000. *Collection of James R. and Diane Cook.*

Pintail drake. Ignatius Valentine Stachowiak (1898-1964), LaSalle, Illinois, Visited often with Charles Perdew who obviously tutored him in the fine art of decoy making, circa 1930. $2,500. *Collection James R. and Diane Cook.*

Little decoy maker diorama, Wendell Sherman (1920-present), Streator, Illinois, circa 1960. $500.

Mallard pair Ignatius Stachowiak, LaSalle, Illinois, circa 1930. $2,000. *Collection Alan and Elaine Haid. Photograph Alan Haid.*

Left:
Slimm Brothers Duck Calls, Harry H. Slinn (1847-1917 and John B Slimm (1863-1945), Chillicothe, Illinois. These were manufactured in Harry's gun shop in black and brown molded gutta-percha featuring a dead-mount scene with braces of shorebirds, ducks, and rabbits, circa 1880. $1,500 each.

Mallard drake, field decoy, Forest John "Jack" Stiles (1908-?), Savanna, Illinois, circa1930. $7,500. *Collection of James R. and Diane Cook.*

Mallard hen, Stephen Tyler (1880-1950), Dallas City, Illinois. Patterned from Charles Perdew decoy patterns, circa 1930. $1,000.

Owl decoy, cast aluminum, Joseph Swisher & James Soules, Decatur, Illinois. Originally created to scare starlings from capital building in Springfield, Illinois, Swisher and Soules eventually sold the rights to their molded decoy to the General Fibre Company, St Louis, who manufactured a papier-mâché model to be used by crow hunters, circa 1950. $300.

Mallard drake, Stephen Tyler, circa 1930. $500.

Pintail drake, unknown maker, Peoria, Illinois, circa 1930. $3,000. *Collection of James R. and Diane Cook.*

Duck call, walnut with etched designs and brass rings, unknown Illinois River maker, circa 1900. $1,500.

Crane, confidence decoy, unknown maker, used at the prestigious Crane Lake Gun Club, Beardstown, Illinois, circa 1900. $50,000.

Coot by unknown maker used in the Canton, Illinois area, circa 1930. $2,500.

Passenger pigeon decoy, primitive, unknown maker. Found in Liverpool, Illinois area, circa 1890. $1,000.

Canada goose, field decoy with wooden head and stuffed canvas body, unknown Havana, Illinois maker, circa 1940. $1,500.

Mallard pair, Michael Vallero (1906-1980), Spring Valley, Illinois. Vallero was a fine carver, but unable to master painting techniques. Edna Perdew painted most of his decoys, circa 1930. $5,000.

Duck calls, unknown maker, central Illinois, circa 1900.Left, $1,000; center, $1000; right Old Bill's call, sold by V. L. & A., Chicago, Illinois, $1,500. Duck hunting brochure, Beardstown, Illinois.

Mallard drake, Charles Walker, #28 rig, circa 1930. $12,000.

Pintail drake, #22 rig, Charles Walker, circa 1930. $25,000.

Pintail drake, Vance Rig #28, Charles Walker, circa 1930. $40,000. *Collection of Alan and Elaine Haid. Photograph Alan Haid.*

Mallard pair, Jolley Rig, Charles Walker, circa 1940. $35,000 pair.

Mallard pair with duckling, miniature. Charles Walker carved these miniature duplicates of his working decoys for family and close friends. Signed and dated to Forest Walker, his son, circa 1937. $10,000 set.

Mallard and pintail drake. Charles Walker designed these folding silhouette decoys so their bases could be joined together in an accordion fashion on the water decoys, circa 1940. $3,000 each.

Canada goose, Gibbs rig (probably from original Walker's personal hunting rig). Circa 1920. Shot shell box, Standard Cartridge Company, Chicago, Ill., Load #714, 10 gauge, circa 1880. Decoy, $50,000; shell box, $1000.

Mallard pair, Glenn Wankel (1923-1991), Lincoln, Illinois. Large oversize decoys were used on the Illinois River near Havana, circa 1940. $3,000.

Mallard pair, #32 (Watson Lawton) rig, Charles Walker, circa 1940. $25,000.

Mallard drake, #22 Rig, Charles Walker, circa 1930. $10,000.

Canvasback drake, John Warren (1831-1912), Liverpool, Illinois, circa 1890. $1,000.

Pintail drake, Fred Weber (1862-1958) and Charles J. Gisler (1892-1953), Peru, Illinois. $1,000. *Collection of Randy and Judy Mayers. Photography Joseph Engers.*

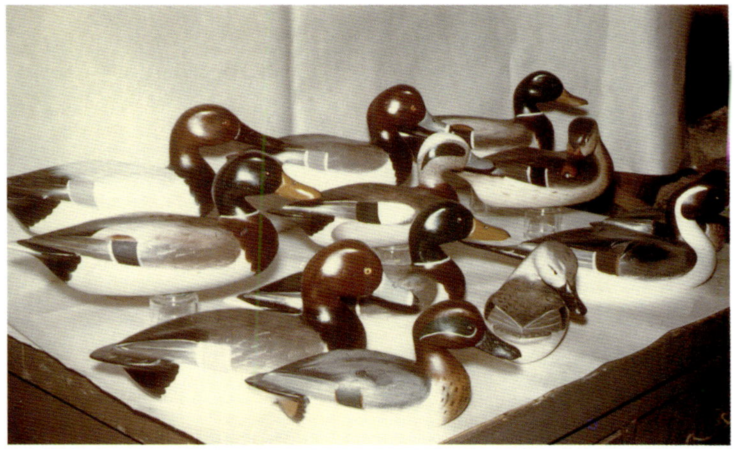

Assortment of Weeks decoys. Photograph by Willis Pennington, 1968.

Robert Weeks (1898-1982), Bureau, Illinois had an appreciation for old working decoys. When a particularly nice decoy came into his workshop to be repainted, Weeks would replace the decoy with a new one of his making. His workshop became a "treasure chest" to the collectors of the 1960s. Photograph by Willis Pennington, 1966.

Green-winged teal drake and mallard hen (background), Robert Weeks, Bureau, Illinois, circa 1950. $1,000 each.

Mallard pair and sleeper hen, 1/3 size miniatures. The Ranch House Lodge, Bureau, Illinois, sold Robert Weeks's decorative working-style decoys exclusively, circa 1960. $400 each.

Pintail drake, Robert Weeks, Bureau, Illinois, circa 1958. $750.

Mallard pair, Robert Weeks. Long after hunters switched to plastic decoys, Weeks continued to sell his working style decoys exclusively through the Ranch House, a favorite resort among duck hunters, circa 1960. $1,000.

Hector Whittington (1907-1981), Oglesby, Illinois carved decoy semi-professionally most of his life. His decoys reflect a strong influence from his regular correspondence with "Shang" Wheeler, noted Connecticut statesman and decoy carver.

These three men were icons of decoy collecting in Illinois during the 1960s: Hector Whittington (carver), Robert Weeks (carver), and Willis Pennington (decoy historian and collector), circa 1968.

Pintail pair, Hector Whittington Oglesby, Illinois, circa 1940. $7,000.

Pintail drake, Hector Whittington, Oglesby, Illinois, circa 1940. A very religious man, Whittington gave the decoys in his personal rig biblical names. $7,000. *Collection of James R. and Diane Cook.*

Mallard pair, Hector Whittington (1907-1981), Oglesby, Illinois, circa 1935. $3,000.

Canada goose, Hector Whittington, Oglesby, Illinois, part of Whittington's personal hunting rig, circa 1942. Canada goose decoys are very rare in Illinois. $7,500. Pointer shot shell box, Clinton Cartridge Company, Chicago, Illinois, circa 1920. $1,000.

Mallard drake, decorative wall hanging, life-size flying, Hector Whittington, Oglesby, Illinois, circa 1938. $4,000.

Mallard hen, decorative wall hanging, life-size flying, Hector Whittington, Oglesby, Illinois, circa 1938. $4,000 each.

Perry Wilcoxen (1862-1954), Liverpool, Illinois, posed with an assortment of his decoys, circa 1940. Canada goose, $2,000; mallard drake, $400; pintail drake, $400; miniature mallard drake, $300; and miniature pintail drake, $300.

Canada goose, Perry Wilcoxen, circa 1940. $2,000.

Green-winged teal drake, Perry Wilcoxen, circa 1920. $4,000.

Mallard Drake, Perry Wilcoxen, circa 1930. $400.

Pintail drake, Perry Wilcoxen, circa 1925. $500.

Green-winged teal drakes; mallard drake; pintail drake, miniatures, Perry Wilcoxen, circa 1930's. $300 each.

Ringbill drake; bluebill drake; canvasback drake; redhead drake; miniatures, Perry Wilcoxen, circa 1930's. $350 each.

Canvasback drake, oversized, Perry Wilcoxen, circa 1930. $750.

Bluebill drake, Perry Wilcoxen, from Wilcoxen's personal hunting rig, marked PW on bottom, circa 1930. $400.

Canvasback drake, Perry Wilcoxen, circa 1930. $500.

Canvasback drake, Richard Wilcoxen (1855-1926), older brother of Perry Wilcoxen, Liverpool, Illinois, circa 1890. $2,500.

Pintail drake, Richard Wilcoxen circa 1890. $4,000.

Pintail drake, Richard Wilcoxen, circa 1890. $3,000.

Mallard pair, William Zarnicki, Oglesby, Illinois, circa 1940. $1,500.

Mallard drake, Joseph Zender (1899-1960), Chicago, Illinois, circa 1940. $1,000.

FISH:.

Black Crappie, 10", Edward Forman, Antioch, Illinois, wood decorative plaque, signed and dated on back, 1948. $4,000.

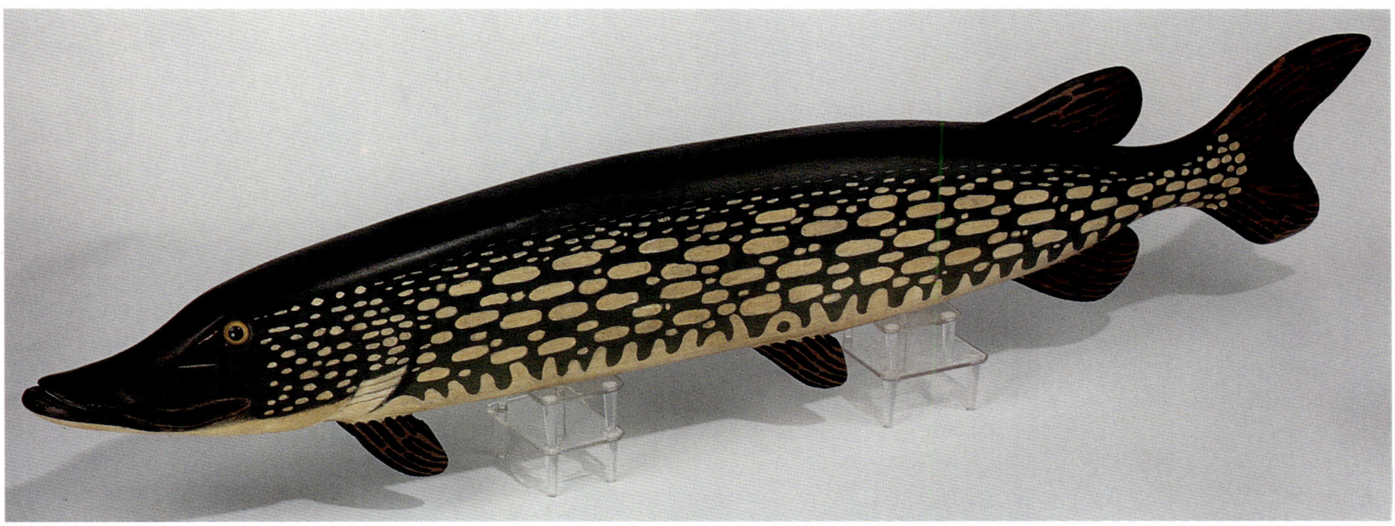

Northern pike, 40"; John Williams, New Boston, Illinois, circa 1950. $2,500.

Bass, wooden decorative carving, 21" (fish, 18"), John Hyatt, Pekin, Illinois, circa 1940. $4,000.

Wisconsin

Wisconsin, originally spelled "Ouisconsin" is derived from the Native American word meaning "gathering waters." Within the state's boundaries are 7000 lakes including the largest land-locked lake in the United States, Lake Winnebago. Migrating waterfowl traverse the state from the north heading towards the Mississippi River. Waterfowlers enjoy a variety of hunting opportunities. The early September migration brings teal darting into the potholes followed by the larger puddle ducks. Rafts of canvasback, redheads, and scaup use Lake Michigan's Green Bay and the larger lakes, Winnebago, Poygan, Butte des Morts, and Koshkonong.

Before the days of drainage ditches that plagued most of the natural waterfowl habitat, the surrounding watersheds provided a wildlife paradise. Though a mere shadow of their former glory, these areas remain good hunting areas. Wisconsin has long been a popular vacation spot. After the Civil War railroad lines were well established and regularly advertised. Reduced rates during the hunting seasons for hunters allowed liberal allowance for game equipment, which was often carried free. Sportsmen traveled from most parts of the country to partake in the waterfowling. Some held memberships in the prestigious clubs that formed during the 1800s, like the Blackhawk Club (est. 1874) and the Carcajou Club (est. 1896) on Lake Koshkonong. To the northeast lay the great Horicon Marsh, 40,000 acres of waterfowl heaven that was home to numerous clubs, most notably the Diana Shooting Club (est. 1883) and Upper Horicon Club. Somewhat farther north was Lake Puckaway, the hunting grounds of historic hunting clubs with interesting names, such as the CawCaw Club (est. 1866) and the Nee-pee-Nauk Club (est. 1882)

The countless clubs and hunting groups that used Wisconsin lakes for outstanding waterfowling spawned many talented decoy carvers, developing several important Schools of carvers. Sportsmen gunning off the historic Stony Blind at the end of Lake Koshkonong's Bingham's Point often shot over decoys made by the brothers, Ferdinand and Mandt Homme from McFarland. Along with Enoch Reindahl, these men created highly realistic Stoughton School decoys, which seem to be captured in fluid motion. The Milwaukee School of carvers was led by Owen Gromme's work. Associated with the Milwaukee Public Museum, Gromme carved decoys, along with his fellow museum associates Walter Dettman and Walter Pelzer, that were used to gather study skins and recreationally for hunting. Together these men ran a training program that taught WPA workers how to carve working decoys. The big waters of Lakes Winnebago, Poygan, and Butte des Morts inspired the deep bodied duck decoys with high heads, especially diver decoys made by carvers like Joe Gigl, Joe Sieger, and Frank Strey. Wisconsin carvers, like August Moak are also famed for their perky coot and stylized canvasback decoys. During the 1920s Walter Evans established his decoy-producing factory in Ladysmith offering sportsmen a complete line of high quality Wisconsin style decoys for nearly 30 years.

Eons ago the Green Bay Lobe of the Wisconsin Glacier scooped out a huge egg-shaped hollow measuring 14 miles north to south and 3-4 miles east to west, which evolved into the Horicon Marsh. After several failed attempts to reduce the great marsh into agricultural land, conversationalists convinced legislators to pass the 1927 Horicon Marsh Wildlife Refuge Bill. By the early 1950s Wisconsin and Federal governmental agencies had created The Horicon Marsh Refuge. In recent years, the Horicon Marsh has been developed into a major staging area for the Canada goose. Geese had always migrated through the state, but now it can hold 300,000 Canada geese until the snow covers the surrounding cornfields pushing the geese south in search of feed. Field shooting geese is most successful over decoys. Canada goose decoys by Owen Gromme, Mandt Homme, and Enoch Reindahl are some of the finest ever created.

Possibly the oldest and finest crafted fish decoys were produced in the LaCrosse area. Here the Mississippi River widens, creating an area dotted with small islands and lush aquatic plant life. The fish decoys used here are called river fish. Although the decoys were suspended through the ice as in other areas, the water below moved in strong currents, thus a decoy didn't need large side fins to stabilize it or any curvature in the body to accentuate the decoy's motion. The current would wiggle the decoy in the natural motion of a minnow swimming upstream. The clear running river waters also encouraged fish decoy makers to use the natural colorations of the small baitfish species. These decoys were usually very small. Some measure less than 3 inches. On the other hand on the large northern lakes, early spear fishermen often hunted for large sturgeon. Unlike most large prey fish, the sturgeon like to congregate and will respond well to large sturgeon decoys. When size limits were placed on the sturgeon a fisherman was allowed to keep, decoys that corresponded to the legal length were suspended below a fisherman's hole so he could tell at a glance if an approaching fish was an allowable catch. Throughout the state individual carvers went about the business of supplying local fishermen and tourists with fish decoys.

Horicon Marsh Sportsmen, Mayville, Wisconsin, embroidered felt patch.

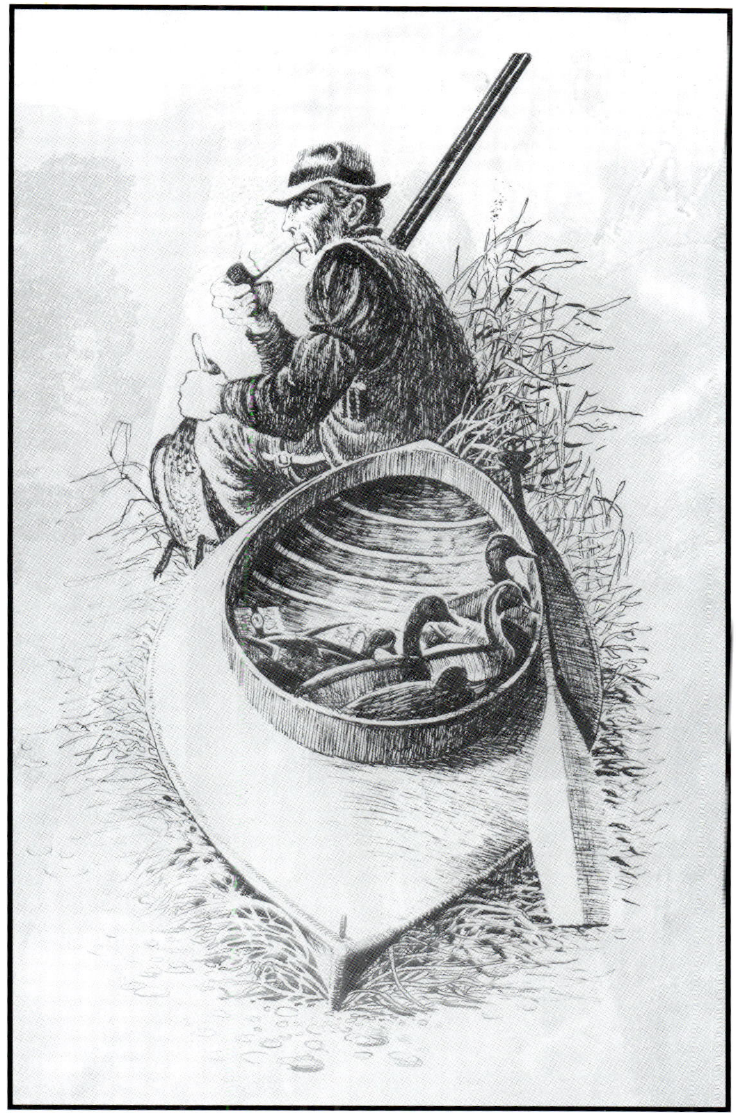

Pen and Ink drawing, Lou Schifferl, Neehna, Wisconsin, originally published by Hal Sorenson in *Decoy Collectors Guide*. *Courtesy Barbara Sorenson and Lou Schifferl.*

Puckaway Rod & Gun Club, Puckaway, Wisconsin, embroidered felt patch.

Duck skiff trade sign, hung outside W. Nourse boat building shop in Fox Lake, Wisconsin, circa 1930.

Horicon Marsh Hunters Club

Herbert Kloeden

Mayville

1942 Is A Member in Good Standing

OFFICIAL MEMBERSHIP CARD

HORICON MARSH HUNTERS CLUB

NAME Herbert Kloeden

ADDRESS Mayville Wis.

SEASON 1945—1946
EXPIRES
SEPTEMBER 1946

No.

Membership cards from Horicon Marsh Hunter Club, 1942 & 1946.

Duck Hunting and Fishing

LAKE WINNEBAGO

Best in the State

NATURAL BLINDS

Decoys - Skiffs - Boats - Guides - Lodging

Drive 8 miles North on Highway 45 from intersection of Highways 41 and 45 at Fond du Lac

TO

Willow Beach Lodge

Leo Roebke

ROUTE 1

OSHKOSH, WISCONSIN

Business card offering guide service and equipment for duck hunting and fishing on Lake Winnebago, Oshkosh, Wisconsin, circa 1940. *Courtesy Shirley, Joe and Dean Dashner.*

Right:
Wisconsin hunters often built stationary blind tucked into the grassy cover of the shoreline. They would set out their decoys in the clear hole about forty yards from the blind leaving an inviting open area for the ducks to land within shooting range.

The flatboat was a popular hunting skiff among early waterfowlers on Lake Koshkonong. The original Koshkonong flatboat measured 16 feet long and 6 feet wide. Similar to the sink boxes of Maryland, the flatboat had a rectangular box that rode beneath the water level. A canvas cover would be stretched over the boat creating a profile that was barely visible at a distance. *Courtesy Barbara Sorenson and Lou Schifferl.*

Frederick Theadore Bohl (1870-1949), seated center, Beaver Dam Wisconsin. Although he never hunted himself, Bohl supplied local hunters with working pintail, teal, mallard, bluebill, and canvasback decoys. He also carved miniature decoratives for the tourists, including swans. *Photograph courtesy Shirley, Joe and Dean Dashner.*

Pintail drake, Frederick Bohl, Beaver Dam, Wisconsin, circa 1920. $1,000. *Collection of Jim Wierzba. Photography Grace Natoli Sheldon.*

Advertising flyer, Carry-Lite decoys. The same graphics were used for a large oval paper label, which was glued to the bottom of early Carry-Lite decoys.

Mallard pair, Frederick Bohl, Beaver Dam, Wisconsin, circa 1930. $1,000 pair. *Collection of Jim Wierzba. Photograph by Grace Napoli Sheldon.*

Coot, papier-mâché , Carry-Lite Decoys, Division Pulp Reproductions Company, Milwaukee, circa 1950. $75.

Carry-Lite DECOYS

No. 700
MALLARD HEN

Actual Color Reproductions ¼ Full Size

No. 700
MALLARD DRAKE

No. 702
BLUE-BILL HEN

No. 702
BLUE-BILL DRAKE

No. 701
PINTAIL HEN

No. 701
PINTAIL DRAKE

No. 703
CANVAS-BACK HEN

No. 703
CANVAS-BACK DRAKE

NO TWO ALIKE! Adds greatly to realism. Attracts birds more readily. An exclusive Carry-Lite feature so far as we know.

DEALERS: Order from your regular sporting goods or hardware jobber. Complete stocks available.

No. 704
BLACK DUCK

See Other Side For Additional Decoys

Fall issues of leading outdoor magazines will again carry our Carry-Lite Decoys advertising messages to hundreds of thousands of sportsmen. From Coast to Coast and from the Arctic Circle to the Gulf of Mexico, duck hunting enthusiasts will be clamoring for "Carry-Lites." Be prepared to meet the demand. Stock orders placed NOW, will be put on our "priorities" list.

Carry-Lite DECOYS

MOLDED CARRY-LITE DECOYS 2601 N. 30th ST. MILWAUKEE, WIS.

Page from wholesale buyer's catalog, Carry-lite Decoys Division, Pulp Reproductins Company, Milwaukee, Wisconsin, circa 1950.

Pintail pair, papier-mâché , Carry-Lite Decoys, Division Pulp Reproductions Company, Milwaukee, circa 1950. $150 pair.

Mallards, salesman sample, papier-mâché, Carry-Lite Decoys, Division Pulp Reproductions Company, Milwaukee, circa 1950. First manufactured in 1939, Carry-Lite decoys are one of the earliest manufactured molded paper decoys. $75 each.

Mallards, pair and single drake. Carry-Lite Decoys with Carry-Lite shipping carton, Division Pulp Reproductions Company, Milwaukee, Wisconsin, unused condition; carton held twelve decoys, circa 1948. $600 set of 12.

Rare example of Carry-Lite black and white label.

Mallards, tip-up decoys; corn decoy; papier-mâché, Carry-Lite Decoys, Division Pulp Reproductions Company, Milwaukee, circa 1950. Decoys, $100 each; corn, $50 each.

Blue-winged teal drake, Stanley Ceman (1902-1976), Berlin, Wisconsin, circa 1930. $1000. *Collection of Shirley, Joe and Dean Dashner.*

Mallard drake, Ora Clough, Peckinstown, Wisconsin, circa 1930. $700. *Collection of Shirley, Joe, and Dean Dashner.*

Blue-winged teal, John Dettman, Milwaukee, Wisconsin, circa 1950. $2,500.

Pintail pair, Warren P. Dettman (1904-1979), Milwaukee, Wisconsin, circa 1960. Dettman carved decoys primarily for his own use for hunting and to assist him in collecting waterfowl specimens for the Milwaukee Public Museum where he worked as a taxidermist. $10,000.

Mallard drake, eclipse plumage, Warren Dettman, Milwaukee, Wisconsin, 1935. $4,000. *Collection of Jim Wierzba. Photography Grace Natoli Sheldon.*

Mallard hen, Warren Dettman, Milwaukee, Wisconsin, circa 1940. $7,500. *Collection of Jim Wierzba. Photography Grace Natoli Sheldon.*

Mallard hen, Warren P. Dettman, Milwaukee, Wisconsin, circa 1950. $5,000. *Collection of T. Thompson Bosworth, Photograph courtesy T. Thompson Bosworth.*

Pintail pair, Warren Dettman, Milwaukee, Wisconsin, circa 1930. $25,000. *Collection of Jim Wierzba. Photography Grace Natoli Sheldon.*

Promotional photograph of carvers Roy E Discher (1899-1977) and Charles Koepsel (1989-1980), Milwaukee, who worked together as a decoy producing team. Discher was responsible for the detail painting and Koepsel the carving. Sponsored by the Blatz Brewing Company, Milwaukee, they often set up at sports shows to demonstrate how to make hunting decoys, circa 1950. *Photograph courtesy John D. Riefenrather.*

Mallard pair, miniatures, Warren P. Dettman, Milwaukee, Wisconsin, circa 1950. $5,000. *Collection of William Rigsbee, Photograph courtesy T. Thompson Bosworth.*

Bluebill pair, Warren Dettman, Milwaukee, Wisconsin, circa 1950. $8,000. *Collection of James R. and Diane Cook.*

Black duck, Discher/Koepsel, Milwaukee, Wisconsin, circa 1940. $300.

Bluebill drake, Discher/Koepsel, Milwaukee, Wisconsin, circa 1940. $300 each.

Redhead drake, Discher/Koepsel, Milwaukee, Wisconsin, circa 1940. $300 each.

Canvasback drake, Discher/Koepsel, Milwaukee, Wisconsin, circa 1940. $300 each.

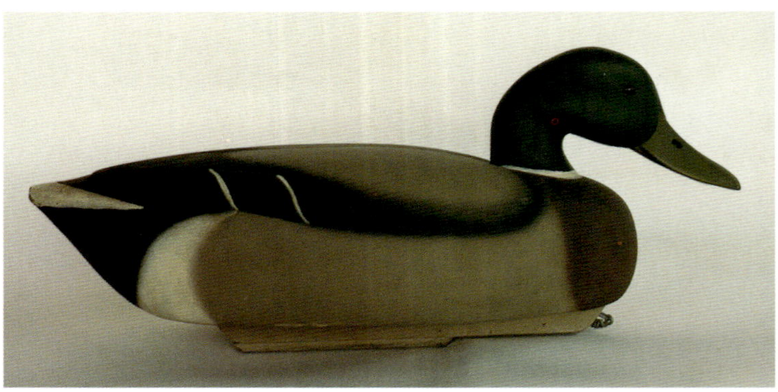

Mallard drake, Discher/Koepsel, Milwaukee, Wisconsin, circa 1940. $300 each.

Koepsel/Discher instruction booklet.

Walter Evans (1872-1948), Ladysmith, established the Evans Decoy Company during the early 1920, offering a complete line of quality wooden hunting decoys in three grades, Mammoth, Standard, and Competitive, until the mid-1930s.

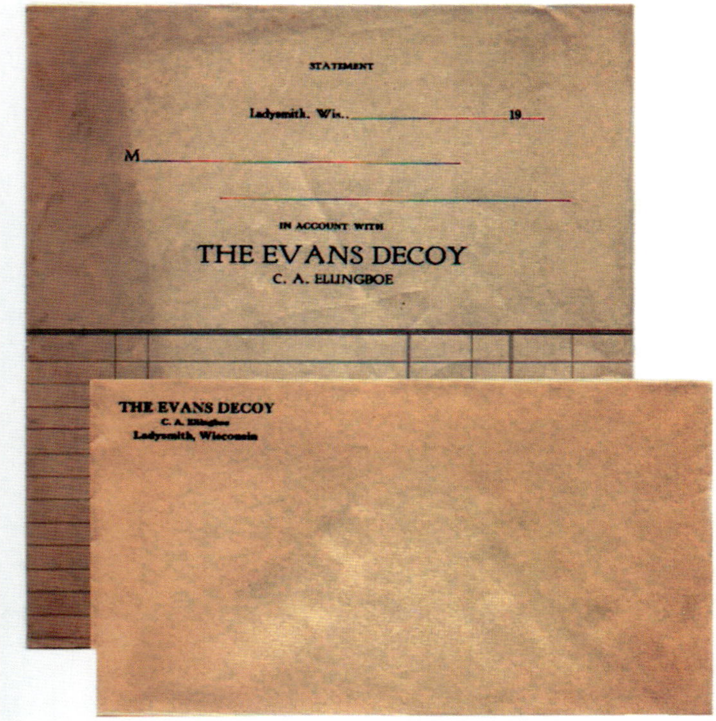

Original billing statement and letterhead envelope, Evans Decoy Company, circa 1940.

Mallard pair, Mammoth Grade, Evans Decoy Company, Ladysmith, Wisconsin, circa 1920. $3,000 pair. *Collection of Shirley, Joe, and Dean Dashner.*

Mallard pair Standard Grade, Evans Decoy Company, Ladysmith, Wisconsin, circa 1920. $1,500. *Collection of Shirley, Joe, and Dean Dashner.*

Black ducks. Top: Mammoth Grade, $3,000; bottom: Standard Grade, $1,500. Evans Decoy Company, Ladysmith, Wisconsin, circa 1920. *Collection of Shirley, Joe, and Dean Dashner.*

Pintail pair, Standard Grade, Evans Decoy Company, Ladysmith, Wisconsin, circa 1920. $3,000, pair.

Green-winged teal, Hollow Competitive Grade, rarest example of Evans decoys, only pair known, Evans Decoy Company, Ladysmith, Wisconsin, circa 1920. $10,000, pair. *Collection of James R. and Diane Cook.*

Blue-winged teal pair, Standard Grade, Evans Decoy Company, Ladysmith, Wisconsin, circa 1920. $4,000 pair. *Collection Shirley, Joe, and Dean Dashner.*

Canvasback pair, Standard Grade, Evans Decoy Company, Ladysmith, Wisconsin, circa 1920. $4,000, pair. *Collection of James R. and Diane Cook.*

Widgeon pair, Standard Grade, Extremely rare, Evans Decoy Company, Ladysmith, Wisconsin, circa 1920. $5,000. *Collection of Shirley, Joe, and Dean Dashner.*

Canvasback drake, Standard Grade, Evans Decoy Company, Ladysmith, Wisconsin, circa 1920. $1,000.

Canvasback hen, Mammoth Grade, Evans Decoy Company, Ladysmith, Wisconsin, circa 1920. $1,000.

Coot, Standard Grade, Evans Decoy Company, Ladysmith, Wisconsin, circa 1920. $800.

Bluebill pair, Mammoth Grade, Evans Decoy Company, Ladysmith, Wisconsin, circa 1920. $3,000. *Collection Herb Desch.*

Redhead drake, Myron Frisque, Green Bay, Wisconsin, circa 1940. $500. *Collection of Jim Wierzba. Photography Grace Natoli Sheldon.*

Bluebill pair, Myron Frisque, Green Bay, Wisconsin, circa 1940. $750 pair. *Collection of Jim Wierzba. Photography Grace Natoli Sheldon.*

Mallard pair, Milton Geyer, Green Bay, Wisconsin, circa 1960. $1000. *Collection of Shirley, Joe, and Dean Dashner.*

Black duck, Milton Geyer, Green Bay, Wisconsin, circa 1960. $300. *Collection of Shirley, Joe, and Dean Dashner.*

Joseph R Gigl (1882-1962), Fremont, Wisconsin, carved hundreds of working wooden and cork decoys as well as miniature decoys and miniature dioramas. *Photograph courtesy Ron Koch.*

Miniature Canada geese flying, mounted in painted wooden bowl. Joseph Gigl, Fremont, Wisconsin, circa 1940. Gigl painted surreal backgrounds, which accented his decorative miniature dioramas. $1,000.

Miniature mallards flying, mounted on painted wooden board, Joseph Gigl, Fremont, Wisconsin, circa 1940. $750.

Bluebill drake, flying, Joseph Gigl, Fremont, Wisconsin, circa 1930. $1,500. *Collection of Shirley, Joe, and Dean Dashner.*

Mallard hen, Joseph Gigl, Fremont, Wisconsin. Gigl rarely produced wooden decoys. Most of his working decoys had cork bodies with inlaid wooden tail, and wood heads, circa 1930. $1,000.

Canvasback pair, rare wooden models, Joseph Gigl, Fremont, Wisconsin, circa 1935. $2,000. *Collection of Jim Wierzba. Photography Grace Natoli Sheldon.*

Owen Gromme, Milwaukee, Wisconsin was the leading force that propelled the Wisconsin's WPA style decoys, circa 1940. mallard hen, $5,000; pintail drake, $5000. Pictured with William Taylor, Sr. *Photograph courtesy William Taylor, Jr.*

Canvasback drake, wooden, Owen Gromme, Milwaukee, Wisconsin, circa 1932. $5,000. *Collection of James Wierzba.*

Canvasback hen, wooden, Owen Gromme, Milwaukee, Wisconsin, circa 1932. $20,000. *Collection of James R. and Diane Cook..*

Mallard hen, wooden, Owen Gromme, Milwaukee, Wisconsin, circa 1932. $10,000. *Collection of Alan and Elaine Haid.* Duck call, Owen Gromme, circa 1932. $2,000.

Ring-bill pair, wooden, Owen Gromme, Milwaukee, Wisconsin, circa 1932. $10,000. *Collection of Mr. and Mrs. Roy Gromme.*

Canada goose, wooden, Owen Gromme, Milwaukee, Wisconsin, circa 1932. $15,000. *Collection of James R. and Diane Cook.*

Canada goose, wooden, Owen Gromme, Milwaukee, Wisconsin, circa 1932. $15,000. *Collection of Herb Desch.*

Canada geese, Owen Gromme, Milwaukee. Gromme molded a rig of papier-mâché geese that were amazingly life-like. The same body pattern was used for geese with several different head positions. Note the single blue goose nestled among the Canada geese. The molds can be seen on the lowest shelf. Gromme cast his decoys solely for his own use in the field as Curator of Birds and Mammals at Milwaukee Public Museum, circa 1940. *Photograph courtesy William Taylor, Jr.*

Goose call, Owen Gromme, Milwaukee, Wisconsin. The only known call of its kind, it shows remarkable attention to detail. The tongue is actually twisted and syriux (voice box) is carved inside throat. Circa 1939. $15,000. *Collection of Mr. and Mrs. Roy Gromme.*

Detail of the goose call.

Mallard drake, unknown W.P.A. worker, Milwaukee, Wisconsin, circa 1934-35. $2,000. *Collection of Shirley, Joe, and Dean Dashner.*

Bluebill pair, August Guhl (1901-1991), Oshkosh, Wisconsin, circa 1930. $2,500. *Collection of Shirley, Joe, and Dean Dashner.*

Black duck, Ferdinand Homme, Stoughton, Wisconsin, circa 1930. $7,500. *Collection of James R. and Diane Cook.*

Canvasback drake, sleeper, Harold Holup, Tustin, Wisconsin, circa 1920. $1,500. *Collection of Shirley, Joe and Dean Dashner.*

Mallard drake, Sleeper, Ferdinand Homme, Stoughton, Wisconsin, circa 1930. $20,000. *Photograph courtesy Gene and Linda Kangas.*

Pintail pair, Howard Homer, Diamond Lake, Wisconsin, circa 1950. $1,200.

Mallard pair, Ferdinand Homme, Stoughton, Wisconsin, circa 1940. $15,000, pair. *Collection of James R. and Diane Cook.*

Mandt Homme, (1905-1964), MacFarland, Wisconsin. Photograph Enoch Reindahl.

Canvasback pair, Mandt Homme, Stoughton, Wisconsin, circa 1920. $25,000.

Canada goose, Mandt Homme, circa 1930. $30,000.

Canvasbacks, Mandt Homme, MacFarland, Wisconsin, circa 1930. $10,000 each.

Dr. Shearer hunted over his rig of Homme decoys, which included spectacular geese and canvasback decoys on Lake Kosgkonong, circa 1950.

Pintail drake, Mandt Homme, MacFarland, Wisconsin, circa 1940. $5,000.

Duck call, black hard rubber, J & M Manufacturing, Oshkosh, Wisconsin, circa 1940. $1,000. *Collection of Shirley, Joe, and Dean Dashner.*

Mallard drake, Mandt Homme, MacFarland, Wisconsin, circa 1940. $7,500.

Jim Crow Call, black hard rubber, J & M Manufacturing, Oshkosh, Wisconsin, circa 1940. $500.

Great horned owl, Mandt Homme, Stoughton, Wisconsin, circa 1935. $35,000.

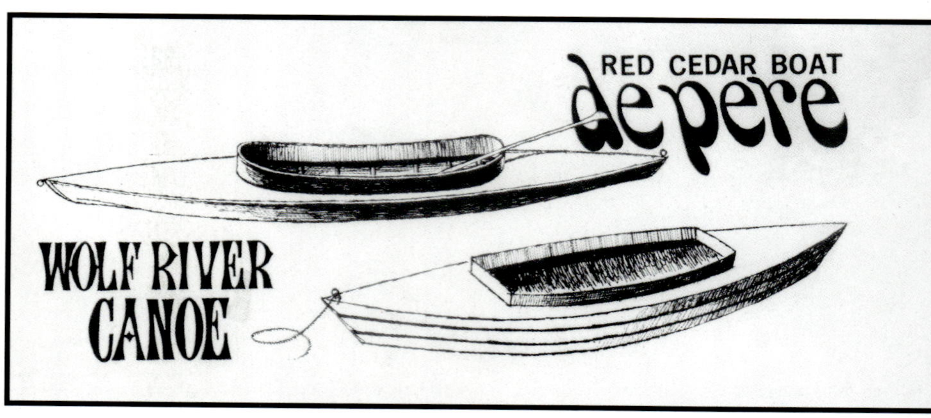

The DePere red cedar boat, Kinney Boat Works, DePere, Wisconsin, measured 15 foot with a 32inch beam and depth of only 9 inches. This lightweight boat was popular with marsh hunters throughout the Midwest. The Wolf River Canoe can be recognized by its simple 2 or 3 horizontal boards that made up the boat's side. Drawings by Lou Schifferl originally published in Decoy Collector's Guide. *Courtesy Barbara Sorenson and Lou Schifferl.*

Louis Loboda, New Lisbon, Wisconsin, was a professional taxidermist who carved a rig of hunting decoys for his own use. He often painted scenic backgrounds on the mount's backboard. *Photograph courtesy of Jim Wierzba.*

Bluebill pair, Louis Loboda, New Lisbon, circa 1930. $4,000. *Collection of Jim Wierzba. Photography Grace Natoli Sheldon.*

Mallard drake, Louis Loboda, New Lisbon, circa 1930. $1,500. *Collection of Jim Wierzba. Photography Grace Natoli Sheldon.*

Top: canvasback hen, only known example, $750. Bottom: mallard hen, $500, Benton "Burt" Lange (1896-1967), Horicon, Wisconsin, circa 1940.

Ringbill pair, Louis Loboda, New Lisbon, circa 1930. $6,000. *Collection of Jim Wierzba. Photography Grace Natoli Sheldon.*

Pintail pair, Benton "Burt" Lange, Horicon, Wisconsin, circa 1940. $1,500. *Collection of Jim Wierzba. Photography Grace Natoli Sheldon.*

Black duck, Walter Lowery, La Crosse, Wisconsin, circa 1930. $4,000. *Collection of Shirley, Joe, and Dean Dashner.*

Mallards, Benton "Burt" Lange, Horicon, Wisconsin, circa 1940. $750 each. *Collection of Jim Wierzba. Photography Grace Natoli Sheldon.*

Canvasback drake, Myron Mackowski, Beaver Dam, Wisconsin, circa 1930. $1,000. *Collection of Jim Wierzba. Photography Grace Natoli Sheldon.*

Mallard pair, Walter Lowery (1878-?), La Crosse, Wisconsin, circa 1920. $5,000. *Collection of Shirley, Joe, and Dean Dashner.*

Mallard drake, Myron MacKowski, Beaver Dam, Wisconsin, circa 1928. $1,000. *Collection of Jim Wierzba. Photography Grace Natoli Sheldon.*

Canada goose, August Moak (1852-1942), Tustin, Wisconsin, circa 1925. $4,000. *Collection of Herb Desch.*

Bluebill drake, August Moak, Tustin. Wisconsin, circa 1920. $2,500. *Collection of Shirley, Joe, and Dean Dashner.*

Canvasback drake, August Moak, Tustin, Wisconsin, circa 1920. $2,500.

Canvasback pair, August Moak, Tustin, Wisconsin, circa 1920. $5,000. *Collection of Jim Wierzba. Photography Grace Natoli Sheldon.*

Coot, August Moak, Tustin, Wisconsin, circa 1930. $4,000. *Collection of Jim Wierzba. Photography Grace Natoli Sheldon.*

Coot, Gust Karl Nelow (1882-1962), Oshkosh and Omro, Wisconsin, circa 1940. $700. *Collection of Jim Wierzba. Photography Grace Natoli Sheldon.*

Redhead drake, Gust Nelow, Omro, Wisconsin, circa 1940. $800. *Collection of Jim Wierzba. Photography Grace Natoli Sheldon.*

Canada goose, Gust Nelow, Omro, Wisconsin, circa 1940. $1,500. *Collection of Jim Wierzba. Photography Grace Natoli Sheldon.*

Canvasback drake, Gust Nelow, Omro, Wisconsin, circa 1940. $800. *Collection of Jim Wierzba. Photography Grace Natoli Sheldon.*

Top: ringbill hen, $3,500. Bottom: bluebill hen, $3,000. Walter Pelzer (1911-?), Milwaukee, Wisconsin, Milwaukee Public Museum School, circa 1930. *Collection of Herb Desch.*

Ringbill drake, Walter Pelzer, Milwaukee, Wisconsin, circa 1940. $4,000. *Collection of James R. and Diane Cook.*

Ringbill hen, Walter Pelzer, Milwaukee, Wisconsin, circa 1940. $4,000.

Pintail drake, Pelzer/Dettman, Milwaukee, Wisconsin, circa 1930. $5,000.

Pintail drake, Walter Pelzer. Milwaukee, Wisconsin, Circl 1930. $5,000. *Collection/ Photograph Gene and Linda Kangas.*

Bluebill pair, Pelzer/Dettman, Milwaukee, Wisconsin, circa 1930. $4000.

Canvasback drake, Realistic Decoy Company, Kewaunee, Wisconsin, circa 1935. $400. *Collection of Shirley, Joe, and Dashner.*

Bluebill drake, Realistic Decoy Company, Kewaunee, Wisconsin. Alois Luker produced mallard, canvasback, and bluebill decoys similar to Evans Decoy Company decoys under the trade name Realistic Decoy Company from 1932-1939. $300. *Collection of Shirley, Joe, and Dean Dashner.*

Mallard Hen, Russell "Razz" Berry, Stoughton, Wisconsin. Berry was a contemporary and hunting companion of Enoch Reindahl. $3500. *Photograph and collection Alan and Elaine Haid.*

Canada goose, Enoch Reindahl (1904-2000), Stoughton, Wisconsin, Carved a limited number of hunting decoys mainly for his own use, circa 1938. $35,000. *Collection of Jim and Diane Cook.*

Canada goose, Enoch Reindahl, Stoughton, Wisconsin, circa 1940. $25,000.

Canada goose, canvas stuffed body with wooden head, Enoch Reindahl, Stoughton, Wisconsin, circa 1940. Reindahl pieced together denim from old Oshkosh bib overalls to create a lighter weight field decoy. The wooden head could be folded over for easier transportation. $5,000. *Photograph and collection Alan and Elaine Haid.*

Mallard pair, Enoch Reindahl, Stoughton, Wisconsin, circa 1940. $25,000.

Self-portrait of Enoch Reindahl with his hunting stool of mallards and pintails, circa 1935.

Pintail drake, Enoch Reindahl, Stoughton, Wisconsin, circa 1940, only three known examples. $10,000.

Mallard pair, Enoch Reindahl, Stoughton, Wisconsin, circa 1940. $20,000.

Pintail pair, Enoch Reindahl, Stoughton, Wisconsin, circa 1940. $20,000. *Collection of James R. and Diane Cook.*

Mallard hen, Enoch Reindahl, Stoughton, Wisconsin, circa 1940. $7,500. *Collection of James R. and Diane Cook.*

Canvasback pair, Enoch Reindahl, Stoughton, Wisconsin, circa 1940. $30,000. *Collection of James R. and Diane Cook.*

Enoch Reindahl holding his miniature jumping mallard, circa 1990. Carving, $4,000.

Canvasback pair, Frank Resop, Berlin, Wisconsin, circa 1930. Although Resop carved decoys mostly for himself, he gave away hundreds of decoys to friends and local hunters. He produced approximately 1000 of these wonderfully folky interpretations of the waterfowl that frequented his favorite hunting spot, Lake Poygan. $2,000 pair. *Collection of Shirley, Joe, and Dean Dashner.*

Canvasback drake, Frank Resop, Berlin, Wisconsin, circa 1920. $700. *Collection of Shirley, Joe, and Dean Dashner.*

Owl striking rabbit, miniature carving, Enoch Reindahl, Stoughton, Wisconsin, circa 1935. $4,000. Photograph Enoch Reindahl.

Canvasback drake, flying, Frank Resop, Berlin, Wisconsin, circa 1940. $5,000. *Photograph and collection Alan and Elaine Haid.*

Pintail pair, Frank Resop, Berlin, Wisconsin, circa 1946. $4,000. *Collection of Ron Koch. Photograph courtesy Oshkosh Public Museum.*

Bluebill pair, Frank Resop, Berlin, Wisconsin, circa 1930. $1,500. *Collection of Jim Wierzba. Photography Grace Natoli Sheldon.*

Canvasback pair, Frank Resop, Berlin, Wisconsin, circa 1925. $2,000 pair. *Collection of Jim Wierzba. Photography Grace Natoli Sheldon.*

Blue-winged teal, Frank Resop, Berlin, Wisconsin, circa 1930. $5,000 pair. *Collection of Jim Wierzba. Photography Grace Natoli Sheldon.*

Blue-winged teal pair, Frank Resop, Berlin, Wisconsin, circa 1920. $4000.

Blue-winged teal drake, Frank Resop, Berlin, Wisconsin, circa 1920. $2500. *Collection of Shirley, Joe and Dean Dashner.*

Bluebill hen, John Roth, Oshkosh, Wisconsin, circa 1930. $400.

Mallard drake Frank Resop, Berlin, Wisconsin, circa 1930. $3000, pair. *Collection of Shirley, Joe, and Dean Dashner.*

Bluebill drake, John Roth, Oshkosh, Wisconsin, circa 1930. $350. *Collection of Shirley, Joe, and Dean Dashner.*

Canvasback pair, John Roth (1885-1948), Oshkosh, Wisconsin, circa 1920. $1,000 pair. *Collection of Shirley, Joe, and Dean Dashner.*

Canvasback drake, Ernest Rothe (1910-1968), Oshkosh, Wisconsin, circa 1930. $1000. *Collection of Shirley, Joe, and Dean Dashner.*

William Schultz, Milwaukee, Wisconsin, painting Avocet in his workshop, circa 1960. Schultz was on staff at the Milwaukee Public Museum and was responsible for most of the waterfowl dioramas.

Walter J. Ruppel (1902-1999), Sheboygan, Wisconsin in his painting room. 1970.

Ringbill drake, William Schultz, Milwaukee, Wisconsin, circa 1940. $1,500. *Collection of Shirley, Joe, and Dean Dashner.*

Black duck, Walter Ruppel, Sheboygan, Wisconsin, circa 1940. $400.

Hooded merganser drake, William Schultz, Milwaukee, Wisconsin, circa 1940. $1000. *Collection of Shirley, Joe, and Dean Dashner.*

Bufflehead drake, William Schultz, Milwaukee, placed first in the National Decoy Carving Contest, New York, 1948. Although considered a contemporary decoy carver his early decoys were made for hunting. $1,500.

Ringbill pair, William Schultz, Milwaukee, Wisconsin, circa 1970. $3,000.
Collection of Jim Wierzba. Photography Grace Natoli Sheldon.

Pintail pair, William Schultz, Milwaukee, Wisconsin, circa 1970. $4,000.
Collection of Jim Wierzba. Photography Grace Natoli Sheldon.

Canvasback drake, Joseph Sieger (1872-2959), Tustin, Wisconsin, circa 1920. $15,000.

Frank Strey (1890-1966), Oshkosh, Wisconsin, started carving decoys around 1910. Carving decoys for his personal use, he would make improvements in his patterns and replace his rigs selling the old decoys to local hunters. *Photograph courtesy Ron Koch.*

Canvasback pair, Frank Strey, Oshkosh, Wisconsin, circa 1920. $2,000. *Collection of Herb Desch.*

Canvasback drake, Frank Strey, Oshkosh, Wisconsin, circa 1930. $1,000.

Canvasback pair, oversized, Frank Strey, Oshkosh, Wisconsin, circa 1920. $3,000. *Collection of Jim Wierzba. Photography Grace Natoli Sheldon.*

Canada goose, Frank Strey, Oshkosh, Wisconsin, circa 1930. $3,000. *Collection of Jim Wierzba. Photography Grace Natoli Sheldon.*

Bluebill pair, Frank Strey, Oshkosh, Wisconsin, circa 1920. $2,000 pair. *Collection of Shirley, Joe, and Dean Dashner.*

Bluebill pair, Frank Strey, Oshkosh, Wisconsin, circa 1930. $2,000. *Collection of Jim Wierzba. Photography Grace Natoli Sheldon.*

Coots. Left: high head, circa 1920, $1000. Right: low head, circa 1940, $750. Frank Strey, Oshkosh, Wisconsin. *Collection of Shirley, Joe, and Dean Dashner.*

Redhead pair, Frank Strey, Oshkosh, Wisconsin, circa 1930. $2,000 pair. *Collection of Shirley, Joe, and Dean Dashner.*

Black duck, Frank Strey, Oshkosh, Wisconsin, circa 1930. $1,000. *Collection of Shirley, Joe, and Dean Dashner.*

Black duck, Frank Strey, Oshkosh, Wisconsin, circa 1940. $1,000. *Collection of Jim Wierzba. Photography Grace Natoli Sheldon.*

Mallard pair, Frank Strey, Oshkosh, Wisconsin, circa 1930. $2000 pair. *Collection of Herb Desch.*

Canvasback drakes, Sylvester "Swede" Swedesky (1905-1971), Neehna, Wisconsin, circa 1930. Swedesky's decoys were solid but often had a core of cork plugged into the body to lighten the decoy. His clean smooth lines are exemplary of classic Wisconsin big water decoys. $1,500 each. SeDUCKtive duck call box, H.E. McMahon Sportsmen Specialties Company, Delafield, Wisconsin, circa 1940. $400.

Duck call, SeDUCKtive, H.E. McMahon Sportsmen Specialties Company, Delafield, Wisconsin, circa 1940. $400 each.

Canvasback hen, unknown carver, found near Madison, Wisconsin, circa 1930. $300.

Canvasback hen preener, unknown maker, Lake Winnebago, Wisconsin, circa 1920. $1500. *Collection of Shirley, Joe, and Dean Dashner.*

Coot, unique silhouette coot decoy with full half-globe shaped wooden keel, wood, unknown carver, Lake Geneva, Wisconsin maker, circa 1940. $400.

Mallard drake, unknown Milwaukee School carver, Milwaukee, Wisconsin, circa 1920. $1,000.

Pintail Drake, unknown Wisconsin maker, found in the Horicon Marsh area. The style is similar to a Mason Decoy but a fine detailed feather design is etched to surface, circa 1890. $3,000.

Mallard pair, unknown maker, Milwaukee, Wisconsin, circa 1920. $3,000, pair.

Mallard drake, sleeper, unknown maker, La Crosse, Wisconsin, circa 1930. $2,000.

Redhead drake, unknown maker, Milwaukee Public Museum School, circa 1940. $3,000.

Goose hunting club sign, unknown maker, found outside Mayville, near Horicon Marsh, Wisconsin, circa 1940.

Ringbill drake, Earl Voelker, Milwaukee, Wisconsin, circa 1940. $2,500. *Collection of Jim Wierzba. Photography Grace Natoli Sheldon.*

Mallard pair, DeWitt Wakefield (1849-1912), Fremont, Wisconsin, circa 1900. $3,000, pair. *Collection of Herb Desch.*

Blue-winged teal hen, DeWitt Wakefield, Fremont, Wisconsin, circa 1900. $1,500. *Collection of Shirley, Joe, and Dean Dashner.*

Bluebill pair, DeWitt Wakefield, Fremont, Wisconsin, circa 1900. $1,500, pair. *Collection of Shirley, Joe, and Dean Dashner.*

Canvasback pair, Harold E. Weickert, Neehna, Wisconsin, circa 1930. $800, pair. *Collection of Shirley, Joe, and Dean Dashner.*

Blue-winged teal pair, Otto F. Weinert (1893-1979), Oshkosh, Wisconsin, circa1920. $5000, pair. *Collection of Shirley, Joe, and Dean Dashner.*

Bluebill pair, C.W. Wells Life-Like Decoys, Milwaukee, Wisconsin, manufactured from 1936-1944. $700. *Collection of Jim Wierzba. Photography Grace Natoli Sheldon.*

Redhead drake, C. W. Wells Life-Like Decoys, Milwaukee, Wisconsin. $500. *Collection of Jim Wierzba. Photography Grace Natoli Sheldon.*

Miniature carvings. Right: bluebill hen; center: pintail drake; left: canvasback drake. Herman Wendt, Sheboygan, Wisconsin, circa 1930. $500 each.

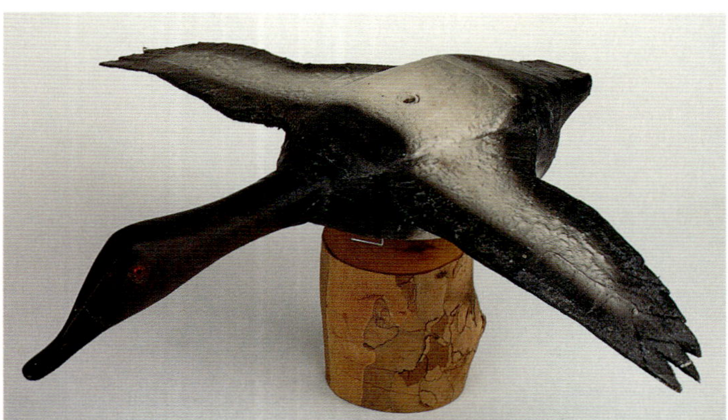

Canvasback drake, flying, C.W. Wells Decoy Company, Milwaukee, Wisconsin, circa 1940. $1500. *Collection of Shirley, Joe and Dean Dashner.*

Blue goose, Herman Wendt (1888-1955), Sheboygan, Wisconsin, circa 1929. $3,000. *Collection of Ron Koch. Photograph courtesy Oshkosh Public Museum.*

Widgeon drake, Herman Wendt, Sheboygan, Wisconsin, circa 1930. $750.
Collection of Jim Wierzba. Photography Grace Natoli Sheldon.

Fish, Anthony Bergans, La Crosse, Wisconsin. Top: white spook, 6"; far left: minnow, 4"; far right: shad, 6 1/4"; bottom: trout, 6"; circa 1930. $750 each.

Mallard pair, Herman Wendt, Sheboygan, Wisconsin, circa 1940. $1,000.
Collection of Jim Wierzba. Photography Grace Natoli Sheldon.

Top: bass, 7", Joseph Gohres, La Crosse, Wisconsin, circa 1925. Bottom: whitefish, 5", wooden tail, Anthony Bergans, guide Goose Island, La Crosse, Wisconsin, circa 1920. $750 each.

Darkhouse box with an assortment of decoys by Anthony Bergans, La Crosse, Wisconsin, circa 1930. $500-$750 each.

Top: trout with jigging stick, 5 1/2", Fritz Kehn, La Crosse, Wisconsin. Bottom: bass, 9", unknown maker. La Crosse School, Wisconsin. $700 each.

Top: minnow, green scaled, 5", unknown maker, La Crosse school. Middle: minnow, Cheater, 4 1/2", Frank Kaufman, La Crosse, Wisconsin, circa 1930. Bottom: minnow, 5 1/2", unknown maker La Crosse School, Wisconsin. $750 each.

Top: northern pike, 5 1/2", unknown maker, La Crosse School, Wisconsin. Middle: minnow, 4 1/2", Floyd "Red" Fischer, La Crosse, Wisconsin. Bottom: minnow, 6", unknown maker, La Crosse, Wisconsin. $400.

Top: brown trout, 5 1/2", unknown maker, La Crosse School. Bottom: minnow, silver on silver paint, 6 1/4", Joseph Gohres, La Crosse, Wisconsin, circa 1925. $500 each.

Darkhouse set. Left: minnow, 3", $300; center: minnow, 3", $300; right: bullhead, 3", $300; foreground: northern pike, 4", $500. Al Rock, La Crosse, Wisconsin, circa 1920.

Top: trout, 5 1/4", unknown maker La Crosse School. Bottom: eelpout, 5 3/4", Gerald Tromey, La Crosse, Wisconsin. $1,000.

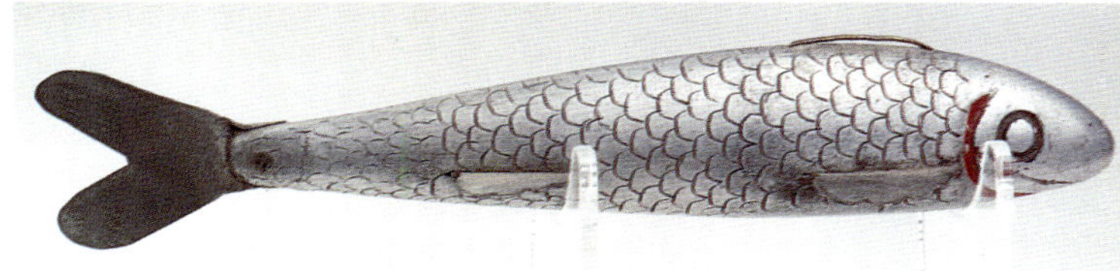

Minnow, 5 3/4", solid aluminum, caste with etched detailing, Unknown maker, La Crosse School, Wisconsin, circa 1930. $700.

Frog, 6", unknown maker La Crosse School Wisconsin, circa 1940. $750.

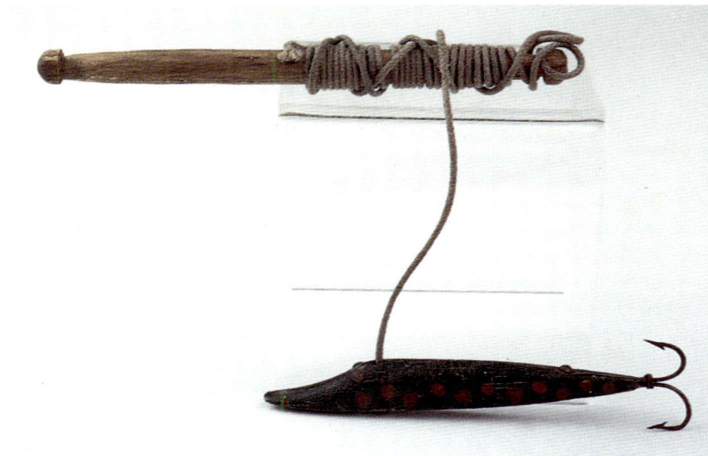

Fish decoy cheater with original jigging stick, northern pike, 4", unknown maker, La Crosse School, Wisconsin, circa 1920. $500.

Top: gray fish, 7"; bottom: minnow, 4"; unknown maker, La Crosse School, Wisconsin. $500 each.

Northern pike, 4 1/2", unknown maker, La Crosse School, Wisconsin. $300.

Top: brown trout, 5 1/2"; bottom: trout, 7". Unknown makers, La Crosse School, Wisconsin, circa 1930. $1000 each.

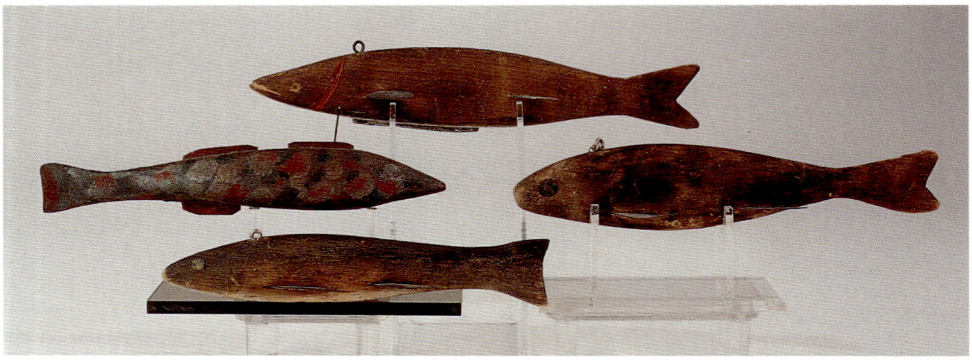

Assortment of minnows, 4 1/2" to 5", unknown makers, La Crosse School, Wisconsin, circa 1930. $400 each.

Top: brown trout; bottom: perch, 8". Unknown makers, La Crosse School, Wisconsin, circa 1930. $500 each.

Sunfish. Top: 3 1/2"; bottom: 4 1/2"; wooden. John Emerson, Superior, Wisconsin, circa 1920. $400 each.

Minnow, 5 3/4", Clarence Zielke, La Crosse, circa 1910. $750.

Assortment of painted metal fish decoys, John Emerson, Superior, Wisconsin. $400 each.

Plaque, brook trout, 15”, circa 1930, Louis A. Loboda (1898-1993), New Lisbon, Wisconsin. $3,500.

Plaque, rainbow trout, 13 1/2””, circa 1930, Louis Loboda, New Lisbon, Wisconsin. $3,500.

Trout, 6 1/4”, unknown maker, central Wisconsin. $300.

Top: trout, 7 1/4”; bottom: trout, 6”, unknown maker, Green Bay, Wisconsin, circa 1920. $500 each.

Top: perch, 6 1/2”; bottom: sturgeon, 9”. Unknown maker, Neehna, Wisconsin, circa 1920. $750 each.

Wisconsin Fishing Licensing Agent porcelain sign circa 1940.

Minnesota

The East-West Continental Divide crosses through the state of Minnesota creating two vastly different types of hunting regions. North-central Minnesota is mostly lowlands, dotted with lakes and ponds surrounded by timberland. The waters move slowly northwest through Lake of the Woods towards Hudson Bay. At the end of the last glacial age Lake Agassis covered most of the western portion of this region. Once the glaciers receded and the waters drained, scores of substantial lakes were formed, including the big waters of Winnigoshish and Leech Lake. Most of these lakes contain shallow areas that support wild rice and other vegetation for waterfowl. Even so, North-central Minnesota is not famous as a duck hunting area There were few organized hunting clubs and most hunting was done during the first couple of weeks of the season when the local waterfowl congregate to feed and rest before they migrate south. Pass shooting was the most popular method of duck hunting so duck decoys were rarely used. The decoys that were produced locally were usually simple silhouettes or crudely carved blocks simply painted black.

Southern Minnesota's landscape is dominated by the Mississippi River, which gradually swells as it flows from its meager origin near Bemidji. Before the growth of the Twin Cities area, the Minnesota River provided a fertile habitat of sloughs and small lakes for waterfowling as it entered the Mississippi at Fort Snelling. The last twenty miles of the Minnesota River was flanked by extensive sloughs. Mallards and wood ducks that prefer this type of habitat made up most of the bagged limits. Prestigious gunning clubs, like the Long Meadow Gun Club, Upgralla Club, and the Minnesota Valley Gun Club, were formed here and the members enjoyed great duck hunting within an hour of their homes. These wealthy businessmen were often able to hunt in the morning and be at their offices by noon. These hunters had little time to carve their own decoys and found a steady supply of factory decoys available through mail order catalogs sent directly from the decoy companies like Mason Decoy Company or large distributors like Sears & Roebuck or at local sporting goods stores. Tuveson Manufacturing Company, St James, Minnesota produced a line of wooden hunting decoys which included a flying decoy with canvas wings. There were several small cottage industries like that run by John Tax in Osakis who produced inexpensive stuffed canvas decoys for the hunter. Tax also created some of the finest full-bodied wooden field decoys known.

The one region of Minnesota that has a well-documented waterfowling history is Heron Lake in the southwestern corner of the state. Known as "the Chesapeake of the West," Heron Lake was an outstanding canvasback marsh in the late 1800s, but during 1890s conditions were favorable for an immense growth of wild celery in the open waters of the hard-bottomed lake. Until the mid 1920, the canvasbacks used this lake in such numbers that hunters could be guaranteed great shooting. During its heyday, Heron Lake and its surrounding watershed that covered an area about 12-1/2 miles long and 2-1/2 miles wide supported 25-30 professional market hunters and numerous gunning clubs. North Heron Lake, the largest open water area, accommodated the most gunning clubs, including Slocum Club, The Ranch, Pohlman Club, St. Francis Club, Burkholz Club, Peters Clubs, Heron Lake Lodge, and the North Shore Club. In addition various market hunting crews, financed by commission brokers for the markets in Chicago and Minneapolis, moved in at the height of the migration to harvest these prime eating waterfowl. Local hunters found they had to set-up on the lake in the dark to secure the best shooting points, often resulting in heated disputes. In 1906, a gentleman's agreement was signed by all the surrounding landowners, which divided the open water into pie shape sections to end the quarreling. Abe Nelson is credited with devising a deadly "pipeline" decoy set-up by arranging two lines of decoys to open water flanked by masses of decoys on each side. The decoys used have been nicknamed "horsehead" decoys because of their unusual head style. Heron Lake "horsehead" canvasbacks in original condition are exceedingly rare because they were made prior to 1900 and most were repainted as bluebills and mallards or transported to the Delta Marsh region of Canada by James Ford Bell, founder of General Mills and member of The Ranch. He started to hunt Canada's Delta Marsh after the canvasbacks left Heron Lake during the mid-1920s.

What Minnesota lacks in quality duck decoy carvers is overshadowed by the sheer number of great fish decoy carvers. Several factors can be considered as reasons for the popularity of fish decoy carving here. Of course the countless number of clear water lakes and the hearty spirit of Minnesotans who relish outdoor winter sports was an important one. The real population of Minnesota started after the Civil War when railroads opened up the state. Land-hungry immigrants from Germany, Sweden, Norway, Demark, and Finland came by the thousands bringing their famed woodworking skills with them. The lakes provided much need food for a people struggling to tame the northern state, with its vast timberland that teemed with peat bogs and swamps barely suitable for farming. Winter spearing was a matter of necessity for many.

The landscape of the state isolated many in small towns or lakefront homesteads. Men had to make their own tools. They whittled out their fish decoys with little influence from other carvers. The resulting fish decoys have strong individual characteristics ranging from highly realistic decoys to fanciful abstractions that are a delight to collect. A few carvers developed small cottage industries marketing their decoys to visiting fishermen through local bait shops, hardware stores, and barbershops. Along with fish decoys, they created practical fishing sticks to hold their extra line when jigging their decoys. Pointed ends and handles made the stick a secure walking cane also. The artistry of these untrained men is outstanding and a true folk art form.

Minneapolis Gun Club, embro dered felt patch, Minneapolis, Minnesota, circa 1940.

Federal Trap Champion, embroidered felt patch, Federal Ammunitions Company, Minneapolis, Minnesota, circa 1930.

INTRODUCTION.

Farwell, Ozmun, Kirk & Company catalog, Saint Paul, Minnesota, offering Premier Grade Mason Decoy and little bluebill decoys that bear a strong resemblance to Illinois's Fred Allen duck decoy.

Market hunting crew pulled on shores of North Heron Lake. Morton W. Smith Sr. is on the far right, 1910. *Photograph courtesy Morton Smith, Jr.*

Mallard drake. Joseph Anderson, Heron Lake, Minnesota, carved his decoys using classic Illinois River design, a hollow three-piece body with finely detail head and bill. His paint pattern is reminiscent of Illinois River greats Catherine Elliston and Edna Perdew, circa 1920. $750.

Mallard hen, Joseph Anderson, Heron Lake, Minnesota, circa 1920. $750.

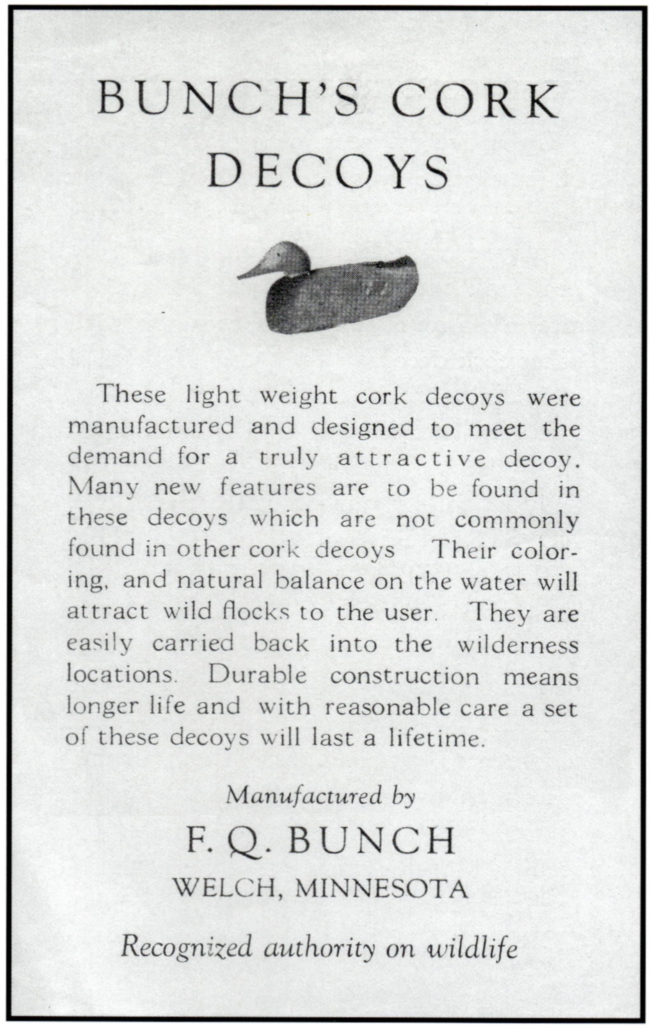

Advertising literature; Bunch's Decoys, F. Q. Bunch, Welch, Minnesota, cork body with wooden head, circa 1930. Most duck hunters in Minnesota found there was little need for fancy decoy rigs and used cheap decoys like Bunch's Decoys or crude black blocks.

Snow goose, metal silhouette decoy, Danz Decoy Company, Jacob Danz, Jr., Minneapolis, Minnesota, patented 1883, circa 1900. $350.

Canada goose, metal silhouette decoy, Danz Decoy Company, circa 1885. $300.

Stencil on underside of collapsible wing of the Danz Snow goose.

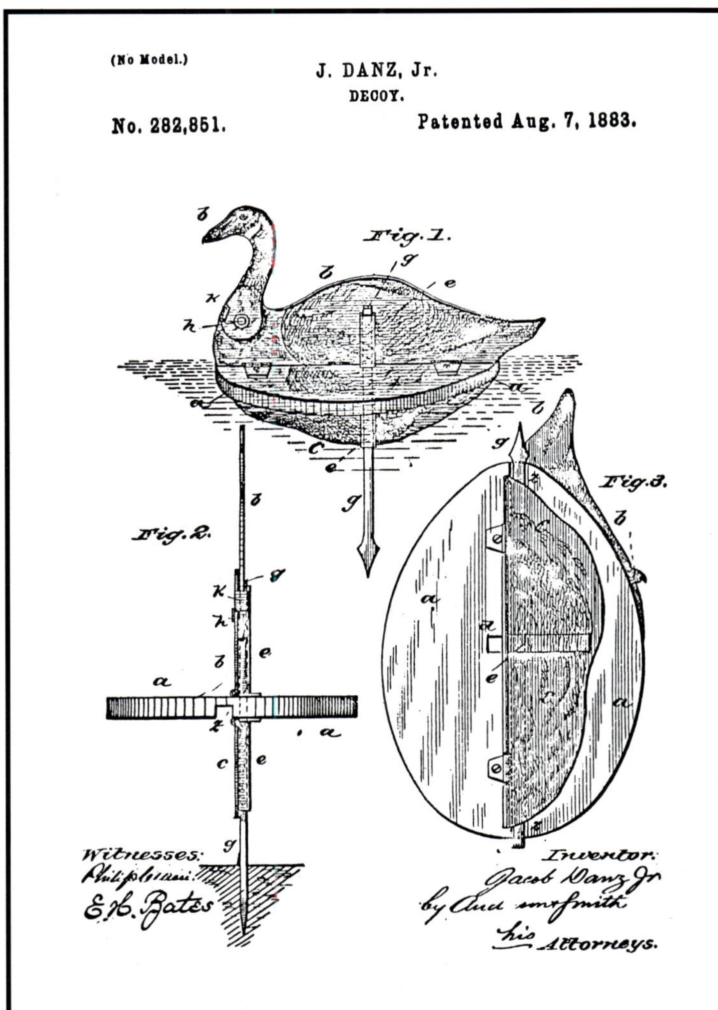

Patent drawing, Danz Decoy, Jacob Danz, Jr., Minneapolis, Minnesota, 1883. One of the earliest known commercial producers of waterfowling decoys in the Midwest, the Danz Company also offered unique silhouette duck decoys. Two silhouettes were mounted perpendicularly on opposite sides of a narrow wooden base. Each decoy had a silhouette of a hen and drake of the species.

Harry's Ear-Toned Duck Call, Harold Edwards, Minneapolis, Minnesota, circa 1940. $150.

Flapping Bill duck call, Natural Duck Call Manufacturing Company, Francis J. Muchlistein, St Paul, Minnesota, patented in 1932, available with glass eye or tack eyes. Early calls are stamped "Patent Applied." Flapping Bill duck calls are often found without the bill's upper mandible because hunters found it distracting moving up and down while they blew the call. $300.

Mallards, tri-fold set, Nels Hansen (1867-1962), N. C. Hansen Company, Zimmerman, Minnesota. Broadbill duck call in box, N.C. Hansen Company, Zimmerman, Minnesota, patented 1914, circa 1920. Decoys, $400; call, $100.

Redhead pair, Marty Hanson, St. Cloud, Minnesota, circa 1980. Hanson is one of a growing number of contemporary carvers that concentrate on producing working decoys. His early working decoys have become collectibles. $500, pair.

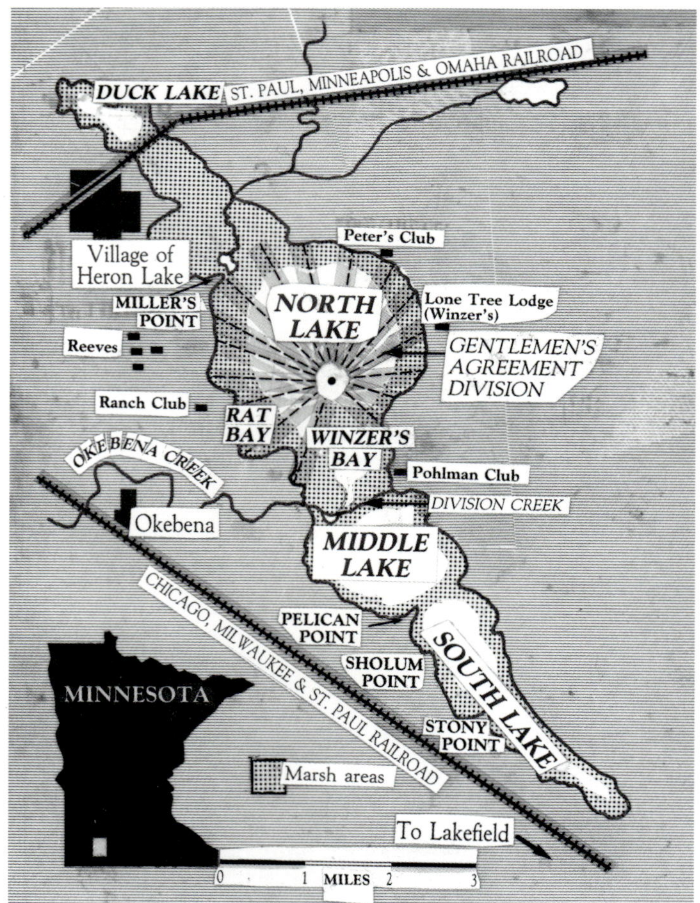

The marshy North Heron Lake was a duck hunting paradise, which was divided by a Gentlemen's Agreement among the surrounding landowners into wedge-shape sections to prevent disagreements among the various hunting clubs, markethunters, and local sport hunters. *Photograph courtesy Morton Smith, Jr.*

Canvasback pair, Harry Converse, Heron Lake, Minnesota, circa 1880. Harry Converse was one of several noted market hunters who shot canvasbacks on Heron Lake. The birds were then iced-down and shipped by rail to the Minneapolis markets. Duck call, early octagon barrel with large label, Oscar Quam, Minneapolis, Minnesota, 1930. Decoys, $1,500 each; call, $350.

Canvasback drake, Joseph Peters, Heron Lake, Minnesota, circa 1880. Duck call, octagon barrel, Oscar Quam, Minneapolis, Minnesota; a special oversized call used by Quam at sports shows, circa 1930. Decoys, $1,500 each; call, $1,000.

Canvasback pair, Joseph Marr, circa 1880. Although Marr was a barber in Sioux Falls, South Dakota, he spent the hunting season in Heron Lake hunting for the market and is considered a Minnesota decoy carver. The blunt-ended bills and the classic Heron Lake "Horse-head" style identify his decoys. Duck call, octagon barrel with metal medallion, Oscar Quam, Minneapolis, Minnesota, circa 1930. Decoys, $1,500 each; call, $300.

Canvasback drake, Robert S. Rank, Wilder (Heron Lake), circa 1890: Heron Lake metal car license plate attachment, circa 1940. Decoy, $1000; plate decoration, $50.

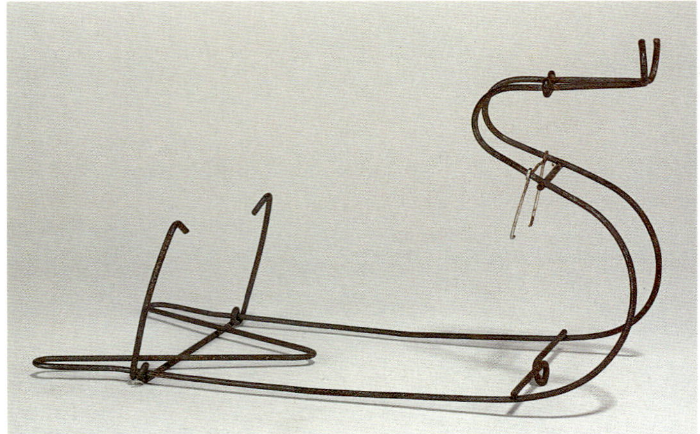

Minnesota Duck Chair, Hersey Sales Company, St Paul, Minnesota, circa 1930. $100.

Duck calls, Jack Grass, Otawatona, Minnesota, circa 1950. $300 each.

Decoy Catalog, Herter's Manufacturing Company, Inc., Waseca, Minnesota, circa 1942. George Herter started the Herter's Manufacturing Company in his father's garage as a teenager sometime during the early 1930s, when he ran a small fly tying supply operation. His business grew into a multi-faceted distribution company with six retail stores throughout the Midwest, which were the major suppliers for hunters, fishermen, trappers, gunsmiths, and taxidermists until the company, near bankruptcy, was sold to the N. Marshall Seeburg & Sons Investment Company, Chicago, Illinois, circa 1970.

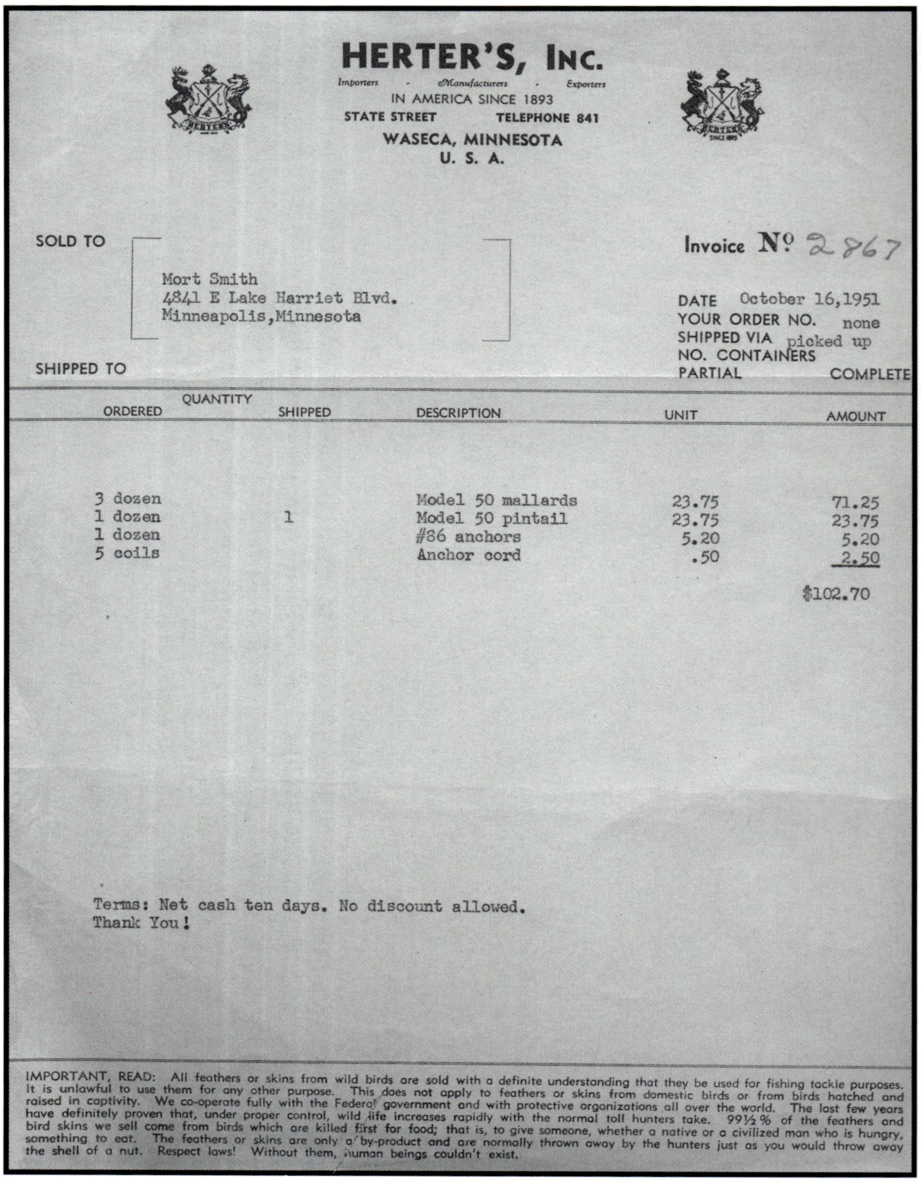

HERTER'S, INC.
Importers · Manufacturers · Exporters
IN AMERICA SINCE 1893
STATE STREET TELEPHONE 841
WASECA, MINNESOTA
U. S. A.

SOLD TO
Mort Smith
4841 E Lake Harriet Blvd.
Minneapolis, Minnesota

Invoice № 2867

DATE October 16, 1951
YOUR ORDER NO. none
SHIPPED VIA picked up
NO. CONTAINERS
PARTIAL COMPLETE

SHIPPED TO

QUANTITY ORDERED	SHIPPED	DESCRIPTION	UNIT	AMOUNT
3 dozen		Model 50 mallards	23.75	71.25
1 dozen	1	Model 50 pintail	23.75	23.75
1 dozen		#86 anchors	5.20	5.20
5 coils		Anchor cord	.50	2.50
				$102.70

Terms: Net cash ten days. No discount allowed.
Thank You!

IMPORTANT, READ: All feathers or skins from wild birds are sold with a definite understanding that they be used for fishing tackle purposes. It is unlawful to use them for any other purpose. This does not apply to feathers or skins from domestic birds or from birds hatched and raised in captivity. We co-operate fully with the Federal government and with protective organizations all over the world. The last few years have definitely proven that, under proper control, wild life increases rapidly with the normal toll hunters take. 99½% of the feathers and bird skins we sell come from birds which are killed first for food; that is, to give someone, whether a native or a civilized man who is hungry, something to eat. The feathers or skins are only a by-product and are normally thrown away by the hunters just as you would throw away the shell of a nut. Respect laws! Without them, human beings couldn't exist.

Left:
Original invoice for rig of Herter's tenite Model 50 mallards and pintail decoys. 1951.

True-to-Life Model canvas owl decoy, Herter's Manufacturing Company, Inc., with complicated three dimensional design including tufted ears and stuffed legs. Life-sized with cork core and kapok fiber stuffing. The bill was an actual black bear claw. Circa 1938. $2,500. Model Perfect Crow decoy, Herter's Manufacturing Company, Inc., cedar, circa 1938. $1,000. *Collection of Rosemary Adamson.*

Dove, Model Perfect, Herter's Manufacturing Inc., Waseca, Minnesota, cedar, circa 1940. $1,500. *Collection of James R. and Diane Cook.*

Mallard drake, Model Supreme, balsa, circa 1940. Redhead pair, Model Supreme, balsa, circa 1930. Herter's Manufacturing Inc., Waseca, Minnesota. $150 each.

Mallard pair, Model Perfect #963, Herter's Manufacturing Company, Inc., cedar, circa 1940. Known as Pothole Mallards these detailed feathered blanks were turned by the Artistic Wood Carving Company, Chicago, Illinois. Once delivered to the Herter's plant their cedar bodies were hollowed and a bottom board was added. For the hens, the tail curlicue was chipped off. Herter's quickly abandoned this time-consuming model. Other Model Perfect species with less detailing were kept in production until 1954. $3,000.

Hunters load their brush that will be used later to camouflage their boat for hunting. Note the Herter's Model Supreme balsa bluebill decoys in their boat and the classic Evinrude motor.

Mallard hen, Market Hunter Series, canvas-covered cork body, pine head, Herter's Manufacturing Inc., Waseca, Minnesota, circa 1938. When customers began to complain that their cork decoys did not hold up to the rigors of hunting, Herter's began to cover the decoy bodies with canvas imprinted with feather designs, eliminating that problem and the need to paint the decoy bodies. $400.

Canada goose, Model Supreme, (balsa wood), Herter's Manufacturing Inc., Waseca, Minnesota, circa 1940. Goose call, Glodo type with brass label, circa 1938. Decoy, $200; call, $1,000.

Canvasback drake, Market Hunter Series, canvas-covered cork body, pine head, Herter's Manufacturing Inc., Waseca, Minnesota, circa 1938; catalog, Herter's manufacturing Inc. 1940. Decoy, $700; catalog, $100.

Canada goose, Model Perfect (Pothole) Model, Herter's Manufacturing, Inc., circa 1945. Goose call in box, Herter's Manufacturing, Inc., circa 1940. Decoy, $400; call, $75.

Duck calls, Herter's Manufacturing Inc., Waseca, Minnesota. Left: early Vit-Glodo Model, brass tag, wooden stopper, with box, $1,000. Center: special edition, Jimmy Robinson Model, $1,000. Right: widgeon call in box, $25. Duck and goose calling manual, $25.

Great horned owl, Model Perfect #90 Feather Weight (balsa wood), Herter's Manufacturing Inc., Waseca, Minnesota. Model Perfect #12 Feather Weight Clutch crow (balsa wood), Herter's Manufacturing Inc., balsa wood, circa 1940. $3500.

Passenger pigeon, Antique 1893 Series (cedar), production year 1967-1978, Herter's Manufacturing Inc., Waseca, Minnesota. $150.

Blue-winged teal, Antique 1893 Series (cedar), production year 1972-1980, Herter's Manufacturing Inc., Waseca, Minnesota. Ever the marketing genius, Herter's recognized the growing interest in collecting old wooden decoys during the 1960s. He commissioned prize-winning contemporary decoy carvers, like Jack Musgrove, Des Moines, Iowa, to create models for a line of wooden decoys, which were marketed as "antique." The date 1893 represented the year that the elder Herter started his business, the Beehive Clothing & Dry Goods Store, Waseca, Minnesota. $150.

Curlew, Antique 1893 Series (cedar), production year 1966-1978, Herter's Manufacturing Inc., Waseca, Minnesota. $150.

Shoveler drake, Antique 1893 Series (cedar), production year 1972-1980. Ruddy duck hen, Antique 1893 Series (cedar), production year 1974-1979. Herter's Manufacturing Inc., Waseca, Minnesota. $200, each.

Common loon, early style with green head, Antique 1893 Series (cedar), production year 1978-1980. Later models had black heads. $400.

Wood duck drake, Antique 1893 Series (cedar), production year 1970-1980. Duck call box. Herter's Manufacturing Inc., Waseca, Minnesota. Decoy, $150; call, $75.

Mallard drake, Leonard LeDebukr (1900-1955) LaCresent, Minnesota, circa 1930. $400.

Bluebill drakes. Left: hunting decoy, Fred Lexow (1888-1971), Balsam Lake, Minnesota. Right: jewelry box, Fred Lexow, circa 1930. Best known for his fish decoy Lexow carved at least one rig of redheads and bluebill hunting decoys for his friend, John Plank, Bovey, Minnesota. The jewelry box was made for Plank's wife. Decoy, $750; jewelry box, $300.

Mallard pair, inflatable rubber decoys, Minnesota Rubber Duck Company, Mound Minnesota, information embossed on bottom, circa 1940. $100.

Bluebill drake, John Nelson (1877-1940), Stare Lake, Minnesota, circa 1930, $400.

Mallard pair, inflatable rubber decoys, Minnesota Rubber Duck Company, Mound Minnesota, circa 1940. $100.

Duck Calls, Oscar Quam, Minneapolis, Minnesota, with instruction booklet and certificate of "Doctor of Quackery." Foreground: special over-sized duck call worn by Quam at sports shows, circa 1930, $2,000. Background: early octagonal barrel call, stamped, no label, circa 1924, $300.

Mallard pair, Alfred Moses, Minnesota, circa 1930. $6000. *Collection of David Henderson.*

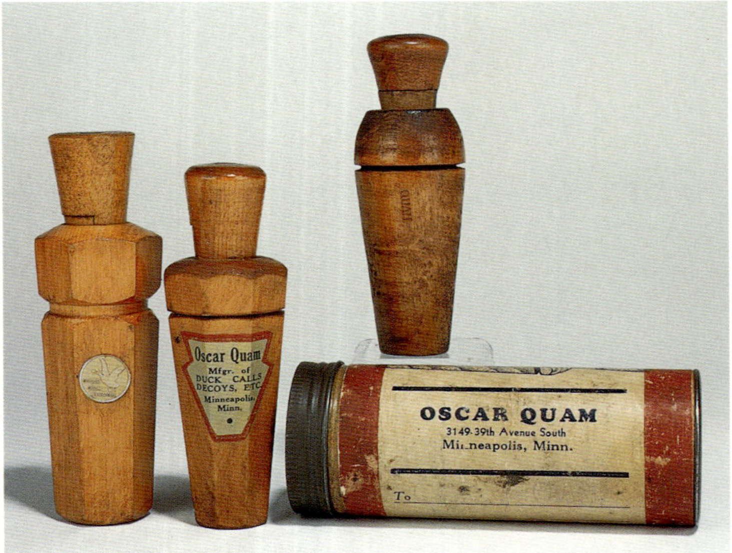

Left: duck call, early octagonal barrel with duck head metal medallion, circa 1930, $500.Center: duck call, octagon barrel with large decal, circa 1935, $400. Right: duck call, round barrel call with original packaging tube, circa 1925, $500. Oscar Quam, Minneapolis, Minnesota.

Decorative plaque, miniature flying quail on painted board, William J. Reinhold, Minnesota, circa 1940. $250.

Oscar Quam, "Professor of Duckology" produced a varied line of duck hunting products, game bird call, instruction records, decoy paints and cork hunting, circa 1940. Left: phonograph record, "Oscar Quam Calling Ducks," 78 RPM; center: booklet entitled *Duck Calling Course;* right: the Oscar Quam Company catalog, Spicer, Minnesota.

Owl and crow set, Swan-Douglas Manufacturing, Minneapolis, Minnesota, canvas covered wooden core. Marketed through Spiegel, Inc. Chicago, Illinois, circa 1900. $800.

Canada geese, John Tax (1894-1967), Osakis, Minnesota, rare standing field decoys, circa 1920. Tax's wooden field decoys present his finest work. His more common line of decoys was constructed of stuffed canvas. He also produced fish decoys and a wide variety of folk carvings like doorknockers and birdhouse. $75,000. *Collection of James R. and Diane Cook.*

Canada goose, John Tax, Osakis, Minnesota, rare standing field decoy, sentinel head, circa 1920. $15,000. *Photograph and Collection Carter Stenburg.*

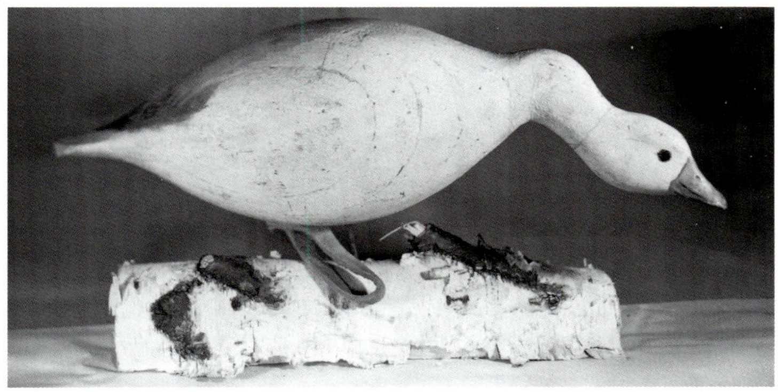

Snow goose, John Tax, Osakis, Minnesota, rare standing field decoy, feeder head style, circa 1920. $15,000. *Photograph courtesy Barbara Sorenson.*

Below:
Mallard pair, John Tax, Osakis, Minnesota, rare standing field decoys, circa 1920. $60,000. *Collection of James R. and Diane Cook.*

Mallard drake, John Tax, Osakis, Minnesota, rare standing field decoys, circa 1920. $25,000. *Photograph and Collection Carter Stenburg.*

Bluebill pair, John Tax, Osakis, Minnesota, circa 1930. $7,000. *Photograph and Collection Carter Stenburg.*

Mallard hen, John Tax, Osakis, Minnesota, circa 1930. $5,000. *Photograph and Collection Carter Stenburg.*

Wood duck drake, John Tax, Osakis, Minnesota, circa 1930. $20,000. *Photograph and Collection Carter Stenburg.*

Blue-winged teal drake, stuffed canvas decoy, John Tax, Osakis, Minnesota, circa 1930. $1,000. *Photograph and Collection Carter Stenburg.*

Left: goose call, in original box, $300. Right: duck call in original box. $400. Ralph True, Minneapolis, Minnesota, circa 1940.

Canvasback drake, flying, Tuveson Manufacturing Company, Inc., St. James, Minnesota, circa 1920. Patented in 1927, Tuveson's flying decoys were constructed with a solid cedar body and wire-framed canvas wings. The company also made cork decoys with wooden heads and bottom board, and a line of wooden floaters. $750.

Duck call, Ralph True, Hopkins, Minnesota, circa 1940. $500

Poster, Tuveson Manufacturing Company, Inc., illustrated a complete set of flying decoys mounted on a floating triangular frame. Set out in the marsh grasses, the decoys gave the illusion of a flock of ducks flying into the hunter's rig of floating decoys, circa 1930.

View inside Tuveson Manufacturing's decoy factory, circa 1920.

Ernest Aamodt (1915-?), Crosby, Minnesota, produced wonderfully abstract fish decoys. He used blotches and wavy lines of color in an attempt to recreate fish scales on his decoys. Some of his decoys have glitter sprinkled into the wet paint to give the decoy an iridescent appearance. Photograph in his garage, circa 1985.

Mallard drakes. Top: flying style, Tuveson Manufacturing Company, Inc., St. James, Minnesota, circa 1920, $600. Bottom: regular model Tuveson Manufacturing Company, Inc., circa 1920, $200.

Sunfish, 5 1/4", Ernest Aamodt, Crosby, Minnesota, circa 1940. $1,000. *Collection James and Mary Richards.*

Coots, unknown Minnesota maker, Used at Cabin Creek Club, Grand Rapids, Minnesota, circa 1920. $750 each.

Perch, 6", Ernest Aamodt, Crosby, Minnesota, circa 1940. $1,000. *Collection James and Mary Richards.*

Top: trout, Unknown maker, Walker, Minnesota, 6 3/4", $700. Middle: northern pike, 7 1/4", Frank Achop, Walker, Minnesota, $400. Bottom: trout, 5", Frank Achop, Walker, Minnesota, $400.

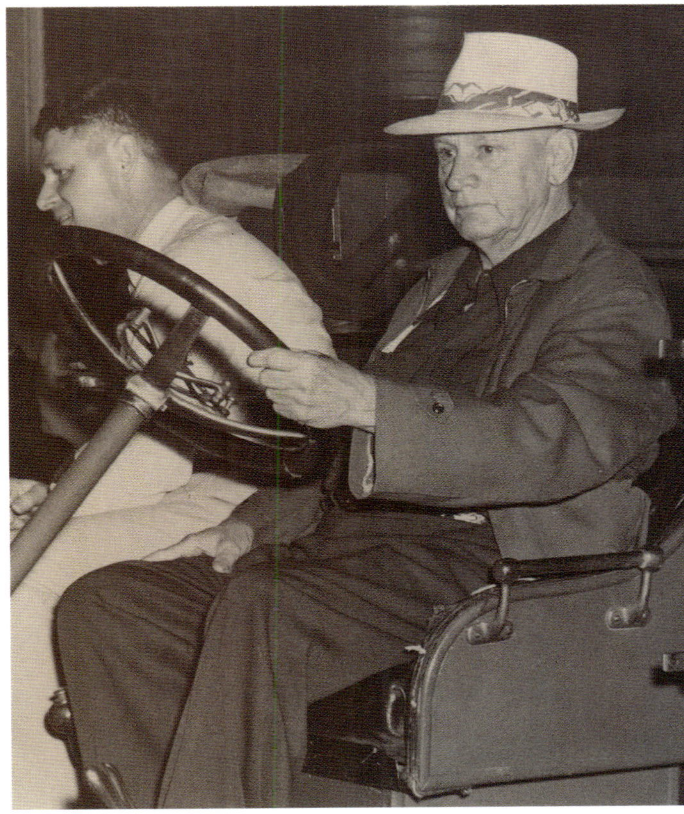

William "Slow" Batter (1882-1957), Little Falls, Minnesota, carved most of his fish decoys at the Little Falls firehouse where he served as a fireman and then Fire Chief for many years. For years his decoys were misidentified as being made by a "Harry Blanchard."

Top: northern pike, 12"; left: green fish, 6"; right: frog, 5 1/2". Ivan Amist, Grand Rapids, Minnesota. He carved fish decoys for his own use, circa 1920. $750 each.

Top: sunfish, 5 1/4", $700; middle: sunfish, 4 3/4", $700; bottom: minnow, 3", $500.William "Slow" Batters, circa 1930. $500.

Below:
Whirl-i-gig, blue fish, wood, polychrome, 44", Carved by Ivan Amist for his yard outside of Grand Rapids, Minnesota, circa 1920. $3,500.

Top: trout, 7"; bottom: whitefish, 10", jointed with leather hinge. Pearl Bethel (1894-1960), Park Rapids, Minnesota, sold his decoys through the Earl Fuller Tackle Shop in Park Rapids for. $1.00 –1.50 per dozen, circa 1930. $750 each.

Top: whitefish, 10"; bottom: trout, jointed, leather hinges, 10 1/2". Pearl Bethel (1894-1960), Park Rapids, Minnesota, circa 1930. $750 each.

Bullhead, 8", Otto Bishop, Sr. (1915-?), Osage, Minnesota, circa 1930. This decoy was purchased out of Otto's personal darkhouse, circa 1979. $1,000.

Minnows, red and white, 7", Art Boelter, LeSueur, Minnesota. These decoys are very thin and have a single long side fin. They are usually painted with an abstract design that incorporates large dots and/or long wavy lines, circa 1940. $750 each.

Top: minnow, abstract, 7", Art Boelter (1896-1989), LeSueur, Minnesota, circa 1940, $750. Bottom: bass, red and white, unknown Minnesota maker, 9 1/4", circa 1920. $750.

Merrill Booth (1892-1966), Minneapolis, Minnesota, in his workshop showing how he soldered the two convex metal forms to create his hollow copper fish decoys. A wood form was used to mold the metal, either, zinc, aluminum, nickel or copper, circa 1940.

Plaque, bass, James Franklin "Frank" Clark (1899-1972), Eden Valley, Minnesota, circa 1940. $750.

Copper fish, Merrill Booth (1892-1966), Minneapolis, Minnesota, copper plated, 10 1/2", $1,000 each.

Copper sunfish. Top: unknown Minnesota maker, sand cast, solid, 5", $500. Bottom: Charles J. Downing (1886-1991), hollow, 5 1/4", Minneapolis, Minnesota, rare example. Downing was only known to have made less than 24 fish decoys. He preferred to make enameled copper decorations like butterflies, circa 1940. $1,500.

Fisherman illustrates how he used an old crank wood drill to suspend his Booth copper decoy.

Bullhead, 8", Merle Falstaff, Park Rapids, Minnesota, circa 1950. This decoy was purchased directly from Falstaff in 1980. $2,000.

Northern pike. Top: red and white, 10"; bottom: natural coloration, 10", Otto Faue (1881-1954), Hanover, Minnesota. Otto's fish decoys are distinguished from his brother William's by their double side fins, circa 1930. $2,000 each.

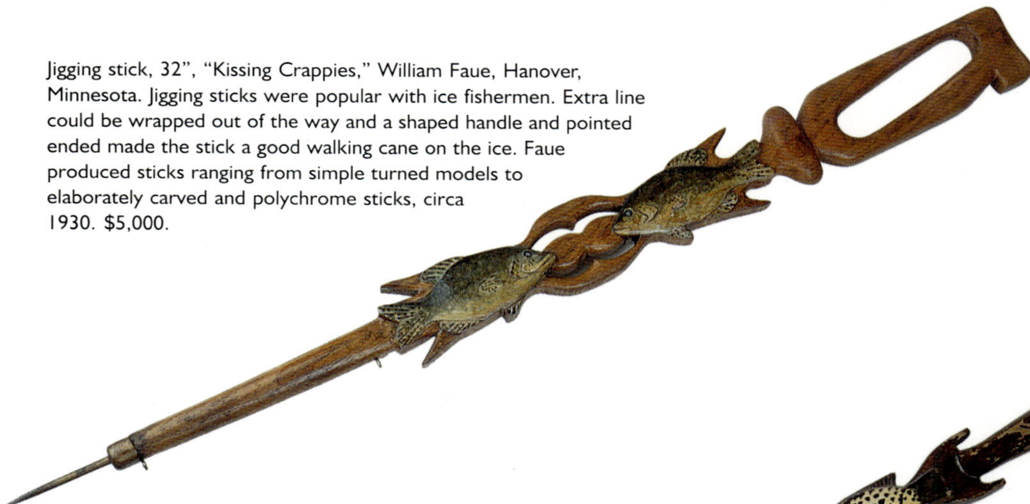

Jigging stick, 32", "Kissing Crappies," William Faue, Hanover, Minnesota. Jigging sticks were popular with ice fishermen. Extra line could be wrapped out of the way and a shaped handle and pointed ended made the stick a good walking cane on the ice. Faue produced sticks ranging from simple turned models to elaborately carved and polychrome sticks, circa 1930. $5,000.

Jigging stick, 31 1/2", "Kissing Crappies" and trout, William Faue, Hanover, Minnesota, polychrome, circa 1930. $4,000.

Jigging stick, 31", "Kissing Crappies" and keg, natural finish, William Faue, Hanover, Minnesota, circa 1930. $1,500.

Top: perch, 8 3/4"; bottom: "Clown" fish, 7 3/4", William Faue (1878-1950), Hanover, Minnesota. William's exhibited more flare and imagination than his brother when he painted his fish, particularly his "clown" fish. He also commonly used a single side fin, circa 1930. $2,000 each.

Sunfish, 6 1/2", William Faue, Hanover, Minnesota, circa 1930. $3,000.

John Greer, Isle, Minnesota, circa 1950. Top: crappie 6 1/2", $750. Bottom: perch "cheater," 5 3/4", illegal hooks were added to a decoy to snag passing fish thus the name "cheater," $400.

Darkhouse box, John Greer, Isle, Minnesota, circa 1950. Like most ice fishermen, Greer carried an assortment of fish decoys with a line saver onto the ice each time he speared, because fish react to different colored decoys under different weather conditions. If a naturally colored fish wasn't attracting fish on a certain day maybe a red and white one would. Set: $3,500.

Minnows, John Greer, Isle, Minnesota, circa 1950. Clockwise from top: 6"; 5 3/4"; 6"; 6". $400 each.

Fish decoys attributed to Fred Gibbon, found in St. Cloud, Minnesota. A relative purposely mislabeled the maker's name to protect his identity, circa 1940. Left: perch, 8"; middle: frog, 4"; right: walleye, 8". $2,000 each.

Charles "Chuck" Hall (1908-1995), Barnum, Minnesota, scratched a living off the land, hunting, fishing and carving a few fish decoys. Photograph, circa 1980.

Charles "Chuck" Hall, Barnum, Minnesota with a nice northern pike, 1947.

Hall's personal darkhouse box with an assortment of his decoys. Hall made decoys using any scrap of wood he could find and paints from paint-by-numbers kits that he bought at the local 5 & 10 store.

Chuck Hall, Barnum, Minnesota, circa 1920. Top: trout, 6"; middle: brown trout, 6"; far left: northern pike, 5 3/4"; far right: sunfish, 3"; bottom: minnow, red, 5 1/2". $500 each.

Leroy Howell (1894-1989), Hinkley, Minnesota. Early examples of Howell's blunt-nose style decoy. Top: flowered abstract fish, green and white, 6 1/2". Middle: flowered abstract fish, yellow and natural, 6 1/2". Bottom: flowered, black and orange. His elaborate over-lapping dot paint pattern is described as "flowered," circa 1920. $1,000 each.

Walleye, Herter's Manufacturing, Inc, Waseca, Minnesota, circa 1950. Top: 5 1/4". Middle: 7". Bottom: 7", George Herter was the main supplier of the needs of fishermen, hunters, taxidermists, and gunsmiths for over 40 years. $500 each.

Left: minnow, solid green, 5", circa 1940. Top: minnow, red variegated, 5", circa 1950. Right: sunfish, natural wood finish, 4 1/4"; Leroy Howell, Hinkley, Minnesota, circa 1930. One way to identify a true Howell decoy is to look at the bottom. All his fish have a coat of heavy white lead paint here, even the natural finish decoy. $750 each.

Plaque, jumping black bass, 14" X17". Signed J. Hodge, found in northern Minnesota. Circa 1950. $1,500.

Top: minnow, yellow variegated, 7 1/4", circa 1950. Middle: minnow, brown variegated, 7 1/4" circa 1950. Bottom: minnow, white spook, 3/4", circa 1945. Leroy Howell, Hinkley, Minnesota, cut double rings to denote eyes in all of his fish. He made his own cutting tool using a spent rifle shell. $800 each.

Abstract fish, 4 1/2", with an exceptional twisting form, Fred Johnson, Bovey, Minnesota, circa 1930. Johnson's decoys are exemplary of the fabulous imaginative style found in many Minnesota fish decoys. Each decoy body curves and twists, giving a flowing form to his decoys. $500.

Leroy Howell, Hinkley, Minnesota. Top: minnow, green and natural finish, flowered, 5", $1,000, circa 1940. Middle: minnow, red and natural finish, flowered, 7 1/4", rare pointed nose style, circa 1920, $2000. Bottom: minnow, red and natural finish, flowered, 4 3/4", $1,000, circa 1940.

Jigging stick, 33", Burdette Jacobs, Glen, Minnesota. Walnut, elaborate multi-design carved handle including a ram's head line guide, relief pattern, pheasant, marlin, sailing boat, winter cabin scene, pine cone, moose head, elk head, four aces, mermaid, pine tree, flying duck, dice, and the name DAVE across top, circa 1930. $3,000.

Abstract fish, 4 1/2" and 6 1/2", Fred Johnson, Bovey, Minnesota, circa 1930. $500 each.

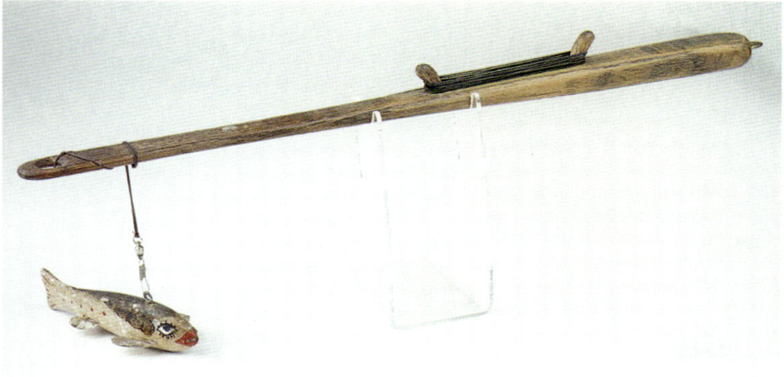

Abstract fish decoy, 4 1/2", original jigging stick, Dr. Lester Johnson (1900-1977), Lakefield, Minnesota, circa 1950. $1,000.

Trout, 8", Dr. Lester Johnson, Lakefield, Minnesota, circa 1950. $1,000. *Photograph courtesy John Banhozer.*

Top: abstract minnow, 5", Dr Lester Johnson, Lakefield, Minnesota, circa 1940, $1,000. Middle: sunfish, 5", unknown maker, Minnesota, $300. Bottom: abstract bass, 5 1/2", Albert Morris, Grand Rapids, Minnesota, circa 1945, $1,000.

Trout, 8 1/2", Dr. Lester Johnson, Lakefield, Minnesota, circa 1950. $1,000. *Photograph courtesy John Banhozer.*

Top: crappie, 8", Stephen Lacni. Bottom: Joseph Lacni, 4". The Lanci brothers, Virginia, Minnesota, both carved very narrow finless decoys, circa 1920. $800 each.

Top: red and yellow perch, 6 1/2". Center: brown trout, 6 1/2". Bottom. two unfinished fish decoys. Albert Larson, Palisade, Minnesota, circa 1950. Finished decoys, $750 each.

Pen and Ink, 16" X 20", Fred Lexow, Balsam Lake, Minnesota. Using colored inks from his daughter, a cell artist at Walt Disney Studios, Lexow created unusual drawings composed of parallel wavy lines much like a French Impressionist painter used dots of color.

Fred "Max" Lexow (1888-1971) was a self-taught artist who had a weakness for alcohol. A recluse after his wife divorced him, his family set up charge accounts for his necessities, but not for beer money. He traded his artwork and decoys at local taverns for drinks.

Plaque set, mirror image fish (2), rainbow trout 9 1/2", Fred Lexow, Balsam Lake, Minnesota, circa 1930. $3,000 each.

Plaque, brook trout, 1”, Fred Lexow, Balsam Lake, Minnesota, circa 1930. Lexow was the most prolific Minnesota fish plaque carver. Unlike less talented craftsmen, he carved his fish in the round often curving away from the backboard. Backboards decorated with painted pondweeds or textured with a graining comb became his signature. $4,000.

Plaque, rainbow trout, 14”, Fred Lexow, Balsam Lake, Minnesota, circa 1930. $3,000.

Plaque, brook trout, 14 1/2”, Fred Lexow, Balsam Lake, Minnesota, circa 1930. $5,000.

Plaque, rainbow trout, 14 1/4”, Fred Lexow, Balsam Lake, Minnesota, circa 1930. $5,000.

Plaque, brook trout, 11”, Fred Lexow, Balsam Lake, Minnesota, circa 1930. $4,000.

Plaque, brook trout, 13", Fred Lexow, Balsam Lake, Minnesota, circa 1930. $4,000.

Plaque, double trout; brook trout with metal fins and tail, 13 3/4"; rainbow trout with wooden tail and fins, 13 3/4", wood polychrome, plaque frame 40" x 13 1/2". Fred Lexow, Balsam Lake, Minnesota. This rare double fish plaque exhibits both types of Lexow plaque fish: one with wooden fins and tail, the other with metal fins and tail. It was commissioned for the Antler Lodge on Balsam Lake, circa 1930. $10,000.

Crawdads, Fred Lexow, Balsam Lake, Minnesota, circa 1930. Top: metal silhouette with wood body, 6"; middle: metal silhouette with wood body, 6"; bottom: carved in round wood polychrome, 6". $750 each.

Northern pike, 8 1/2", Fred Lexow, Balsam Lake, Minnesota, circa 1930. $1,000.

Sucker, 10", Fred Lexow, Balsam Lake, Minnesota, circa 1930. Lexow carved trout almost exclusively, making this sucker extremely rare. The distinctive sucker mouth is carved complete with suction ridges. $2,000.

Top: green trout, 8 1/2’: middle: trout, 8”; bottom: silver and red minnow, 8”; Fred Lexow, Balsam Lake, Minnesota, circa 1950. $1,000 each.

Top: green trout, 8 1/2”, $1200; middle: trout, 8”, $1500; bottom: silver and red minnow, 8”, $1000; Fred Lexow, Balsam Lake, Minnesota, circa 1950.

Top: green trout, 5 3/4”, $1000; middle: white spook, 5 3/4”, $500; bottom: trout, 5 3/4”, $1,000. Early fat examples, Fred Lexow, Balsam Lake, Minnesota, circa 1940.

Top: green trout, 7 3/4”: middle: red trout, 7 3/4”; bottom: green trout, 7 3/4”. Early fat examples, Fred Lexow Balsam Lake, Minnesota, circa 1940. $1,000 each.

Top: green trout, 6 1/2”; middle: brown trout, 7 3/4”; bottom: yellow minnow, 7 3/4”. Early examples are usually fatter and have fins that are more pointed. Fred Lexow, Balsam Lake, Minnesota, circa 1935. $1000 each.

Very early examples, Fred Lexow, Balsam Lake, Minnesota, circa 1930. Top: yellow minnow, 7 3/4"': middle: trout, 5 3/4"; bottom: trout 8". $1000 each.

Three variations of Fred Lexow's commercial grade fish. Approached by financial backers, Lexow designed this flat-sided trout for commercial production. Unfortunately, Lexow did not have the dedication necessary for a commercial enterprise and few flat-sided Lexow fish decoys have been found. Circa 1940. $400 each.

Frank Mizera (1898-1969), Ely, Minnesota, was a popular local fishing guide and decoy carver on the Boundary Waters of northern Minnesota. His decoys were marketed and distributed throughout the state by a local barber usually selling for $1.00-$1.50 each.

Red and white fish, 8 3/4" each, Frank Mizera, Ely, Minnesota, circa 1920. Early examples are fatter than his later work. $500 each.

Black fish with fish designs. Top: early fat decoy, 7 3/4"; circa 1920. Bottom: classic Mizera "fish-on-fish" design, 9", circa 1940. $750 each.

Ernest "Ernie" Newman (1908-1976), Carlton, Minnesota, circa 1940. Top: foiled white and red, 9"; middle: red and white open mouth, 8 1/2"; bottom: sucker, 8 1/2".; $500 each.

Top: sucker, 8 1/2", $700; bottom: trout, 4 1/4", $300; Ernie Newman, Carlton, Minnesota, circa 1940.

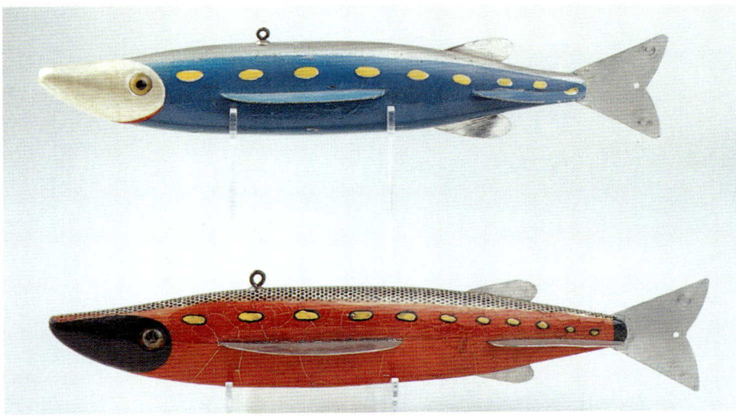

Top: pearl head, blue body, 9", $800; bottom: orange with black head, 9", $700, circa 1940. Ernie Newman, Carlton, Minnesota, who also produced fine trout lures, used commercial fishing lure enamel paints on his fish which were carved of redwood. These quality materials held up beautifully and examples of his fish, although over 60 years old, can look like they were made yesterday. Besides using pearlized enamels, Newman adapted other lure painting techniques like painting over plastic netting to create a scale effect on his fish decoys.

Trout lures: red, 4"; yellow 4 1/4"; Ernie Newman, Carlton, Minnesota, circa 1940. $300 each.

Top: red head, white body, 9"; bottom: orange with blue head, 9"; Ernie Newman, Carlton, Minnesota, circa 1940. $700 each.

Decoys by Wilbur "Willie" Peterson (1921-1986), Brainerd, Minnesota, circa 1935. Clockwise from the top: gray fish, 5", $400; sunfish, 3 1/2", $300; frog, 5 1/2", $1000; northern pike, 6", $500; sunfish, 4 1/4", $700.

Right:
Oxley, an amateur photographer, often captured his fishing experiences on film. These two northern pike were speared over his decoys, shown here in a special carrying case Oxley used to protect his decoys. Decoys, $500 each. *Photograph courtesy Rosemary Adamson. Collection of Donald J. Peterson.*

Elmer Oxley (1902-1919), Fergus Falls, Minnesota circa 1920. *Photograph courtesy Rosemary Adamson.*

Color flyer, Randall Decoys and Spears, Wilmar, Minnesota, circa 1940.

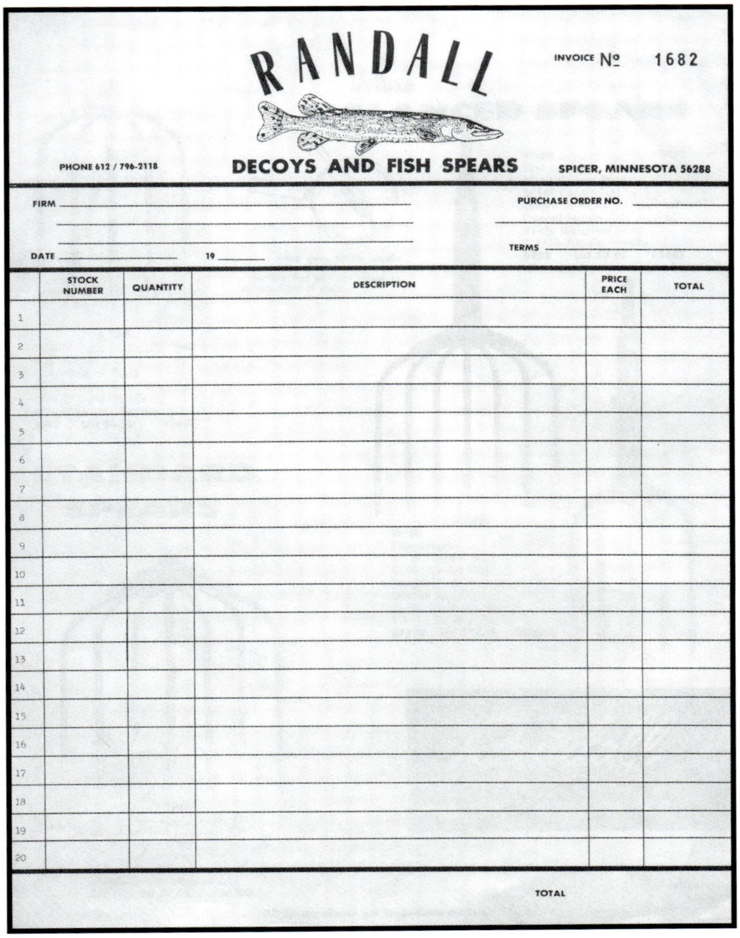

RANDALL

INVOICE № 1682

PHONE 612 / 796-2118

DECOYS AND FISH SPEARS

SPICER, MINNESOTA 56288

FIRM

PURCHASE ORDER NO.

DATE 19

TERMS

	STOCK NUMBER	QUANTITY	DESCRIPTION	PRICE EACH	TOTAL
1					
2					
3					
4					
5					
6					
7					
8					
9					
10					
11					
12					
13					
14					
15					
16					
17					
18					
19					
20					

TOTAL

Order form, Randall Decoys and Spears, Wilmar, Minnesota, circa 1940.

Top: northern pike, "Come-on" northern, Natural Pickerel R-500, in box, George Randall (1921-1979), Randall Decoys & Spear Company, Wilmar, Minnesota, 15", circa 1940, $400. Bottom: sucker, Golden Sucker RS150, Randall Decoys & Spear Company, Wilmar, Minnesota, 6", circa 1940, $100.

Top: crappie, 5 1/2"; bottom: sunfish (bluegill), 6". John Ryden (1897-1982), Aitkin, Minnesota, was a craftsmen who created fish decoys, miniature furniture, and toys that he sold out of the back of his pickup in the Aitkin City Bank's parking lot during the summer months. Circa 1920. $1,000 each.

Department of Natural Resources Officers pose with confiscated ice fishing spears, spotlights, and landing nets used by poachers. One can see by the size of their spears that Minnesota spear fishermen were after big fish. Their decoys were usually small to represent small baitfish which northern pike and muskellunge fed upon.

Top: sunfish, hammered copper insets on sides, 4 /12", $1000; middle: sunfish, 5"; bottom: northern pike, 9 3/4". John Ryden's decoys all have a distinctive mouth carving that makes them easy to identify. Circa 1920. $700 each.

Top; brown trout, 6 1/4"; middle: green trout, 5 3/4": bottom: brown trout, 6 1/4", John Ryden, Aitkin, Minnesota, circa 1920. $700 each.

Top left: brown trout, 5", $500; top right: brown trout, 5 1/4", $500; bottom left: walleye, 5 3/4", $500; bottom right: natural wood finish, wood burned detailing, 5 3/4", $500, John Ryden, circa 1920.

Brook trout, 4 1/2" to 6 1/4", John Ryden, Aitkin, Minnesota, circa 1920. $700 each.

Top: white spook, 5 3/4", $800; middle: bluegill (sunfish), 5 1/2", $1200; center: northern pike, 5 1/2", $1000; gray fish, 7 1/4", $700, John Ryden, Aitkin, Minnesota, circa 1920.

Top: trout, 5 3/4", $1,000; middle: walleye, 5 3/4", $1,000; bottom: walleye, 6 3/4", $1,500, John Ryden, Aitkin, Minnesota, circa 1920.

Jigging stick, sculpted walnut form, John Ryden, Aitkin, Minnesota, circa 1920. $250.

Top: shad, 11 1/4", $1000; middle: sunfish, 7", original. $2.50 price on side, $750; bottom: sunfish, 6 3/4", $500, carved and painted by Chester "Chet" Sawyer, Duluth, Minnesota, circa 1940.

Trout, 6", Chet Sawyer decoy with original Fred Lexow paint. Sawyer and his friend Fred Lexow work together to produce a finished fish decoy during the 1940s. $700.

Chester "Chet" Sawyer (1904-1994), Duluth, Minnesota, worked many odd jobs including caretaker of the Gray Wolf Lake Lodge, a private resort with three land-locked lakes outside of Grand Rapids, Minnesota. Family members there recall Chet taking them out onto the ice as children with a coffee can filled with his decoys and teaching them how to spear fish, circa 1930. Photograph circa 1980.

Top: shad, 11", carved and painted Chet Sawyer, circa 1920, $700.bottom: trout, 6 1/2", $400, Chet Sawyer, painted by his daughter. Fred Lexow taught Sawyer's daughter how to paint Chet's fish decoys, circa 1920.

Copper fish, Charles "Charlie" Slechta (1872-1965), Spring Park (Minneapolis), Minnesota, 10 1/2", circa 1930. Slechta was the most prolific of the "copper" fish decoy makers producing aluminum, galvanized steel, chrome, and copper fish decoys for nearly 30 years. His earliest models were soldered together and had glass eyes, but as demand increased he rolled and crimped the seams to save time. He also developed a special tool to press double ringed eyes into the metal replacing the glass eyes. Another identifying feature was his use of punching line of dots to detail his fish. $1000 each.

Copper fish. Top: northern pike, unknown Minnesota maker, and 10". Middle: northern pike, Charles Slechta, Spring Park, Minnesota. Bottom: northern pike, unknown Minnesota maker, 10". $750 each.

Top: perch, wooden tail, 9 3/4", Raymond Stotz. Stoltz, a house painter and guide during the summer months, built a local reputation as a fly fisherman, yet it would be his fish decoys that gave him immorality among collectors. This early example of his realistic fish renderings is a classic, circa 1920. $2000. Bottom: perch, metal tail, 8" unknown Minnesota maker, possibly Stotz, $700.

Frogs, Albert Eugene Storrs (1911-1986), Amboy, Minnesota, 5", circa 1950. Frogs were Storrs's specialty and over the years his design changed little. Many are stamped "A.E. Storrs" on their belly as were his fish. Storrs's fish decoys were simple minnows and had the same fin design as his frogs. Frogs, $300 each.

Top: perch wooden tail, 53/4", Raymond Stotz, Cleveland (Scotch Lake), Minnesota, circa 1945, $1,000. Bottom: bass, 7", Lawrence Bethel, circa 1960, $300.

Frog, John Tax, Osakis, Minnesota, circa 1930. $3,000. *Photograph and collection, Carter Stenburg.*

Right: walleye; 6 1/2". Left: trout, 5 1/4"; John Tax, Osakis, Minnesota, circa 1930. $2,000 each. *Photograph and collection, Carter Stenburg.*

Right: trout, 5 1/4"; left: trout, 5 1/4', John Tax, Osakis, Minnesota, circa 1930. $1,000 each. *Photograph and collection, Carter Stenburg.*

Right: blue trout, 5 1/2"; left: red trout, 5 1/4"; John Tax, Osakis, Minnesota, circa 1930. $1,000 each. *Photograph and collection, Carter Stenburg.*

Bluegill sunfish, decorative carving, John Tax, Osakis, Minnesota, circa 1930. $4,000. *Photograph and collection, Carter Stenburg.*

Birdhouse, rainbow trout, 17 1/2" x 7", John Tax, Osakis, Minnesota, circa 1930. $5,000. *Photograph and collection, Carter Stenburg.*

Birdhouse, largemouth bass, 16" x 10", John Tax, Osakis, Minnesota, wood, polychrome, circa 1940. $7,500.

Plaque, rainbow trout, Raymond "Hair-lip" Albert Thompson, (1887-1966), Park Rapids, Minnesota, circa 1920. This is an early Thompson plaque was found in Park Rapids in the home of a family friend. $1,500.

Brown trout, 8 1/2"; rainbow trout, 8 1/2"; Raymond Thompson, Park Rapids, Minnesota, circa 1930. Even the tongues are carved in these open mouth decoys with metal teeth. $7,000 each.

Speckled trout, 8"; rainbow trout, 8 1/2"; Raymond Thompson, Park Rapids, Minnesota, circa 1930. Ends of dental tools were used as metal teeth in these open mouth decoys. $5,000 each.

Copper fish. Top: minnow, sunfish, unknown Grand Rapids, Minnesota maker, copper "scales" over wood, 7". Bottom: bass, sunfish, unknown Mille Lac, Minnesota maker, 8 3/4". $350 each.

Copper critters. Top: beaver, hollow, 7 1/2", unknown Minnesota maker. Bottom: turtle, lead-filled copper, 4 1/2", unknown Minnesota maker. $750 each.

Copper fish. Left: sunfish, hollow copper, 4 1/2", unknown Minnesota maker. Middle: northern pike, sheet copper silhouette, 5 3/4", unknown Minnesota maker. Right: northern pike, hollow copper, painted, 6 1/2", unknown Minnesota maker. $400 each.

Trade-vane, Fisherman with fish on the line, wood, polychrome, Found Longville, Minnesota, maker unknown, circa 1930. Boat and man: 30"L x 25"H; fish 36", $3,000.

Northern pike, bi-colored, leather tail, unknown Native American maker, Red Lake Reservation, Bemidji, Minnesota, 16", circa 1930. $2000.

Frog with moveable legs, unknown Native American maker, Red Lake Reservation, Bemidji, Minnesota, 7" X 3 1/2", circa 1930. $4000.

Left: frog, 5 3/4" x 1 3/4"; center: painted jigging stick. 12"; right: tadpole, 5 3/4", same unknown Native American maker, Red Lake Reservation, Bemidji, Minnesota, circa 1930. $4,000, set.

Bluegill (sunfish), unknown Virginia, Minnesota maker, 8 1/2" x 5 3/4", circa 1920. $2,000.

Perch, 6", unknown Mille Lacs, Minnesota maker, circa 1920. $3,000.

This close-up of the Mille Lacs decoy shows that a seed pearl was set inside decoy's open mouth to depict the perch's common practice of stealing eggs off bluegill spawning beds.

Brown trout, natural finish, hinged, moveable copper tail, copper fins, 5", circa 1920. $1,000.

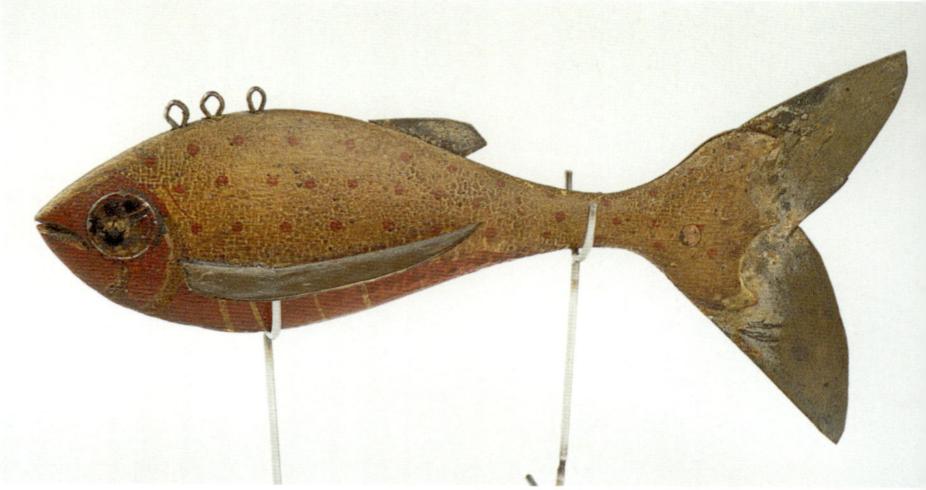

Sunfish, 6", unknown Minnesota maker, strong Scandinavian influence in coloration and design. Copper tail is inset into a sculpturally carved tail, circa 1900. $3,000.

Top: trout, 6 3/4", unknown Grand Rapids, Minnesota maker, gold metallic paint, circa 1920. Bottom: trout, 7", moveable fins, unknown Grand Rapids maker, circa 1920. $750 each.

Jigging stick, 20 1/2", carved duck head handle, unknown maker, Park Rapids, Minnesota, circa 1950. $1,000.

Bait sign, double sided, wooded, polychrome metallic gold, Grand Rapids, Minnesota, circa 1930. $2000.

Store display, brook trout, 16", wooden with cardboard fins and tail, unknown maker, Deer River Sports Shop, Deer River, Minnesota, circa 1940. $3,000.

Miscellaneous ice fishing button, Minnesota, circa 1950. $100 each.

Perch, "cheater," 6", unknown Aitkin, Minnesota maker. $500.

Top: northern pike, 10", unknown Crosslake, Minnesota maker, circa 1940, $800. Bottom: northern pike, 9 3/4", unknown Brainerd, Minnesota, maker, circa 1940, $500.

Abstract fish, 9", unknown Virginia, Minnesota, maker, circa 1940. Minnesota fish decoys are known for their strong individual style and flare. With its blue and black color pattern and open mouth full of metal teeth, this is a good example of the wild imaginary fish some makers created. $500.

Trout. Top: trout, 9 1/2", unknown maker, Bovey, Minnesota, circa 1930; middle: trout, 10", unknown maker, Grand Rapids, Minnesota, circa 1920; bottom: trout, 9 1/4", unknown maker, Bovey, Minnesota, circa 1930. $500 each.

Frog bait sign, double-sided, sand paint, Grand Rapids, Minnesota, circa 1940. $500.

Miscellaneous frog decoys, 4 1/4" – 5", unknown makers, Aitkin, Minnesota area, circa 1940-50. $500 each.

Miscellaneous frog decoys, 4 1/2" -5 1/2", unknown makers, Brainerd, Minnesota circa 1940-50. $400 each.

Miscellaneous frog decoys, 4 3/4"- 5 1/2", unknown makers, Grand Rapids, Minnesota each, circa 1940-50. $300 each.

Miscellaneous frog decoys, 4 1/4" -6", unknown Minnesota makers, circa 1940-50. $400 each.

Miscellaneous frog decoys, 4 "-6", unknown Minnesota makers, circa 1940-50. Top right: Mille Lac frog, attributed Fred Waltham, Brainerd, Minnesota. $400 each.

Attributed to Fred Waltham, Brainerd, Minnesota, circa 1940-50. Clockwise from the top: northern pike (abstract yellow), 8 1/2";. $700; catfish, 4 3/4", $1000; frogs, 4"- 6", $1000 each; frog, 4 1/2", $1000.

Top: sunfish, 4 3/4", unknown maker, circa 1950, $300; middle: perch, 6", circa 1940, $300; bottom: minnow, 5 3/4", unknown maker, circa 1950, $200.

Frog, unknown Cass Lake, Minnesota maker, moveable metal forelegs, 6 3/4", circa 1940. $500.

Selected Readings

Books

Alexander Henry's Travels & Adventures in the Years 1760-1776 edited by Milo Milton Quaife, Chicago, Il, Lakeside Press, 1921. If you can find it this is a good source for many interesting insights into the transfer of fish spearing techniques from the Native Americans to early explorers and settlers.

The American Sporting Collector's Handbook Edited by Allan J. Liu, Tulsa, Winchester Press, 1982. The late Robin Starr was one of the first collectors to document the fish decoy as a viable folk art form in his chapter in this literary collection.

Barber, Joel, *Wild Fowl Decoys*, New York, New York, Dover Publications, 1934: *Wild Fowl Decoys* was the first book published on vintage decoys and is considered a classic.

Baron, Frank R., *Commercial Fish Decoys*, Paducah, Kentucky, Collector Books, 2002. This is a comprehensive study of commercially produced fish decoys.

Baron, Frank R., Carver, Raymond L., *Bud Stewart, Michigan's Legendary Lure Maker* Hillsdale, Ferguson, 1990. Although this text is primarily about Stewart's lures, his fish decoys and also discussed and beautifully illustrated in full color.

Baron, Frank R., *One Fish, Two Fish, Green Fish, Blue Fish*, Livonia, Baron Inc. Frank Baron is one of the leading authorities on Michigan and factory decoys. His books are a must for any fish decoy collector.

Barrett, Harry B.; *Lore & Legends of Long Point,* D'Anjou, Lenore, Don Mills, Ontario, Burns & MacEachen Ltd., 1977. Long Point is still one of the most prestigious waterfowling clubs of the Midwest and this text is filled with a rich history that any duck hunter would appreciate.

Bosworth, T Thompson and Hayes, Jeffery R., PHD; *Whistling Wings, Whittled Ducks & Wetlands*, (museum catalog); Milwaukee, Wisconsin, Milwaukee Public Museum, 1996. After years of devoted research into the archives of the Milwaukee Public Museum's fine collection of waterfowling decoys (which was compiled during the early 1960s with the help of Wm. Mackey and other collectors) T. Thompson "Tom" Bosworth orchestrated a one time exhibition which brought to light decoys that had been stored for years. This museum catalog is a must for any collector of Midwest decoys.

Cheever, Byron, *Mason Decoys*, Spanish Fork, Utah, Hillcrest Publication, 1974. *Mason Decoys* is a classic decoy book on the Mason Decoy Factory, Detroit, Michigan.

Christensen, Robert D., *Duck Calls of Illinois*, DeKalb, Illinois, Northern Illinois University Press, 1994. Christensen has compiled the most extensive and detailed resource book on the Illinois duck calls and makers. It is filled with good illustrations, lots of accurate biographies of Illinois' finest call makers and a detailed history of call making in this state, *Duck Calls of Illinois* is the perfect companion book for *Decoys and Decoy Carvers of Illinois*

Crandell, Bernard, W. "Barney", *Decoying St Clair to the St Lawrence*, Erin, Ontario, The Boston Mills Press, 1988. Solid reference book on Michigan decoys and their makers.

Coykendall, Ralf, *Duck Decoys and How to Rig Them*, New York, Chicago, San Francisco; Holt, Rinehart and Winston, 1955. Written as a how-to book this has become a classic decoy book with vintage photography from the 1951 North American Decoy Makers Contest sponsored by Nash Motors as well as then contemporary decoy makers and commercial decoys.

Delph, John & Shirley, *Factory Decoys of Mason, Stevens, Dodge and Peterson*, Exton, Pennsylvania, Schiffer Publishing Ltd., 1980. This full color publication is still one of the best resources for collectors of early factory decoys and a must for every collector.

Earnest, Adele, *The Art of the Decoy: American Bird Carvings*, New York, New York, Bramhall House, 1965. Earnest presented an interesting view of decoy collecting from a folk art collector's perspective. It heralded the recognition of the hunting decoy as a functioning art form.

Engers, Joseph, ed., *The Great Book Wildfowl Decoys*, San Diego, California, Thunder Bay Press Inc. 1990. Engers brought together under one cover the expertise and knowledge of some of the country's foremost decoy collectors who each supplied chapters about their regional specialties.

Fleckenstein, Henry A. jr., *American Factory Decoys*, Exton, Pennsylvania. Schiffer Publishing Ltd., 1981. This fact filled text is a must for anyone who collects factory decoys. Whether the decoys are wooden, plastic or paper, Fleckenstein has documentation and illustrations of most of the known commercially produced hunting decoys.

Goldberger, Russ J, and Haid, Alan G., *Mason Decoys*, Burtonsville, Maryland, Decoy Magazine, 1993. Haid and Goldberger have set a new standard for decoy books with this volume with high quality photography and comprehensive study of the Mason Decoy Factory and their production line.

Guyette, Gary and Schmidt, Frank, private printings. Each year the Guyette & Schmidt presents three major auctions to the collecting world. Each is preceded with a fully illustrated catalog with good photography and detailed descriptions. Combined with the follow-up price guide this catalogs are invaluable as references.

Haid, Alan G., *Decoys of the Mississippi Flyway*, Exton, Pennsylvania, Schiffer Publishing Ltd., 1981. This has joined the works of Wm. Mackey and Joel Barber as a classic decoy book that belongs in every collector's library.

Hall, Michael and Swanson, Ronald, *Decoys as Folk Sculpture*, exhibition catalog, Bloomfield, Michigan, Cranbrook Academy of Art Museum, 1987. This is a great resource for Michigan decoys.

Harlan, Howard L. and Anderson, W. Crew, *Duck Calls- an Enduring American Folk Art* Nashville, Tennessee, Harlan-Anderson Press, 1988. Harlan and Crew have compiled a comprehensive, well-illustrated study on the call makers, which includes many makers from the Great Lakes regions. Their book is a worthy companion for any decoy collector's library

Harrell, Loy S. Jr., *Decoys, North America's One Hundred Greatest*, Lewes, Delaware, *Decoy Magazine*. Whether one agrees with Harrell's selection of 100 best decoys or not, this book stirred more serious discussion on the qualities of decoys than any published to date.

Jackson, Lowell, ed., *Benj J. Schmidt: a Michigan Decoy Carver* private publication. Excellent source for Michigan decoys.

Johnsgard, Paul A. ed., *The Bird Decoy*, Lincoln, Nebraska, University of Nebraska Press, 1976. Although primarily illustrated with black and white photographs this hardcover exhibition catalog is very well written and contains excellent examples covering the broad spectrum of waterfowl decoys.

Johnson, Archie, *Canvas Decoys of North America*, Burtonsville, Maryland, Decoy Magazine, 1994. Today's growing interest among collectors in canvas decoys makes this book a must for very collector and dealer. Johnson deals with these fascinating decoys in a very knowledgeable manner.

Kangas, Gene & Linda, *Decoys*, Paducah, Kentucky, Collector Books, 1992. A beautiful tabletop book that takes a look at waterfowling decoys from a different point of view. By arranging the decoys by species rather than regions. Gene and Linda have concentrated on the individual interpretations of the various species that were hunted.

Kangas, Gene & Linda, *Decoys: a North American Survey*, Spanish Fork, Utah, Hillcrest Publications, Inc., 1983.This is the first book I pick up when I'm need basic information on a carver. It is well written and organized making it an excellent reference book for the decoy collector.

Kimball, Art, Brad & Scott, *The Fish Decoy: Volume I* Boulder Junction, Aardvark Publications, Inc. 1986. Kimballs' three-volume text has done more to establish the fish decoy as a viable collectible that any other books. Volume I was the first major hardcover publication devoted entirely to fish decoys. Subsequent volumes continue to document the emerging information about this fascinating art form.

_____. *The Fish Decoy, Volume II*. Boulder Junction, Aardvark Publications, Inc. 1987

_____. *The Fish Decoy, Volume III*. Boulder Junction, Aardvark Publications, Inc. 1998.

Kohl, Johanna, *Kitaki Gami (Wanderings Round Lake Superior)*, London, Chapman & Hall. Another interesting old text, which recounts early interaction among Native Americans and early explorers and their use of fish decoys.

Lacy, Ann Tandy, *Perdew: an Illinois River Tradition*, Baxter, Nancy, ed., Muncie, Indiana, David Galliher, (private printing) 1993. David Galliher generously provided decoy collectors with a beautiful book on the master artisans, Charles and Edna Perdew. No costs were spared to research and develop this project and the book has set a standard for all future decoy books.

Lacy, Tandy, *The Wooden Bird*, Washburn, Illinois, Sun Foundation, 1989. This is more than an exhibition catalog for *The Wooden Bird*, Lakeview Museum, Peoria, Illinois, 1998. The text discusses the transition of the wooden working decoys into the contemporary floating sculptures of present-day carving competitions by Illinois cavers with lush full color photography.

Leitch, Jay A., *Darkhouse Spear Fishing Across North America*, Tri-College University, Center for Environmental Studies, North Dakota State University, Fargo, North Dakota, 1992 Excellent reference book which documents the sport of spear fishing through the ice. Every fish decoy collector should read this text to gain a better understanding of the use of the fish decoy. Excellent chapter on spear fishing history.

Mackey, William J. jr., *American Bird Decoys*, New York, New York, E. P. Dutton & Co., 1965. A must for every decoy collector's library, this is one of the great classics.

Mackey, William J. jr., *The Decoy Maker's Art*, exhibition catalog, Minneapolis, Minnesota, St Paul Art Center & Oshkosh, Wisconsin, Paine Art Center, Heikenen, Patricia, St. Paul, Minnesota, North Central Publishing Company, 1967. This exhibit was representative of displays fostered by Mackey's desire to expose collectors to a newly recognized fort art form, the decoy. Although all the illustrations are black-and-white photographs, the decoys are exquisite.

McGrath, Brain J., *Duck Calls and Other Game Calls*, Plano, Texas, The Thomas B. Reel Company, 1988. Duck calls go hand-in-hand with duck decoys. This book is a classic among call collectors.

Parmalee, Paul W. and Loomis, Forrest D., *Decoys and Decoy Carvers of Illinois*, DeKalb, Illinois, Northern Illinois University Press, 1969. Considered by collectors to be the bible of Illinois River decoys, the first hardcover and subsequent soft-cover editions quickly sold-out and are out-of-print.

Peterson, Donald J., *Folk Art Fish Decoys*, Schiffer Publishing Ltd., Atglen, Pennsylvania, 1996. A comprehensive study of vintage Minnesota fish decoy carvers and their work. Also includes information on fish spear makers from the state.

Peterson, Donald J., *Fish Decoy Makers Past and Present*, Lewes, Delaware, *Decoy Magazine*. Although there are some vintage fish decoy makers discussed in this text, the major emphasis is on contemporary Minnesota fish carvers.

Ridges, Bob, *Decoy Ducks*, New York, New York, W.H. Smith Publishers Inc., 1988.

Robarts, Ronnie and Birkbeck, Bill, *The Red Book of Sporting Collectibles*, Birkbeck, Bill, ed., Conway, New Hampshire, private printing, 1996. Though price guidelines are out-of-date, this is still a good reference for quick identification.

Robinson, Jimmy, *Forty Years of Hunting*, Jimmy Robinson, Minneapolis, Minnesota, 1947. Interesting tales from a veteran sportsman and outdoors writer, Jimmy Robinson

Saliva, Marcel L., *Ice Fishing Spears* Potomac, Marjac Publications1993. This comprehensive study of the fishing spear is the prefect complement to any fish decoy library that gives a fuller understanding to this folk art form.

Swanson, Ronald S., *Fish Model: An Exhibition* Manchester, American Museum of Fly Fishing, 1992-93. This exhibition catalog provides a fact filled history of the origins and development of fish decoy plaques as an American folk art form. Exquisite examples are beautifully illustrated.

Sorenson, Hal, ed., *Decoy Collector's Guide*, Burlington, Iowa, Hal Sorenson, 1963- 1977. At one time this was the only link among decoy collectors nationwide. Sorenson's unselfish efforts were characteristic of the very nature of decoy collecting during the 1960s. There was a camaraderie that few collectors share today. This remains a major source of information about decoys for the student of the art form. No library is complete without the complete set of volumes.

Tonelli, Donna, *Top of the Line Fishing Collectibles* Atglen, Pennsylvania, Schiffer Publishing LTD. 1997. This full-color book presents an overview of vintage collectibles related to sport fishing; decoy, lures, reels, folk art.

Tonelli, Donna, *Top of the Line Hunting Collectibles* Atglen, Pennsylvania, 1999. This book covers the field of waterfowl collectibles from decoys and calls to advertising and powder tins. Descriptive information is supplemented with estimates of current values.

Traff, Cliff jr., and Lindgren, John, *Last of the Prairie Carvers*, private printing, 1970. This small black & white pamphlet is a tribute to one of the Midwest's finest decoy carvers, John Tax, Osakis, Minnesota.

Walsh, Clune, Jr., and Jackson Lowell G., ed., *Waterfowl Decoys of Michigan and the Lake St Clair Region*, Detroit, Michigan, Gale Graphics, 1983. Chapters were written by the top Michigan collectors of the day, who provided superb examples and invaluable information on Michigan decoys and decoy carvers.

Webster, David S. and Kehoe, William, *Decoys at Shelburne Museum*, Burlington, Vermont. The Lane Press, 1961. This black & white pamphlet is a catalog for the first permanent decoy collection in a major folk art museum, the Shelburne Museum, Shelburne, Vermont.

Periodicals

Decoy Magazine, P. O. Box 787, Lewis, Delaware 19958. Editor, Joe Engers has developed a highly informative and timely publication for the vintage decoy collectors with market analysis, top quality photography and authoritative articles.

Hunting & Fishing Collectibles Magazine, P.O. Box 40, Lawsonville, North Carolina 27022. This new publication offers coverage of a broad range of sporting collectibles.

Wildfowl Carving and Collecting, 500 Vaughn Street, Harrisburg, Pennsylvania 17110. The main emphasis of W C & C is contemporary wildlife art and bird carving.

Organizations

American Fish Decoy Association (newsletter), c\o John Shoffner, 624 Merritt, Fife Lake, Michigan 49633

Canadian Decoy & Outdoors Collectible Association, 22-635 Richmond Road, Ottawa, Ontario, Canada K2A-0G6

Duck Call Collector and Makers Association, 5145 Deland Road, Flushing, Michigan 48433

Great Lakes Fish Decoy Collectors & Carvers Association (newsletter), c\o Frank R. Baron, 35824 West Chicago, Livonia, Michigan 48150

Midwest Decoy Collector's Association, Herb Desch, 3006 Fox Glen Court, St. Charles, Illinois 60174

Minnesota Decoy Collector's Club, 1515 Byrd Avenue South, Golden Valley, Minnesota 55422

National Fishing Lure Collectors Club (quarterly magazine), PO Box 13,Grove City, Ohio 43123

Ohio Decoy Carvers and Collectors Association, P.O. Box499, Richfield, Ohio 44286

Wisconsin Decoy Collectors, 3792 Leonard Point Road, Oshkosh, Wisconsin 54904

Auction houses

Decoys Unlimited, Incorporated, 2320, Main Street, West Barnstable, Massachusetts

Dixie Sporting Collectibles, 1206 Rama Road, Charlotte, North Carolina 28211

Gary Guyette & Frank Schmidt Decoy Auction House, RR #1, Box 540, West Baldwin, Maine 04091

James Julia, PO Box 830, Fairfield, Maine 04937

Frank & Frank Sporting Collectibles, 424 Lakewood-Farmington Road, Howell, New jersey 07731

Lang's Sporting Collectibles Incorporated, 30 Hamlin Road, Falmouth, Maine 04105 Massachusetts

Victorian Images, PO Box 284, Marlton, New Jersey 08053

Index

N

O

P

Q

R

S